T0365714

ALSO BY BRUCE JOHNSON

Flexible Software Design: Systems Development for Changing Requirements, with Walter W. Woolfolk, Robert Miller & Cindy Johnson, Aeurbach, CRC Press, 2005.

Information Systems Technology for Quality Improvement, Editor with Sam Pinto, Xavier University, 1992.

Professional Programming in COBOL, with Marcia Ruwe, Prentice-Hall, 1991.

Managing the Professional Programmer, editor, course packet, 1987.

MY YEARS IN THE INFORMATION TECHNOLOGY
TRENCHES,
FROM DATA PROCESSING TO INFORMATION TECHNOLOGY

THE REMINISCES OF A CRUDmudgeon

Bruce Johnson, PhD

Order this book online at www.trafford.com
or email orders@trafford.com

Most Trafford titles are also available at major online book retailers.

Print information available on the last page.

ISBN: 978-1-4120-9984-4 (sc)

Library of Congress Control Number: 2015916338

Trafford rev. 10/06/2015

 www.trafford.com

North America & international
toll-free: 1 888 232 4444 (USA & Canada)
fax: 812 355 4082

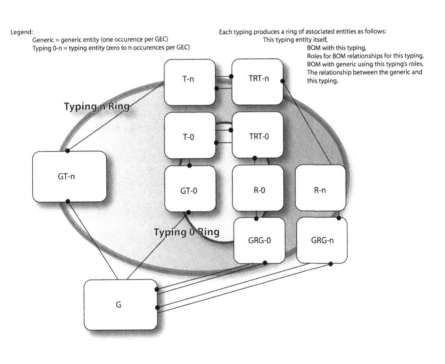

Legend:
Generic = generic entity (one occurence per GEC)
Typing 0-n = typing entity (zero to n occurences per GEC)

Each typing produces a ring of associated entities as follows:
This typing entity itself,
BOM with this typing,
Roles for BOM relationships for this typing,
BOM with generic using this typing's roles,
The relationship between the generic and
this typing.

CONTENTS

Introduction

Why these reminisces? How did all this get started? Portraying an overview of my background (including my parents), education, career, and retirement. How the book is developed and organized. Sets the stage for the following chapters.

Why These Reminisces?
How Did All Of This Get Started?
College: Washington State University
Background

Chapter 1: Insight/Ingenuity Into Computer Hardware & Software Operation

Chapter 2: Curmudgeon

Chapter 3: CRUDmudgeon: Let The Data Do The Work

CRUD the data cycle: **C**reate, **R**ead, **U**pdate, and **D**elete. The centrality of data is demonstrated through incidents, systems, and their ramifications. Stories about superrecond, "if the data only looked this this," along with unique and innovative file designs for systems such as technical recruiting and personnel records, demonstrate the importance of data. Most of these incidents occurred while I was at General Computer Services Corporation (GCSC) and thus also give insights into the nature of GCSC's business. (chapters 8 & 9).

What Is A CRUDmudgeon?
If Only The Data Looked Like This
Sales Reporting
Time And Attendance System
Technical Recruiting System
Side Bar: P&G Recruits Bruce
Side Bar: Contrasting Computing Results
Personnel Records System
Side Bar: Ralph: "Reverse Your Collar..."
SuperRecord
Conclusion

Chapter 4: Bruce Has A PhD

It was June 10, 1990 when my PhD was officially conferred. In June of 1985 I had been awarded my master of business administration; in June of 1962 I had received my masters degree in civil engineering. And in February of 1959, thirty-one years earlier, I had earned my first degree—a bachelors degree in civil engineering. I had attended none of the first four graduation ceremonies.

Chapter Bibliography

Chapter 5: Technical Distance

Introduction
Washington State University Car/Expense Account

Chapter 6: (In)Flexible Systems

This chapter includes stories demonstrating the detrimental effect that inflexible systems have on organizations and the benefits of flexible systems and how flexible systems are developed.

Chapter 7: teaching technology

Teaching as creativity along with impediments to teaching. Presenting stories about teaching experiences, specific students from industry, trade schools, and at universities, shows these experiences as both positive and not so positive. Several innovative teaching techniques are explored—some that worked, some that didn't.

Chapter 8: The Rise And Fall Of General Computer Services Corporation

My involvement with General Computer Services Corporation (GCSC) was a watershed time in my careers. This chapter based upon a Masters if Business Administration case study presents how GCSC came to be and how it was destroyed in a boardroom coup.

Chapter Bibliography

Chapter 9: GCSC Days And Nights

General Computer Services Corporation (GCSC) days ... and nights... were some of the most intense, stressful, and interesting periods of my life. In many ways it all blends together —the projects, the people, the terror, the excitement—the stress on my marriage and family life. The rise and fall of GCSC and some insights into the nature of the business were presented in chapter 8. This chapter presents my life during the existence of GCSC—from 1968 to 1976. The following chapter covers GCSC's largest project system for planning electrical construction.

Introduction
CULTURE
Our Salesman
Back Side Printing
354 CALL—Customer Satisfaction
Projects Are Finished On Fridays
Inventory Policies
Nepotism
Fire At The Backup Location
OFFICES
Musical Desks
The Beauty Parlor
Odd Fellows
Cincinnati Branch Office
RELATIONS WITH IBM
Inadvertent Financing
Software Bugs
BUREAUCRACY
Spouse's Salary
Who Is Responsible For The Financials?
Wage And Hour Laws
THE IBM 1401
IBM 1401 And The Investment Tax Credit
IBM 1401 Incidents
DEALING WITH LIMITED STORAGE
Add Feed-A-Card To Counter
Not A Millennium Bug!
Card Overlay
Tape Overlay
PROJECTS
Federal Home Loan Bank
Marrying Republicans
Fuel Oil

Chapter 10: System For Planning Electrical Construction

This chapter presents my multiplicity of roles in the development of System For Planning Electrical Construction (SPEC). Though my participation ended in 1976, 22 years before I retired, SPEC is certainly one of my most significant career accomplishments. SPEC was done for the engineering division of Procter & Gamble, a very demanding customer. SPEC was done on a tight budgets and time schedules—-as we preceded incrementally $25,000 (in 1970 dollars) at a time through many deadlines and several budgets. While this start-stop hectic environment is, unfortunately, not unusual for it projects, what was unusual was that this was also a leading-edge endeavor in which the implementation team had little or no application knowledge and the client team had no experience in developing computer systems.

Chapter 11: Some Advice

What does this all mean? What advice does it yield for todays it professionals? This chapter places the previous chapters in perspective and tries to make sense of it all. No attempt is made to predict the future—as a great deal of said future it is already here.

BE AWARE OF IT MYTHS

- The Myth Of Perfect Knowledge
- The Myth Of Methodology
- The Myth Of Reuse
- The Myth Of The Solution
- The Myth Of The Isolated System
- The Myth Of The Naive Customer
- The Myth Of Outsourcing
- The Myth Of Classification
- The Myth Of Rapid Application Development (Rad)
- The Myth Of OO As A New Technology And A Silver Bullet
- The Myth Of Retroactive Documentation

SOME WISDOM

- Get An Education—Not Just Training.
- Continue Your Education And Training.
- Be Ware Of Technical Distance
- Never Be Bored.
- Have Fun—Enjoy What You Do—And Be Good At It.
- Learn And Practice The First Law Of Wing Walking.

- Keep On Top Of Technology Progression.
  - Look For The Constants In Ever-Evolving Technology.
  - Don't Be Afraid To Start Over.
  - Design For Flexibility.
- Choose The Right Bosses.
- Follow Stupid Rules Exactly.
- Be Patient.
- Pay Attention To Detail.
- Don't Get Outsourced.

AGAIN

DEDICATION

This work is dedicated to my 5th, 6th, and 9th grade teachers who set me on the straight and narrow and recognized my abilities. And to my bosses at Washington State, Procter & Gamble, and Thoman Software who made such valuable contributions to whatever success that I have had. I alone am responsible for my failures.

ACKNOWLEDGEMENTS

I am deeply indebted to my numerous book coauthors, without whom these works would not have occurred: Marcia on our *COBOL* book; Walt, Bo, and Cindy on our flexible systems book. Others have helped me in writing journal articles—both published and rejected. I am also beholden to several colleagues who reviewed portions of this tome.

INTRODUCTION:
WHY THESE REMINISCES?

I have observed and been intimately involved in the world of computers since 1956. I thought it useful to set down some of my experiences, observations, and adventures from these years. Though I am officially retired I continue to be actively involved in using, writing about, and study information technology (as it is now called) or IT and related subjects. While describing this project to a friend, I was asked, "Have you kept a journal of these happenings?" The answer is no. This has all been reconstructed from memory. When I have discovered inconsistencies, I have reported them. Thus this work: *My Years in the Information Technology Trenches: From Data Processing to Information Technology—Reminisces of a CRUDmudgeon*[1]. The events, people, and places described and presented herein are true as I remember them to the best of my ability.

A great question first introduced by Sam, one of the professors in my PhD program is: "Who cares?" Sam said that when we wrote or spoke, the first question to ask was, "Who cares?" I am not sure what the answer is in this case. But I care and William Zinsser in *On Writing Well* [2006] says that is whom I am supposed to write for. Recording my adventures has been fun and instructive. Part of the history of information technology is contained herein, which, I hope, will make it interesting to others. By the way, Sam was the only faculty member in my PhD program who was older than I!

My knack for and insight into computer operation led me on this wild ride. What enabled me to 1) gain such insight to computer operation and capabilities: 2) to do a PhD Dissertation on technical

---

[1] A take off on curmudgeon using **C**reate, **R**ead, **U**se, **D**elete the basic operations on data, the data life cycle, that are underrated in current computing (IT) in favor of fancy Graphical User Interfaces (GUIs) and other much over-hyped techniques. As goes the data, so goes the system. One of may favorite mantras: "Let the data do the work."

distance, and 3) to coauthor books on COBOL and computer systems flexibility? Early on I was wired for these three tracks. Though, this did not all come together until relatively late in my careers[2].

Was it my early math and computing inclination: My knack for math, aided by rigorous math fact drilling in 6th grade, by baseball with its statistics, grading IQ tests in high school and a sidetrack during college from math into computing caused by a perplexing math class? Did being left-handed with dyslexia help?

Much of my computing career was spent forcing inflexible computer systems into compliance with current business practices. It would have been more satisfying and productive to make the systems flexible in the first place; hence, computer system flexibility became my mantra and my main research interest in the later years of my careers.

I made several computing innovations in both processing and data design and was often ahead of my time. I taught math—mainly quantitative methods: such as, optimization, linear programming, and simulation and often helped students overcome their fear of statistics, by calling it "variation."

The clash between two different logical systems, what I came to call "technical distance" has been an important part of my careers. Technical distance is the gap between the technologist and the manager. One person who has knowledge of the technology involved in a given decision situation; another person has the power and authority to make the actual decision. In a way, it's like the ruling and the governed. This phenomenon often impedes the technologist from accomplishing his or her duties. It took me too long to fully understand the technologist-manager dichotomy, which I now believe will never be fully overcome. My failure to understand this sometimes caused me to be too outspoken and to be out of a job. But I always recovered, generally with a better, more interesting, job with increased salary.

I am a computer programmer, I enjoy computer programming, and all modesty aside, I am good at it. In addition, I enjoy the challenge, the creativity, and the test of wills that occurs while programming and developing computer systems. In addition, while computers often seem arbitrary in that they do exactly what they are told, unlike humans,

---

[2]   I say careerS because as I look back, I really did have more than one career.

they act rationally and predictably. I do better dealing with computers than I do with people.

I started in civil engineering, partly because my father was a civil engineer, partly because I was good at math and science and enjoyed them. I am a numbers guy—frequently, counting, keeping track, and the like. Like I was my grade school grandsons are enamored with math—because numbers are not abstract as they are so often in math teaching—they relate specifically: counting trucks, determining the age of grandpa and the like.

While not entirely leaving engineering, I morphed into becoming a computer programmer and a techie. I am also left-handed, which while often an advantage in sports is not always an advantage in life.

With my left-handedness goes self-diagnosed mild dyslexia. Although my understanding that I have mild-dyslexia came late in life, I can now look back and trace its effects and recognize the effects that it continues to have. My most notable episodes with dyslexia were in high school while taking ROTC. When the command left face or right face was given I had a 50 percent chance of turning the correct way. So a brick was put in one of my hands, but I could not remember which hand. Next a cinder block—same (non) result. It was not until I was retired in Estes Park that I could instinctively tell left from right when during water exercise we would place our left/right side adjacent to the pool wall.

I also have tinnitus (ringing in the ears) though I am not sure when or how it occurred. In addition to these internal attributes I am a husband, father, grandpa, peace activist, and conservationist, particularly interested in sustainability via reduced parking and driving.

These identities have shaped and colored my life and my careers. With them my careers have been successful and satisfying even though I have encountered bumps along the way. These bumps have been due to differences between myself and my managers or my colleagues or the IT industry itself and/or by being an *innovator*. Actually in many ways my career has been like a roller coaster with many ups and downs. I have been really scared at times when things appeared to be over my head—but I have never been bored.

I have often been out of touch with the industry, or the industry has been out of touch with me in, at least three specific areas. 1) The all-to-often ignored issues of flexible/inflexible computer systems. 2) The necessity of computer programming for the success of individuals in the IT field and corporate IT endeavors. And 3) technical distance— the gulf.

How Did All Of This Get Started?

I was born with math and computing in my genes and during my academic and professional careers additional math and computing DNA was spliced into these genes. I was steered into *My Years in the Information Technology (IT) Trenches* and becoming a CRUDmudgeon by the juxtaposition of events, talent, knack, and interests, as set forth herein. My interest and ability in math was nurtured by baseball. Baseball, like most sports, has almost endless statistics: averages of all kinds including the, not so intuitive, earned run average (ERA).

In Junior High and early high school, my friends and I avidly followed professional baseball, including the class A Denver Bears. We played street baseball all over our part of Denver's Park Hill neighborhood. We also played the *All-Star Baseball* spinner game where each player had his stats represented by segments of a circular card (disk, dial). We not only kept statistics from the games we played, we made our own cards for players not included in the purchased game.

At Denver's Smiley Junior High I worked with Mr. Parsons, my math teacher, grading IQ tests. When I took the test for fun, I was so familiar with its contents that I registered an IQ of 200+. Genius! Mr. Parsons was the teacher who told my parents, "Since Bruce can compute earned run averages (ERAs) in his head, let's not worry about his math ability."

Mr. Parson's comment is only one example of how my parents and teachers nurtured and supported my academic development. While I was learning to read, my parents and teachers allowed that reading such things as comic books was—reading. Miss Hunt and Miss Gleesner in 5th and 6th grades were strict disciplinarians who took no nonsense and set me (and others) on the straight and narrow path of classroom decorum necessary for effective learning.

Every day at the beginning of Miss Gleesner's 6th grade class we performed an elaborate multiplication facts ritual—thus splicing basic math DNA into my genes. How could one not know one's multiplication tables after a full school year of this? Much the same approach was taken in my beginning chemistry class regarding learning the periodic table of the elements. (Though there were a lot fewer elements then.)

In my last semester at East Denver High, I took an advanced math class in which we spent the entire semester discovering integral calculus. I do not remember the exact process except that it was tedious and we were so relieved when we discovered the formula and did not have to do the work by hand. In college this material was covered in a matter of days—but calculus DNA, which causes so much trouble for many, was spliced into my genes.

I was a "lazy" student through early high school until I went to Woodstock, a boarding school, during my middle two years of high school, when Dad's job took the family to India. There I had to buckle down since the competition was stiff. Most of the students' parents had advanced degrees. Our class, the class of 1954, has more PhDs than any other of Woodstock's almost 162 gradating classes. While at Woodstock I learned the value of a reputation having gone steady with the valedictorian who occasionally received better grades than I, when we agreed my work was clearly superior. So I applied my self, improved my study habits, and pulled myself into a higher academic realm. The nature of my Woodstock education was demonstrated when returning to East High in mid first-semester of my senior year I achieved 125% out of 100% in chemistry (due primarily to extra credit assignments). Early in my college career I worked to establish a favorable academic reputation, which I could occasionally use to ride over a rough spot.

Technically I'm a junior—Bruce Maxwell Johnson Junior or Bruce M. Johnson Jr. My Dad just plain Bruce Johnson suffered a massive stroke in 1978 and died in 1990 six weeks after Mother. After dad died I dropped my middle name and the junior and am now "just" Bruce Johnson. Our family moved every two to four years as I was growing up. I was often the new kid on the block and experienced many nick names: Brucie; Bruce, Bruce, tomato juice; Jackknife Johnson; and some not printable. I was subject to a great deal of teasing. When I delivered the Denver Post while in high school, I was called "Average Carrier." This occurred while being harassed by older paper carriers, I was asked, "How good a paper carrier are you?" And I replied, "About average.

I am left-handed, a late bloomer, a survivor, an engineer (and a Luddite). I am an IT (Information Technology) professional. I am outspoken which is partly responsible for me being fired twice. I am an entrepreneur and a family man. I have been ahead of my time. I am a somewhat softer version of my father.

While being left-handed is not particularly an advantage in life, it is an advantage in tennis. Being left-handed may be at least partly responsible for my self diagnosed dyslexia (which materially complicates my efforts to play the piano) and my "preposition generator." You ask, "What is a preposition generator?" When I am typing and a preposition is called for apparently one just jumps out at random. When I go back a read a passage I say, "Yes, a preposition was called for there—but this is not the right one."

I am a late bloomer—entering my final profession, that of university professor, at the age of 46; receiving my PhD at the age of 54; taking up the piano (again) at the age of 66. I did retire "early" at age 62 —actually I was put out to pasture by Xavier for too often saying, "The emperor has no clothes."

I am a survivor. I had quadruple bypass heart surgery in 2002. This surgery was instrumental in my taking up the piano that I had briefly studied in junior high. I also count my PhD, which took eight years, a change in minor study area, and multiple dissertation topics. I survived the process. I have been fired twice—and ended up better off each time.

As an engineer, I tend to see things in black and white, right and wrong, and I am outspoken about what I see. I am not a politician and this has been instrumental in both of my firings. Many times I have not held back when "the emperor was naked." I have battled (and often lost) bureaucracy and administrivia (not in the spell checker) most of my career. Also being an engineer has caused me to recognize the phenomena of technical distance, which was the subject of my PhD dissertation.

As an engineer I am a techie. I used to wear a nerd pack[3]. While I took extra university courses to broaden myself, as I get older I regret not having a fuller background in the liberal arts, especially music for studying the piano.

I taught in Xavier's College of Business Administration (CBA) and sometimes was caught up in "engineer bashing." In the IT field I wore many hats among them: computer programmer, systems analyst, and database designer. Being the only Xavier IT faculty member with actual IT experience, I felt that I knew what was required to be successful in the field. Therefore I fought for more technical rigor in Xavier's IT programs—more math, more true/hard sciences such as chemistry and physics, machine-level programming, a better understanding of economics and the like. As I frequently said, "Fewer hand-waving courses and more substantial courses!"

Even as an IT professional I often "go against the grain." I coined the term CRUDmudgeon to counteract the over emphasis on flashy screens and lightweight systems. The basis of IT (it used to be data processing) is data: Its Creation, Reading, Updating, and Destruction—hence CRUD and then after curmudgeon—CRUDmudgeon. I and my colleagues are still going against the grain in our struggles to have the IT industry understand the problem of inflexible computer systems and, even better, the solution. The industry, however, would much rather concentrate on buzzword methodologies.

But in spite of being a techie I am, in many ways, a Luddite; for example, I was planning to get through life without a cell phone—but in October of 2014 I succumbed. And while much of my working life was a technical whirl, I marveled at how I could go on week or ten-day backpack trips with just what I could carry on my back and not need or use it all while having a wonderful time. On these trips I was able to get away from the high-pressure technology-driven world in which I worked much of the time.

I am or, at least, have been an entrepreneur—forming and running my own company for eight years. I am also a husband and father of two children and grandfather to five. It is hard to think of anything

---

[3] Nerd Pack: A plastic pack that fits in a shirt pocket and holds pens, pencils, maybe a small ruler, and such. May also include a small slide rule.

more fun and more rewarding than being a grandparent. But at times being an entrepreneur and a family man were not entirely compatible.

Often I was ahead of my time. Fighting for software preventive maintenance while at Procter and Gamble (P&G), coining the term "demotivation" (which still in not recognized by the spell checker) while studying for my PhD. I developed the pseudo computer concept utilizing the 7.8 (a take off on the 1401 to make the 7080 easier for students to ease into to computer programming), my colleagues and I used email and word processing before they were actual applications—or aps as they are known today.

In many ways I take after my father—after all I AM a junior. He was outspoken, did not suffer fools, he was blatantly honest, he had an all-encompassing love of children—all of which I have inherited from him. But, believe it or not, I am a little mellower.

College: Washington State University

When it came time to attend college, I took the easy route and went to Washington State College (now University) (WSU) in Pullman, Washington, where my parents had gone. I planned to major in Civil Engineering (CE) like my Father. My reasons for Civil Engineering were not very strong—basically it was all I knew and it just seemed the natural thing to do. I really liked math and was good at it. I was not as interested in writing at the time and I told my Dad, "Engineers don't do much writing." Of course, he knew better and I soon found out how wrong I was. That was an early demonstration of *my* "technical distance."

"Lazy" as I use the word here means basically "taking the easy path." For example, I say that honesty is the easy or "lazy" way because one does not have to remember what was said. I characterize engineers as "lazy"—because they desire to do things right the first time and not have to do them over and over again. I was able to get acceptable grades in high school without much effort. In fact I said, "An A was twice as much work as a B—so why work for an A?" I planned to go to college but did not think much about it, so when Dad sent to WSU for literature it was an easy choice.

In the fall of 1956 I took a class in differential equations. I was a Civil Engineering student who wanted to take as much math as possible. The professor, Dr. Rechard[4], had come from Los Alamos Atomic Labs to set up the first computing center at the school. But the entire class found differential equations to be obtuse, difficult, and elusive. So we diverted Dr. Rechard and got him to talk about the new marvel—the digital computer. My careers in IS/IT were, in one of my favorite phrases, "Accidents of history." If I had not taken differential equations I might have spent a good deal of my life at a drawing board working for low wages for other civil engineers as civil engineering graduates often did in those days.

Dr. Rechard truly peaked my interest in computers, so the next semester I signed up for the first offering of "Introduction to Digital Computers." Again, like my advanced math class, the class started at a very basic level splicing an understanding of computing into my genes. The class included the progression from IBM 650 machine language, to Symbolic Optimal Assembly Program (SOAP[5]), to FORTRAN, the use and development of subroutines, program optimization, and debugging. This introduction has enabled me to stay close to the computer. I went on to take all the computer courses WSU had to offer. This sparked my interest in computers and computing. I have been at it ever since.

This, in depth foundation, was in stark contrast to the approach at Xavier years later where we taught, "high level computing" and I was unable to install a introductory course that would have provided our students with the foundation such as I found so valuable in both computing and in engineering—it would have been so valuable to our students.

I have two degrees in Civil Engineering, yet I have never done any actual Civil Engineering. I did, however, work on engineering-oriented systems. One was in mechanical engineering—a heat exchange application. The other was System for Planning Electrical Construction (SPEC) chapter 10. Looking back, however, engineering was a near perfect course of study for my many careers. My WSU years preceded specific courses of study labeled computer science, information systems, and IT, but my civil engineering training in technical knowledge, management skills, mathematical analysis, how

---

[4]   Dr. Richard subsequently served on my masters thesis committee.

[5]   As opposed to the acronym's usage today "Simple Object Access Protocol."

to think, and how to tackle problems may have been even better. There was a downside too. I often fell into an engineering trap (and still do) seeing things as black and white and failing to see or understand their shades of gray[6]. My overriding weakness has been lack of political savvy demonstrated by the frequency with which I was fired.

In many undergraduate classes I used the computer, on my own, as unlike most students I had access the computer and knew how to use it. For my CE masters degree I applied the computer to each of CE's sub-fields such as: hydraulics, transportation, highways, structures, and economics. For my master's thesis I developed a computer program to determine intercity travel desire factors for the Washington State Highway System. For a short time I was the computer guru for WSU's Division of Industrial Research. In this position I developed an "ahead it its time" graphical application for power transmission line sag.

The unfolding of these three themes: ahead of the IT curve, technical distance, and inflexible computer systems, is presented in the following chapters. But first a little more background.

Background

Like many of you I owe who I am to my parents. Mother was a homemaker. Dad was a civil engineer. We moved every several years as Dad designed hydroelectric dams. Mother provided the family's stability. My Father was not a patient man, either at home or at work. He was honest to a fault and did not suffer fools gladly. He disputed the Peter Principle, which stated that people rose to one level above their level of competence: he felt that it was two levels. Dad loved his family and children in general. In retrospect, my first glimpse of "technical distance" came from my father, who distained computers. Dad was a highly respected expert, particularly on thin arch dams so; in that sense he was a technical personat least early in his career. But then I was most aware of his career; he was in high-level decision-making positions. It was during this time that he stopped assigning responsibility for mistakes to engineers and assigned them to computers. See the side bar for an inside glimpse of my parents.

---

[6]   But I did enjoy the *Fifty Shades of Grey* books.

Glimpses Of My Parents

Both of these incidents deal with our time in India from 1951-1953.

When Dad had the opportunity to go to India as Director of Design of Bhakra Dam in the Punjab we had a family vote. Dad, my sister Linda, and I voted to go. Mother voted not to. We went. After we had been there about a year things were not going well (I do not remember what the problem was) so we had another family vote—to stay or leave. Dad, Linda, and I voted to leave. Mother said, "We came for two years, we are staying for two years." We stayed. Mother was right, things really worked out for the rest of our time in India.

Dad had a cadre of engineers that tended to follow him from job to job (dam to dam). Part of this cadre was with us at Bhakra. One time when Dad was back in the states recruiting additional engineers for the project a portion of this cadre who were not on the project visited and were given a tour of the dam by the local cadre. I toured along and when they thought I was out of earshot one of visiting cadre asked, "How is Bruce (Sr.) to work for on this project?" The answer was, "He is as big a bastard as ever." I could not have agreed more. But the engineers followed him. He was fair, the work was interesting, and they competed to work with and for him. And that said he was a great dad.

Mom and I had several fun go-arounds. I claimed that we went to Arizona from Denver every summer to see the cactus when I would rather have stayed home and played baseball. Mother's response was: "Bruce, we did that once!" She also noted on occasion that I was engaged in an unsavory activity and called me on it. I responded that I was sampling life. She replied: "Yes, but you don't have to wallow in it."

Dad was a taskmaster, His ultimate compliment was: "You could have done worse." My son has a

follow on: "Dad, you are forceful but you are wrong."
Times changed I never would have said that to my Dad.

I had my formal growing up when the summer before college I had a construction job in a Chicago suburb while the family was living the North Chicago. I spend the week on the job and came home for the weekend. One week it was my birthday and while I was reading my cards Dad repeatedly called me for supper and I kept saying: "I will come when I finish reading my cards." That was the first time I really stood up to him.

In December 1958, while still completing my B.S. degree, I married Carmen, who was also a Johnson—so being ahead of my time I took her last name. Our families were best friends. Right after graduation with my BS degree in February 1959, I spent six months on active duty with the army. Upon my return, I completed my MS degree. I was accepted into graduate school with a 3.06 grade point average—a 3.00 was required. Again my "lazy" way was good enough. While in graduate school I worked for the Highway Research Section of the University's Division of Industrial Research. This was a great job. Reid[7] became my first boss and mentor—teaching me about technical writing, how to deal with politicians, and about running an office.

In 1962, after receiving my MS in Civil Engineering, I felt that I was inadequately compensated, receiving a raise of $10 per year more than the year before. So I told the head of the division, "If your masters degree is worth only 86 cents per month, I quit." This made me person non grata, as no one had quit the division before without having obtained another job, in essence "being lured away by industry."

I subsequently accepted a job with Procter & Gamble's (P&G) Data Processing Systems Department (DPS) in Cincinnati, Ohio. By this time I had a two-year-old son and a daughter due in a few weeks. This was the first of many times that I had a job transition because of standing up for what I believed in. The move to P&G definitely was a step up.

---

[7]   Reid was also on my MS thesis committee.

Procter & Gamble

At Procter & Gamble (P&G) I had a great early job. I learned a lot. I was well treated and respected by my management and my colleagues. I had an almost unbelievable amount of freedom and discretion to do my varied jobs. At a relatively young age I had a great deal of responsibility, authority, a significant budget, and several persons reporting to me.

At P&G I followed the progression of computer technologies, now called information technology or IT that I observed while at WSU. The progression at this time included: two generations of computers, going from punched cards and tape to disk storage: the succession from card-to-card data transmission, through tape-to-tape, and finally computer-to-computer data transmission. Multi-processing, character-oriented terminals, and online processing were just beginning when I left. I had two great boss/mentors at P&G: Jack who nurtured my creative and technical skills and Bob who furthered my managerial skills. But never the less I encountered technical distance, trying my limited patience, which, however, was not as limited as my Father's. DPS's decision-making managers often did not understand the ins and outs of computing—nor did they understand the nature of the programmer's trade.

Many interesting assignments came my way at P&G. I made improvements in the teaching of the introductory programming course including techniques that I was told were impossible. I implemented important computing innovations for the firm: implementing code relocation on a machine without index registers—which, again, I was told was not possible. I loaded programs into memory without utilizing a memory buffer—enabling larger programs. The dichotomy between technical computing and corporate production computing provided opportunities to innovate as well as compounding technical distance. Corporate commercial production took precedence over the development of programs and the running of technical computing jobs. I have said, somewhat tongue in cheek, "I did not know that computers ran during the day," for several years after I went into computing." I often had to come in during the middle of the night in order to obtain computer time to test my programs. But I yet was expected back at my desk the next morning at the regular starting time.

I improved P&G's technical division's access to computing capabilities while "Manager, Winton Hill Technical Center Regional

Data Center," the longest title in the company. The Winton Hill Data Center provided nearly immediate turnaround for engineering, statistical, and scientific computing. Often users were allowed hands-on access to the console—that was anathema to the corporate data processing culture.

At Winton Hill we installed P&G's first time-sharing computer operation utilizing the time slicing process control computing capabilities of the IBM 1800 computer. A typewriter terminal was set up in a conference room adjacent to the computer center and several statistical and engineering programs were modified to operate in the time-shared environment. At the time several divisions were using a remote dial-in time-sharing service provided by GE.

But in many ways the job seemed stifling. I knew almost precisely what I would be making from year to year. P&G's personnel management was based upon the maximum developmental potential or MDP, which, in my judgment, tended to pigeonhole people—and I felt pigeonholed. I wanted what I called an online wallet—pay that reflected more directly my performance—good or bad. The chance to go out on my own and form General Computer Services Corporation (GCSC) was too tempting to refuse. Several times in subsequent years, after the GCSC blowup and after being fired from Billboard, I thought about going back to P&G (that is, if they would take me). But I did not want to be pigeonholed again and thus such thoughts did not go very far. And each time that I was fired I eventually landed on my feet with an even more rewarding job.

P&G And Managed News

When I first wrote this I read that Apple Computer had pulled from their stores and web site all the books from the publisher who issued the unapproved biography of Steve Jobs. But I first became very aware of the managed news phenomenon long ago while working at P&G. I attribute this to P&G being a very large advertiser that the press did not want to alienate.

The first instance happened during programming class. The Sunday after our first week of class a very small piece appeared on an obscure inner page of the *Cincinnati Enquirer* regarding one of the members of our programming class – he had robbed a neighborhood savings and loan. He was not in class on Monday or thereafter—nothing was ever said and I could find no more news reports regarding the robbery.

After being transferred to Winton Hill Technical Center, I encountered another instance. One Saturday morning, when I went to my office I parked in the front visitors lot—since it was Saturday and the offices were officially closed. In the middle of the parking lot there was a significant pool of blood. I was curious but went on about my business.

When I came out to my car later that day the parking lot had been scrubbed clean—one could eat off of it. I found out on Monday via the grapevine that as one of the secretaries came out to the parking lot the preceding Friday night—her boyfriend was waiting for her and shot her dead on the spot.

Nothing at all ever appeared in a Cincinnati—or any other that I know of —newspaper regarding this incident! This lack of reporting was very suspicious, given the sensational nature of such an occurrence.

Another experience with "managed news" was when I lived in Estes Park, our local paper, which publishes "all" letters to the editor did not publish the letter that a tennis colleague and I wrote about gas-price gouging in our community. The price of gas where we lived in the mountains was up to 52 cents more per gallon than a mere 20 miles away on the plains.

My Offices At Winton Hill

My office in the original data center at Winton Hill was enormous—several hundred square feet. But I was hardly ever there as my job was a hands-on job. I belonged in the machine room or at client sights helping them use the data center. I did have a large black board that was helpful for brainstorming and design sessions. But most of the space was wasted.

Since I worked long hours and occasional weekends, from time-to-time I would take our young children to the data center on Saturdays. They loved to watch the lights blinking on the computer and to draw on the blackboard. One Saturday I did not erase the blackboard after they had drawn on it. When I came to work on Monday, the building manager accosted me about my messy blackboard. "What would people think if they saw that? What do you think we are running here? A kindergarten? This is a professional installation." I was dumbfounded and erased the blackboard. "Where was he on Saturday?" I thought to my self. I understand that businesses are much more family friendly today.

In the new data center I designed the manager's office to hold a desk and chair, a conference table with two or three chairs and a blackboard—all of 97 square feet. Not much for stature—but perfect for getting the job done. This provided enough space for confidential meetings with employees and provided maximum space for the computer and auxiliary equipment.

Even though in the original data center I had a large office, it and the technical center had a considerable limitation—offices and labs were non-smoking areas and we all smoked. So starting shortly after 8:30 am our programming and writing projects would migrate to the adjacent lunchroom where smoking was allowed. We would start with our notebook and coding pad, and then we would go back for a manual, then a computer printout, etc. At lunchtime, which, because of staggered starting times within the technical center, began at 11:15, we would have to haul all our stuff back to our office. After lunch the process would be repeated until quitting time. The office-smoking ban did have one benefit. Bob, my boss downtown smoked and thus infrequently came to Winton Hill.

General Computer Services Corporation

I left P&G in 1968. With four other principals, including one from P&G, we formed General Computer Services Corporation (GCSC) with a plan to become the General Motors of Computing. GCSC was headquartered in Middletown, Ohio, the home of Armco Steel, which had employed several of the principals, and was our first customer. The driving force behind this move was to obtain what I called, "an online wallet." Remuneration at P&G was all too predictable and somewhat limited. I wanted my rewards to be more directly tied to my efforts and talents. This again turned out to be a step up.

GCSC was the right thing to do at the time and I am really glad that I did it. But once was enough. I was uniquely qualified technically for the systems and programming and project management jobs that I was called upon to do. At GCSC I really obtained my online wallet making good money, but occasionally not getting paid for long stretches of time.

Technology continued to progress, character-oriented terminals, online processing, multi-programming came into their own, yet the punched card hung on. During the later GCSC years, I was the chief architect and project manager of the System for Planning Electrical Construction (SPEC), which was done for P&G's engineering division. SPEC's champion, Jim, was an important figure in my life both personally and technically. Jim's emphasis was on "getting the job done." If you told Jim that something could not be done his mantra was, "Who is your boss?" SPEC is presented in detail in chapter 10.

Even at GCSC, where I was Executive Vice President and later President, I encountered technical distance, which caused me to chafe. Clients were frequently unaware of the ramifications of technology trade offs. My colleagues and board of directors were often not as technically knowledgeable as I. My technical skills far out weighed my political savvy and persuasive powers. I had to work through other people—so being in charge was not fully enough.

Unfortunately, in 1976 I was ousted from GCSC in a bitter boardroom coup due to personality and ethics related clashes. This coup eventually led to the demise of GCSC and its successors. A very big question is where would I be now if the company had stayed together and we had executed the SPEC contract with P&G and the McAuto division of McDonald Douglas Aircraft? I continue to think that that operation could have been really big. Another Microsoft or

Google? The mutineers may have really blown it with their boardroom coup. The GCSC saga is presented in chapters 8 and 9.

Independent, Thoman Software, Billboard

The next stop on my computing journey was with Thoman Software established by Dick Thoman a former P&G colleague— and as Manager of Systems and Programming (S&P) for Billboard Publications bracketed by two stints as an independent IT professional. Dick, an Olympic swimmer, was the best systems designer and programmer I have known. He was notorious for writing his programs in ink and for his squeaky shoes. His early death was a loss to the profession as well as to his family.

I never chose to be self-employed—which I frequently call "self-unemployed" but it had some upsides as well as downsides. At times I made a great deal of money—but then the taxes were very high (over 93% as I remember with federal, state, city and self-employed social security combined). The demands of the clients were paramount and more than once I missed a party at my own home.

Some of the work was interesting—but frankly, a great deal of it was maintenance programming, which was generally due to inflexible computer systems or being called in to rectify screw ups by a client's staff. One reason for going into university teaching was to have a financial base for consulting and design. I wanted to be in on projects from the beginning so that they would be done right. I also wanted to help technical personnel to be professional and to help managers understand technology. The eight-year quest for the PhD killed my contacts and I did not accomplished that goal.

The inflexible computer system phenomenon was present when I was Systems & Programming (S&P) manager for Billboard. Maintenance programming—more properly fire fighting was generally the order of the day. Technical distance was rampant. I was attempting to provide information technology support for this company managed by marketing types who had no knowledge of technology and, furthermore, wanted none. My non-political responses to their technical distance led to my being fired. (And then hired back as an independent contractor.) My ousting from Billboard seemed like a step down at the beginning but, in the long run, it was actually another step up.

Thoman Software had many interesting and original projects although there was also fire fighting and handholding. Thoman Software was very progressive and often ahead of its time and was on the cusp of developing flexible computer systems. When we thought we had perfected the design we asked the question: "What are the next three things the client is likely to want to do that are not specifically covered in the design? And does our design handle that?"

It was during this time that the technology really bloomed: database management systems, formatted screens (now called Graphical User Interfaces or GUIs)—punched cards were relegated to note taking. It was during this time that the first PCs came to be. I built my first PC from a Heathkit in 1982. The tension between the rapid technological innovation and organizational inertia often made for slow technology adoption, as managers were most comfortable with what they knew. Technical distance became more of a problem as technology progressed, leading to the concept of flexible systems. In some ways, flexible systems exist to save bad management from itself. Flexible systems represent a high degree of technical sophistication and therefore can cause even more technical distance. In another way flexible systems design is an antidote (maybe the ultimate antidote?) to technical distance. If this "logic" appears to be circular—it's because it is!

Xavier University

As an independent consultant, having a flexible schedule, I drifted into part time adjunct teaching at several proprietary schools, Xavier University, and a branch campus of the University of Cincinnati. I was drawn to teaching for several reasons. 1) I thought that I had real world experience knowledge and abilities to share. In so doing I could help bridge the gap between technologists and mangers, thus reducing technical distance. 2) I truly enjoyed the teaching that I had done at P&G and at GCSC. 3) As one of my colleagues said, "Bruce, there are four good reasons for teaching: May, June, July, and August!" But for years I could not make the switch. I would have to take a large drop in remuneration. Most teaching positions available to me were temporary sabbatical replacements and the like. So by opportunistically taking teaching assignments at proprietary schools I was able to "drift" into adjunct part-time teaching. When I did take the full-time position at

Xavier it was at one-fourth of what I had previously been earning. Now that the kids were out of college and "off of the payroll" and my wife had a long-term stable position, I felt free to take the leap.

In 1982 Xavier hired me as a full-time Assistant Professor of Information and Decision Sciences. Tenure and increase in rank were dependent upon acquiring a PhD. I was awarded tenure just days before my terminal contract expired and I became an associate professor the following year.

Mistakenly I thought that my real world experience, insight, and knowledge would stand me in good stead. Not so! They worked against me causing a great deal of turmoil. Now I thought that I would have a chance to address technical distance by teaching managers about technology and technologists about the demands of management. I had hoped to become a cultural translator between the worlds of technology and management. While I gave it a serious go, there is no real evidence that I succeeded in helping to bridge the gap. I choose not to believe that my efforts (and this phase of my career) were a failure. I had many MBA students who accomplished outstanding money saving IT projects for their employers. I actually learned a number of important and valuable lessons, such as perseverance and a modicum of patience in dealing with adversity. I also learned that student learned best when I taught least. Both my students and I really thrived in the project based, experiential courses or phases of courses.

In 1990, with my colleague Marcia, I published a COBOL programming textbook[8], which I planned to be an inroad to enlightened programming and to help overcome technical distance from the technical side. Technical distance frustrated this effort, from the reviewers' reaction to the publisher's failure to promote the book. But it did allow me to obtain tenure and become an associate professor.

The seventeen years at Xavier, ending in 1998, was my longest time in one job. I truly enjoyed the students. But, like elsewhere, the administration/the management took a lot of fun out of the job. There was way too much administrivia, too much paper work, not enough understanding of the challenges of teaching—technical distance actually. I had experienced technical distance in large Fortune 500 firms, in small firms (where I was a principle in one), and now in

---

[8]   *Professional Programming in COBOL.*

academia. I know very few active or retired faculty members who are/were not bummed out by the politics and bureaucracy. I miss the teaching and the students but not the administrivia. Over all I am glad to be out of the fray.

At this time my colleague Walt and I began serious exploration of the theories and concept behind Flexible Systems – planning to publish a book on the subject. My retirement from Xavier placed that project on hold until 2005. Sadly, I did not achieve the rank of full professor due to the eight-year quest for the PhD, the demands of teaching, hassles with the administration, and thwarted attempts at publishing.

While at Xavier "always online" to the Internet and email from the office became possible. Windows became the platform or operating system of choice for Intel-based computers. Desktop computers became much more powerful and much more common.

Doctor Of Philosophy

In order to obtain tenure, which was required to keep my position at Xavier, I needed a doctor of philosophy degree a PhD in a related subject. In 1982, at the age of 46, I went back to school. This time at the nearby University of Cincinnati (UC) where I had taken a few courses at while an adjunct, to earn my PhD.

When I started at Xavier "all I had" was a BS and MS in Civil Engineering. I did not have the "terminal" degree required for tenure—a PhD. Since I was switching careers from doing to teaching, I thought a doctorate in education would be appropriate. But—it would not be. Education degrees are looked down upon in most of academia. I would have to obtain a PhD in a "related" field. I chose operations management (OM) and organizational behavior (OB)—eventually adding information technology (IT) for my minor, as I could not conform to the way of thinking of the OB faculty. Being a middle-aged successful professional with a large ego made the PhD process even harder than it normally is.

After many struggles and dead ends I was able to obtain my degree at the age of 54 by defending my dissertation, on technical distance in April 1990 after 8 long years. I received my PhD one month before my terminal contract at Xavier was due to expire, after which I would have been out of a job—again. I obtained an MBA along the way. Technical distance continued to rear its ugly head during my PhD studies. As a result, I chose the topic of technical distance for my PhD thesis research. My research showed that technical knowledge leads to better decisions.

My PhD was my fourth degree. I had not attended graduation ceremonies for my first three degrees. But I almost caught up here as I attended the business college ceremonies, the departmental hooding, and the all university graduation.

Retirement

Retirement is special. It does not pay well—but neither did teaching. I have kept my hand in the IT field by writing, reading, and learning JAVA, Sentences, and other packages.

I have often said, "I don't mind working. I just mind having to." So now I work when I want to at my own pace and it is fun and keeps my mind (and fingers) active. I am enjoying retirement so much that I often tell my friends, "Retirement is vastly UNDERATED."

As remembrances of my career, I have had hanging on my office wall from time to time the following some of which are shown in later chapters.

- A plague-mounted cassette I/O circuit board.

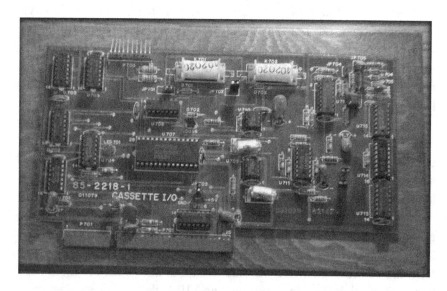

- "The Essence of Communication" the mental health collage I made during the tense days of the SPEC project. (SPEC chapter 10).

- A plaque upon which I had mounted seven slide rules: some mine, some my Dad's, and some my father-in-law's—we all were engineers (and engineering students) in the days when slide rules were our computers.

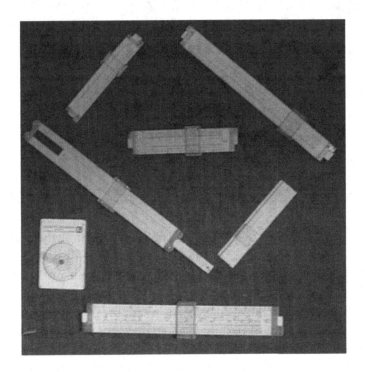

- A plaque with my four bronzed degree certificates: BS and MS in Civil Engineering, MBA and PhD in Operations Management, Information Systems, and Organizational Behavior

I liked and still like to solve problems, primarily technical problems. But there is a tension between technical and human problems. Almost every enterprise today has a significant "technical" component. Yet, many managers do not understand technology. Even, or maybe specially, business schools, in my experience, shun technology. For the most part, technology behaves rationally (basically consistently) and humans irrationally (basically inconsistently). Thus I have had more success with technological problems than with people problems.

Our 2005 book on designing flexible computer system was in a way a culmination of my technical distance inflexible computer systems journey.

These reminisces are just that—reminisces. They are based on recollections—some over 60-years old. While the details may not always be exact—any errors or biases do not change their essential nature. In fact, I have told many of these stories both in oral and written form over the years. Thus these recollections are often not actually as old as they would otherwise seem. The telling may have reinforced the "real" story or embellished it—we will likely never know.

This reminds me of a great story. In the spring of 1996, I attended the Cincinnati Red's baseball fantasy camp in Orlando and Plant City, Florida. One evening before supper several of the retired Major Leaguers were answering questions from the campers about the game and their careers over a few beers and popcorn. Near the end of the session several of the players' wives showed up to go to join them for supper. One of the campers turned to the wives and asked, "Don't you ladies ever get tired of hearing these same stories year after year?" To this one of the wives replied with a straight face "No. They are not the same stories." In turn, one of the retired players piped up and added, "Yea, I seems that the longer ago we played, the better we were!" I hope that has not happened to my stories.

Engineering In Training Exam

In fact here is an example of almost the opposite of the story recounted above. With my BS in Civil Engineering I was eligible to take the Engineer in Training (EIT) exam as the first step toward becoming a professional engineer. Normally the exam was only given in the spring and I graduated in February. Though intervention by our department chair, another February graduate and I were given the exam under special circumstances.

We both felt that we did really well on the exam—but neither of us passed. During the exam, I went so far as to derive an important formula relating to structural stability so that I could solve one of the problems – but to no avail. I distinctly remember not passing the exam!

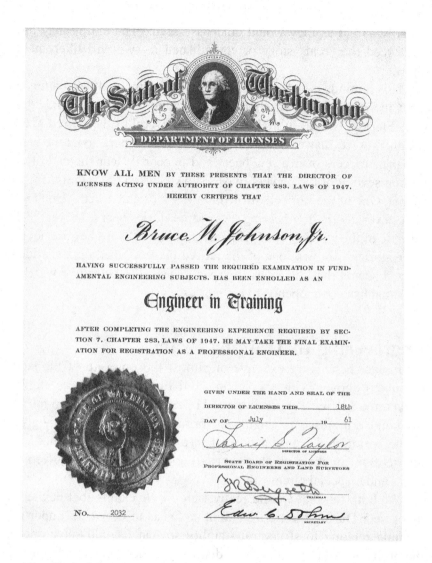

Grading of the normal springtime exam was passed around with a different professional engineer grading each question. However, given that there were only two of us who took the exam, the department felt that one person did all the grading. They also felt that they knew whom it was and that he was a really hard grader.

As I was never really in engineering per se I did not retake the EIT or the actual professional exam.

Some how my memory failed me because in May 2005, while cleaning out my files I found my EIT certificate, shown here, issued July 18, 1961.

Job Transitions (Driving Forces)

In retrospect it is interesting to look back at my job transitions and see what the nature or driving force for each was.

- From WSU, Division of Industrial research to P&G out of displeasure at not having the value of my Masters Degree recognized with a commensurate raise.
- From P&G to GCSC—the on line wallet and the chance to make big bucks.
- From GCSC to self-employed—the illegal boardroom coup and my unwillingness to just be an employee.
- From self-employed to Thoman Software—more security and more interesting work.
- From Thoman Software to Billboard—an easy transition to a client and what appeared to be an important position.
- From Billboard back to self-employed—a matter of speaking out too vigorously regarding untenable situations.
- From self-employed along with part time teaching to Xavier presented a culmination of a life-long desire to teach and write.
- Then from Xavier to retirement —it was time to climb out of the trenches (at least partly).

My Most Significant Accomplishment(s)

My most significant accomplishment was System for Planning Electrical Construction (SPEC). My part of SPEC was completed in 1976. Since this was many years ago. I find this somewhat sad. SPEC was a monumental system that saved P&G and others a great deal of time and money. I was uniquely qualified to manage, design, and implement the project and in the process to overcome significant technical, managerial, and political roadblocks. But the question is, what have I done for encores?

Hopefully our 2005 (seven years after retiring) book *Flexible Software Design: Systems Development for Changing Requirements,* will impact the IT world so that I may be able to look at it as at least my second most significant accomplishment. This was my second book. My first book *Professional Programming in COBOL* was a significant accomplishment as, while it was not well promoted by the publisher Prentice Hall and did not sell well, it was a basis for my achieving tenure and promotion to associate professor.

Particularly under the circumstances achieving a PhD so late in life was also a significant accomplishment—but it was not an end in itself. Certainly relocation without index registers; scatter read and the locator librarian were significant accomplishments—particularly for so early in my career.

Promotion to full processor was a significant accomplishment that I did not achieve. The eight-year struggle for the PhD caused my scholarship to dry up and it did not really get going again until after I retired. Professor emeriti would have been even better but even if my accomplishments were recognized politics would prevent such a occurrence.

Common Threads

Across these various employers and types of jobs there have been several common threads including technical distance and bureaucracy. A sample of others follows.

Two rights make a wrong.

When people are conscientious and diligent—but do not communicate adequately two rights can make a wrong.

Unwillingness to prototype or to accept partial results.

Customers of IT systems generally don't know what they want until they (almost?) see it. Then they want it different. But they are often unwilling to try the system before it is "finished." In other words they are not willing to prototype or to critically use and review partial results.

Failure of parallels

Frequently computer system parallels fail to accomplish their purpose in cutting over to a new system. Several instances and possible reasons for these failures are reported as they occurred during my careers.

Beating up on PhD students

From what I hear via the grape vine things have not changed much since I was a PhD student. Since today's graduate faculty was persecuted when they were students and they can't go back and "get even" with the faculty that persecuted them, they persecute their students and pass it on. This is a trend that should be stopped.

Outstanding Systems/Programs

College
-Backwater curve
-Dimensionless unit hydrograph
-Intercity Travel Desire Factor
-Transmission line sag curves

P&G
-Relocation w/o index registers
-Moore algorithm
-Scatter read (implementation)
-Winton Hill interactive terminal and accounting system
-1620 to 1800 conversion?

GCSC
-4 to zero/DMIOS (1401 to 1440)
-Technical Recruiting System
-Personal Records System
-System for Planning Electrical Construction Independent
-(Calling Answering Listening Linking) CALL

About This Work

As IT (information technology) developed from the plug board, mainframe computer, and punched cards to the Internet with streaming video and beyond, I was there—experiencing the trials, tribulations, the exultations, the highs and the lows. I saw it happen in big corporations, small companies, consulting firms, as an entrepreneur, in a research university, in a teaching university, and as an independent consultant and author. I experienced the development of the IT field in the role of programmer, system designer and developer, data base designer and developer, employee, manager, consultant, educator, author, and user.

This work presents an **historical perspective** in parallel with the **human drama**, as I saw the field of IT evolve, as problems were created and solved with often-elegant solutions.

As the field developed the human drama personified by **technical distance** between the IT professional with the understanding and knowledge of the technology and the leaders and managers with the authority to make technological decisions unfolded, I was there. This unfolding is a major theme of the book and my career. Some of the humans consist of managers, who failed to seek advice from and/or listen to their technologists. By not understanding technology or not taking technical advice these managers made bad decisions. Other players are technicians who could not or would not explain technology to their managers so that they could make intelligent decisions. The finger points both ways. I believed that university teaching could provide an anecdote to technical distance and I experienced eight years in the quest of the required PhD—but there is little or no evidence that the anecdote took.

While the language of this work is geared toward the lay reader, the young IT professional who is interested in the history, issues and problems of her field is the **primary audience**. First hand experience of the IT evolution is not an option for today's IT professional, or layperson for that matter. Thus the rich anecdotes describing early computers, programming practices, management practices, and other aspects of the developed field are the only way to experience, albeit vicariously, the early days—the supposedly "golden era" of computing—the progression from data processing, to information systems, to information technology, to everything technology.

This work points out that in many instances **technology may not have progressed as far or as fast as might be thought** and some cases may have even taken a step or two backwards. As Shakespeare's Horatio said to Petronius, "Is there really anything new under the sun?" For example, IT has become over enamored with fancy GUIs (Graphical User Interfaces), flashy screens and the like at the expense of data—its accuracy, its integrity, its safety, and its security. Hence CRUD!

During my careers I encountered bosses, colleagues, and, unfortunately, nemeses. The stories of their influences and interactions are described in and around the events in which they participated. Other stories include how, in some ways, I was often ahead of the technology curve—doing things with computers that others said could not be done.

In addition to the above these reminises also include my reflections on happenings along the way together with my analysis of common threadssituations that happened in many venues and appeared to be location, and maybe even situation independent. I analyze my career and offer advice to those who follow—advice I often did not take — but should have.

Technical distance deserves a little more treatment here. If one is tuned in one can detect signs of technical distance all around. When this distance, often a gulf is not bridged bad decisions and courses of action often resultto wit the Challenger explosion January 28, 1986. Technical distance was at work at P&G when programmers could not get adequate key punching support. It was evident at Billboard Publications when the wrong consultant's advice was followed.

Technical distance has followed me all the days of my careers. It is one of the reasons that I went into academia. I wanted to improve the technical skills of the technologists and the managerial skills, including understanding of technology, of managers.

Many of today's managers are lawyers not engineers. MBA programs are often devoid of the necessary understanding of technology. Because the value of understanding technology is often not made clear to today's students and managers, students and managers at all levels tend to lack the ambition and interest in technical subjects to become qualified to make decisions regarding them.

One of the outcomes of technical distance is inflexible computer systems. When a computer system is not flexible, inflexible—its keepers say, "Sorry Sir/Madam we cannot do that. The computer system has not kept up with our business changes and there is no way for us to do that." When a computer system is flexible they say, "Yes Mam, we can do that." Or better yet, "Yes you can do that yourself."

The dominant activity during the latter stages of my careers and during retirement has been in depth research regarding the design and implementation of flexible computer systems. In 2005 my colleagues and I published a book on this subject.

Organization Of The Book

In early drafts of these reminisces the material was organized chronologically, which in the judgment of some caused excess material to be presented. A memoir writing class convinced me that the topical presentation would be better than chronological.

The following seven chapters are organized by subject matter as follows:

Chapter

1 Insight/Ingenuity into Computer Software Operation
2 Curmudgeon
3 CRUDmudgeon
4 Bruce has a PhD
5 Technical Distance
6 (In)Flexible Computer Systems
7 Teaching Technology

The material covered in each of the above chapters should be self-explanatory. I have done my best to place material under the most appropriate heading, but often the same material impinges on more than one topic, which caused some duplication. But I trust that I have kept duplication to a minimum.

The next three chapters:

8 The Rise and Fall of General Computer Services Corporation (GCSC)
9 GCSC Days and Nights
10 System for Planning Electrical Construction

Focus on two seminal events in my careers: The Rise and Fall of General Computer Services Corporation (GCSC) and the multi year tense project called System for Planning Electrical Construction or SPEC.

Finally the last chapter
11 Some Advice

Draws conclusions and lesson from my adventures in Information Technology and its predecessors.

Along the way I have had many insights into IT and done many innovative things, which are covered in the next chapter.

Chapter Bibliography
Johnson, Bruce, Walter W. Woolfolk, Robert Miller, Cindy Johnson 2005: *Flexible Software Design: Systems Development for Changing Requirements,* Auerbach Publications.

Zinsser 2006: *On Writing Well: The Classic Guide to Writing Non Fiction—30th Anniversary Edition*, William Zinsser, Collins 2006.

Time Line
Several readers of this work, who were not fully IT literate suggested that a time line of important/representative IT events would be helpful. To that end a time line is furnished below.

YEAR	EVENT
1890	Punched Card
1944	First Electro Mechanical Computer
1945	Magnetic Tape (First medium to allow searching)
1946	First Digital Computer
1950-53	Korean War
1951	First Mass Produced Computer (Thomas Watson: "The world will only need 5 computers.")
1953	IBM 650 computer

1954	FORTRAN FORmula TRANslator ("First" higher level language)
1954	Bruce starts college uses the IBM 650
1954	IBM 705 computer
1955-1975	Vietnam War
1959	Bruce obtains Bachelor of Science in Civil Engineering
1959	IBM 1401 computer
1961	COBOL (COmmon Business Oriented Language)
1961	IBM 7080 computer
1962	Bruce starts as programmer/analyst at Procter & Gamble (P&G) in Downtown Cincinnati with Master of Science in Civil Engineering
1964	IBM System 360
1964	PL/I (Programming Language One)
1968	Bruce leaves P&G and helps form General Computer Services Corporation (GCSC)
1971	Nixon's Wage Freeze
1976	GCSC blows up and Bruce becomes self employed independent data processor
1978	Bruce with Thoman Software and then Billboard Publications
1979	Fired from Billboard and becomes self employed independent data processor AGAIN
1980s	CD, VCR, cable become common
1982	Accepts position with Xavier University as assistant professor of information and decision sciences, starts work toward PhD
1990	Obtains PhD degree and awarded tenure, promoted to Associate Professor the next year
1990	Bruce Coauthors with Marcia Ruwe *Professional Programming in COBOL*
1993	World wide web
1998	Retires from Xavier after sabbatical
2000s	Cell phones become common

2001	9/11
2005	Bruce coauthors *Flexible Software Design* with Woolfolk, Miller, & Johnson
2015-16	Bruce publishes *My Years in the Information Technology Trenches From Data Processing to Information Technology: Reminisces of a CRUDmudgeon*

CHAPTER 1
INSIGHT/INGENUITY INTO COMPUTER HARDWARE & SOFTWARE OPERATION

Introduction

Somehow I gained or just had an innate understanding of computers and how to program them. As a result of this I was able to use ingenuity to accomplish some insightful and innovative results with computers. Often I was "ahead of the times," or "ahead of the information technology curve."

While today these accomplishment may not seem like much, remember when these were done there were no spreadsheets, no word processors, no disk drives, no personal computers, no Internet.

East High Advanced Math Class

Math came easily to me. In high school at Woodstock in India and Smiley Junior High in Denver my math interest and ability was way head of my interest and ability in other subjects. In my last semester at East Denver High, I took an advanced math class in which we spent the entire semester discovering integral calculus. We drew laborious graphs, charts, and did minute calculations and literally during the last week we divined the formula for integrating the area under a curve. Wow!

In college this material was covered in a matter of days—but calculus DNA, which causes so much trouble for many, was spliced into my genes.

Basic Computer Literacy

In the first semester of my senior year at Washington State University I took the course "Theory of Digital Computers." After this I was hooked on computers. I learned computers from the ground up—starting with machine language programming on the IBM 650. One of our assignments was to write a program to calculate square roots. Once the square root routine was working we converted it into a subroutine and when that worked correctly we optimized its performance. It was amazing to observe the effect of optimization. The subroutine ran about 25 times faster after the optimization than it ran before. Writing subroutines and/or optimization are so automatic today that programmers hardly ever think about it—or even know what it is! But back then it was an integral part of the programming task.

The computer used was the IBM 650—its memory, rather than magnetic core or flash semi conductor memory as in today's computers, was a rotating magnetic drum. The machine instructions, which had four parts: an operation code, two data addresses, and the address of the next instructions to be executed, and data were stored on the rotating drum. While an instruction was fetched from the drum and executed, the drum was rotating. When the instruction execution was finished, the next instruction was fetched. In the absence of optimization there would be an average delay of one half a drum revolution before the next instruction could be fetched for execution.

The drum had two thousand ten digit memory locations. These were arranged in 40 columns of 50 rows. Thus there were 40 locations that could be accessed at the same time in the revolution. So the process of optimization involved knowing how long, in terms rows of revolution, each instruction required and then placing the next instruction in column one at the appropriate row. If that location had already been assigned then column two and so on. As each instruction was completed the next instruction would be right under the read head and could be fetched with minimal rotational delay—thus speeding up the computing by up to one half a rotation or 25 times.

What Exactly Is Computer Programming: Then And Now?

What exactly is computer programming all about? How has it changed during the course of my careers and into my retirement?

Computer programming is, and always was, and I expect always will be, an exacting, detailed, often tedious, and occasionally exhilarating endeavor. I have likened developing computer programs to hitting one's self over the head with a hammer—it feels so good when you stop. The stopping part, the exhilarating part, is getting your program to work the way it's intended. Unlike children, and even adults, computers do EXACTLY as they are told. Every step, every eventuality, intended or not, has to be accounted (programmed) for so that the computer (program) does not produce, untoward —or dangerous results.

Next to teaching, computer programming is the ultimate form of creativity. And like teaching, computer programming requires a confident ego. Computer programs can take an infinite number of forms for any given task. Choosing the appropriate form and implementing it is truly a creative challenge. The ability to acknowledge along the way that one is going down a wrong track and to turn back and start over requires confidence in ones ability. I often said that, "I am proudest of code that I threw away. It is not around to haunt me."

The nature of computer programming is exemplified by the following story: When I worked for Procter & Gamble (P&G) as a programmer I often rode the bus to and from work. A neighbor's attractive sister occasionally rode the same bus. One time we sat next to each other and while talking she asked me, "What do you do for a living?" I replied, "I am a computer programmer with P&G." She then looked admiringly at me and appearing impressed asked another question, "Do you ever make errors?" Grinning I replied, "Oh, about 35 on a good day!" The admiring look immediately disappeared.

During my years in the IT field, some aspects have changed dramatically—some have not. The human adventure of technical problem solving remains constant. Here is an example of how the steps in a process (in this case program development) have not changed but their nature is vastly different and much more efficient and effective. But the technical distance and managerial ineffectiveness presented unfortunately still exist.

"Oh, I see the problem," I say to myself." I have just finished entering the initial version of my routine to update the bill of materials structure (BOM)[9] using the source code editor in my Integrated Development Environment (IDE[10]). But it does not work as I intended: it went into an endless loop. Using the IDE, I force the program to stop using a break point[11]. After I studying my code on the screen for some time, I say to myself, "I need another check right here to avoid an endless cycle."

So to avoid the endless cycle, I add three lines of code, which are checked for correct syntax as I enter them. After they are entered and checked I click RUN. The program chugs away for a few seconds and yes the endless cycle is gone. But, now I have what is called a data exception. The data as it exists does not conform to the program/computer expectations. After a few moments of inspection, I mumble, "Damn the variable HASH-KEY was supposed to be declared as floating point." With a click of the mouse and a few keystrokes HASH-KEY is now a floating-point variable. I again click RUN and the program goes to normal end-of-job and thus passes this initial test and is ready for more extensive testing before I add the next feature. This is all accomplished in an hour or so in my home office on my personal computer using an IDE with the JAVA programming language.

As I test further, and all goes well, I contemplate entering code for the next feature. I think back to my initial programming days in the early 60's. What a difference! Back then my first step in coding was to hand print the instructions on coding sheets for the language being used such as Autocoder, COBOL, or PL/I. When that was done I sent the sheets off to the keypunch section and waited, often for a day or more, while they were punched into cards. (See chapter 9 for a picture of an 80-column punch card.)

---

[9]   An example of a bill of materials (BOM): An auto has 4 wheels; each wheel has a tire, rim, bolts, and hubcap that belong to the wheel, which belongs to the auto. A BOM represents a hierarchy of items, which makes it a useful structure for organization charts and like constructs.

[10]   An integrated development environment: A computer system that incudes modules to enter source code and check its syntax, convert the code to an executable form and to execute it under operator control so as to easily check for its correctness.

[11]   A means of stopping a program during its execution in order to examine intermediate results.

When the cards came back from keypunch I had to check them carefully for accuracy and interpretation of my printing. The keypunch operators were trained to efficiently and effectively enter production data, such as orders, payroll hours, and shareholder records—but not program code; thus the results were often far from perfect, so frequently corrections needed to be made to my program deck. Then I had two choices: either develop another set of coding sheets with the corrections and submit them to the keypunch section and repeat the cycle or try to find a keypunch somewhere and make the corrections myself.

Once the deck passed my inspection—often after a week or more, I filled out a job card, and attached it to my program deck with a rubber band and dropped it off at the job-submission window, to be compiled, the next step in the program development process. The code that I had written and had keypunched was not in a language that the computer could "understand." Since the language that the computer understands called machine code or object code is very tedious and error prone for humans to use, higher-level languages, such as FORmula TRANslation (FORTRAN) or COmmon Business Orientated Language (COBOL) have been developed. Humans can more easily and accurately produce computer programs in these languages. To bridge this gap. programs (compilers) have been written to convert the higher level code to machine instructions. This, of course, adds another step in the process of program development.

And now another wait while my program is compiled: if I was lucky it was only overnight. Back then we often said, "Computers, mainframes—big hunks of iron, only ran at night." The truth is that they generally ran around the clock—but "production" such as: orders, payroll, shareholder dividend check printing had the highest priority. Program development: compiles and testing were run if and when the production was finished—often late at night if at all.

When my job came back, along with my original deck of cards was a printout reporting on the results of my compile run with information about any syntax errors in the source code. The instructions containing these syntax errors had to be replaced with corrected syntax, which meant another round of coding sheet preparation and subsequent punching either by going back into the keypunch queue or hunting down a vacant keypunch and doing it myself.

When no syntax errors were encountered, after one or more resubmissions of the compilation job, an object deck of machine-readable code was produced. The program was now ready for testing. During this process of obtaining a clean compile test data had been acquired or prepared —often again by keypunching, this time from 80-column data sheets.

The object deck with an appropriate job card along with data was then submitted to test the program's logic. This submission, again generally after a day or more, yielded a print out of the results of the test run, which included a memory print showing the contents of the computer's memory when the job terminated – either via normal end of job or due to some abnormal interruption.

If the results shown in the printout were not correct, the cause needed to be determined (the bug found) and corrected. Once the correction was made, another submission was required. This continued until, after extensive testing, the results were deemed correct. Then the program was placed into production.

When required, there was two means of making corrections. The most obvious was to change the source code, recompile, and resubmit the tests. However, as has been shown, compiles required a day or more. They also were expensive in terms of computer time. So an alternative was to patch the program by directly entering source code. To patch the program, the programmer recorded the source code change for an eventual recompile and then mentally compiled it into corresponding machine code and punched cards to load said machine code into the appropriate memory address. This was called a "patch."

Today the syntax is checked line-by-line as I key my JAVA program into my PC. The code is entered, in a few hours, with correct syntax. I then make several test runs changing my program and running the new version, reacting to logic errors, in a matter of minutes. This is all done in part of a morning; more than 60 years ago it would generally take several weeks. Another striking difference was that in the current case was that there was really no pressure and it took only a part of a day. Writing this program was basically part of a hobby – a demonstration program for a book that I was writing. Whereas way back then the pressure was intense to place programs into production so they could start earning money for the company– yet the various turn around delays and lack of support (technical distance) caused frustrating hold ups that could have easily been avoided.

One source of pressure was that programs in production were making money for the company. Programs under development were costing the company money in both salaries and computer time. In the case of our programming group there was additional pressure as we were developing system programs and tools. Our programs made it easier, quicker, and less costly for the commercial and technical programmers to develop their programs and to analyze their data. Some of these programs were compilers and early versions of IDEs or pre-IDEs.

One result of this pressure was that I often came in during the middle of the night to obtain test time or to observe one of my programs running. Because of the nature of our programs the remote testing described above was often inadequate to validate them. But given managements lack of understanding of the programming process (technical distance) I had no choice. Since programmers were "management," and thus exempt from the wage and hour laws we received no overtime pay or compensatory time off. And if I came in "late" the morning after was in during the middle of the night I was often reprimanded by the Powers-That-Be with "What will the secretaries think when they see you coming in late?" My response, which did not go over well with The Powers-That-Be, was "Where were the secretaries last night at two am?" This is just one example of how being outspoken caused me trouble and eventually caused me to be fired twice.

While the program development process described above was quite common in most programming shops back then, the culture at P&G exacerbated the situation.

Data Processing Systems (DPS as it was called then) management declared that, "programmers are not keypunch operators." At the same time they were oblivious to the fact that the keypunch operators were unable to reliably produce accurately keypunched programs. Nor were they fully aware of the nature of the programming task. Thus we programmers were stymied. We could not obtain reliable keying of our programs and there were too few keypunches available to us—even for just punching changes. We made repeated requests, including the famous P&G "one pager" report. We asked for a keypunch operator who was trained in and dedicated solely to keypunching programs and test data—to no avail. As an alternative, we requested that at least one keypunch machine be set aside for use by programmers and no one else. This also fell on deaf ears. Blind eyes? Even though keypunch machines cost around $100/month and programmers were about $1,000/month. Was this an example of technical distance, or was it just mismanagement? Either way, technical distance and (mis)management issues were responsible for much of the tension during my career.

It would have been so much more effective to have one or more keypunch operators trained to keypunch program code and and/or to have more keypunches for programmers to access. Many times, we tried to get management to install keypunches for programmer access but they said, "Programmers are not paid to keypunch!" Today that would be like saying "Programmers are not paid to sit at a PC and use the keyboard and mouse!" This is just one more early example of "technical distance." See chapter 5.

When keypunch services were not available and we could not get access to "normal" keypunches we would resort to 010 keypunches and red patches. The keypunches normally used were IBM 026/029 alphanumeric printing punches, which would punch the multiple holes for a character and print the character above the holes on the card. Printing the character above the holes was called interpreting. These were machines that one sat at while operating. A handy feature of the 026/029 was card duplication. There were two stations, a read and a write. Holes, representing data in the card read from the read station could be reproduced into the card in the write station. If a correction needed to be made then at the appropriate point the duplication could be interrupted and corrections could be punched directly into the card and the old card thrown away. This process alleviated the need to repunch the entire card.

The 010 was a little machine about the size of a breadbox, which sat on a desk or counter and punched one hole at a time and did not interpret. Not being able to see directly what had been punched and having to make multiple punches in the same column, since some symbols, such as letters and special characters required multiple punches further reduced the desirability of using the 010. Also there was no way to reproduce and if a correction required that a hole in a given column no longer be present, then a little red patch could be placed over the hole so that it would not be sensed during a subsequent read operation. But, occasionally the little red patch would come off and either causes an erroneous read or the card reader to jam —or both.

Word Processing

I used forms of word processing before there were formalized packages. At P&G we used punched cards and numbered lines as we did for programs. At Billboard we had a full-page online text editor, which we used to produce and maintain documents as well as computer programs. Neither of these had fancy formatting, spell checking, or other such features. But they both facilitated documentation creation and, more importantly, documentation maintenance – keeping documents current.

Conversion Of Transportation Program From 705 To 7080 Machine Language

One of the first projects that I worked on at P&G was to bring the 705-transportation problem up on the 7080. It should have been a snap given the upward compatibility of the 7080. But it was not. I struggled and struggled. There were several complications with the assignment. First there was no source code listing or source program card deck – only a well patched machine language object deck. Second what little documentation existed was a highly marked-up multi-generation Xerox copy that was hard to read and understand.

One night after work, in desperation, I took the well-worn multi-generational document home. With a scotch and soda, I studied it in excruciating detail. Low and behold I found a clue. Buried deep in the hard to read text was mention of console sense switch settings.

During the recent programming class we had been told over and over to never, to never, ever use the console sense switches. Options, when needed, were to be supplied by control cards or via data input. But this program was not written by a P&G programmer and was written long before our class.

The next day with fear and trembling (after all I was just recently out of programming class), I approached the operations manager and

9

requested permission to be at the computer console when a test of my transportation program was run. (Testing was done remotely with the programmer submitting a job and picking up the output and never going near the computer.) He reluctantly agreed after an impassioned discussionI was under the gun to get this working as the program was needed to recalculate freight rates due to a new warehouse alignment.

After a few tests setting the console switches based on my research from the night before —the program actually worked. Based upon my findings I modified the program with a few machine language patches so that it would read a control card and use it to choose processing options and thus bypass the console switches. After additional testing, I placed the program into production and the freight department began using the "new" transportation program to help them route their shipments.

Backwater Curve

Shortly after my undergraduate class, "Theory of Digital Computers" course I took a course in hydraulics. One of our major assignments was to calculate a backwater curve.

Contrary to popular opinion and "common sense," the water behind a dam is not level or at a uniform height. Due to energy dissipation, there is a slight upward curve from the dam to where the reservoir meets the stream or river that is dammed up.

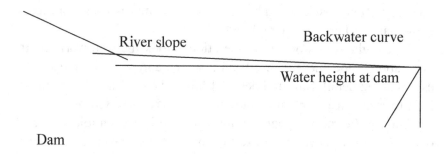

As shown in the above diagram, the water level meets the river flow at an elevation above the actual height of the dam. This can be very significant because while your house upstream from the dam may be at a higher elevation than the dam —it still may be flooded if it is below the level of the backwater curve.

Deriving the backwater curve is a relatively simple, but repetitious iterative operation where 1) each step uses the result of the previous step (and thus an error at any step affects all subsequent steps) and 2) the smaller the increment (going up stream from the dam) the more accurate the calculation. However smaller increments require more work and take longer —and when done manually introduce more opportunities for error. This makes deriving the backwater curve a tedious and error-prone operation when done manually.

Our backwater curve calculation was a major assignment – by and large my classmates spent 40 hours doing the tedious calculations by hand. I also spent 40 hours calculating my backwater curve—however I wrote a computer program using the IBM 650 to do the calculations.

The advantage to my approach was that the next backwater curve would have taken much less time. All I would have had to do was plug in the new data. The professor used my results as the answer key.

Dimensionless Unit Hydrograph

A useful tool for storm runoff estimation was (is?) the dimensionless unit hydrograph. This is because it is easier to predict rainfall than it is to predict flood flow. A unit hydrograph can be represented as the volume of water flowing by a given point plotted against time for one inch of rainfall. As show below.

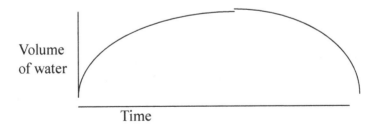

Dimensionless Unit Hydrograph

The graph above represents the flow at a given point over time from one inch of rainfall. To estimate the runoff at say a dam site, the storm rainfall pattern is applied to the unit hydrograph. So if a storm had the following rainfall pattern (in inches) over a four-hour period 1, 2, 2, 1, four unit hydrographs would be calculated offset by an hour each and then the stream flow summed. The hydrographs for hours two and three are doubled before summing. This is shown in the following table:

Hour	1	2	3	4	5	6	7
Rain	1	2	2	1			
Hydrograph 1	1	2	1	0.5			
Hydrograph 2		1	2	1	0.5		
Hydrograph 3			1	2	1	0.5	
Hydrograph 4				1	2	1	0.5
Flow 1	1	4	2	0.5			
Flow 2		1	4	2	0.5		
Flow 3			1	4	2	0.5	
Flow 4				1	4	2	0.5
Resultant Flow	1	5	7	7.5	6.5	2.5	0.5
Hour	1	2	3	4	5	6	7

This is a readymade application for the computer. I wrote a program to do this for two of my professors and ended up getting graduate credit plus two conference presentations—one in Washington D.C.

Remote Terminal System

The 1800 used at P&G's Winton Hill Data center that I managed was designed primarily as a process control computer. In fact, its operating system was called Time Sharing eXecutive (TSX), but we acquired the 1800 for stand-alone processing. However, P&G was buying considerable time from GE for engineering processing on their remote time-sharing system. Also at this time P&G did not have experience with an environment where the operations staff did not have absolute control over machine operations. We felt such experience would be useful as, at least at P&G at the time absolute control of the operating environment was almost a religion.

In the vein of nothing is really new, as I write this IT staffs are suffering lack of control over Wi-Fi and other networks—such as the Internet. Now there is the additional issue of security that we did not face. But with employees and other accessing corporate data from anywhere and at any time the IT staff is loosing, or has lost, at least some modicum of control over corporate networks and data.

Thus we initiated a time-sharing research project. We acquired a typewriter terminal and hard wired it to the 1800 and placed it in the conference room next door to the machine room. We converted several of the more popular programs to run in time-shared mode using this terminal. When programs were initiated and run from the terminal, the main batch-oriented program was swapped out of memory and the terminal program was swapped in and run. Thus the operator at the 1800 console did not have control over this "interruption" and a computer room job that normally took 10 minutes might take 12 or 15 minutes.

The project was a limited success. However it gave P&G valuable experience, as it was the first time that a P&G operation had given up absolute control of what went on in their machine. And beside those of us involved had a lot of fun with this learning experience.

The swapping of programs in an out of memory resulted in some overhead that would not normally be accounted for with our online accounting system. Before going into the effect of the time-sharing system on accounting, we need to step back a notch and describe the accounting system(s).

P&G cross-charged departments for their computer resource usage. Cross charging was done semi-manually with time sheets upon which the operator recorded the charge number and the start stop time. The accounting month ended four working days before the end of the calendar month so that all such charges could be keypunched and submitted to the corporate data center for consolidation by the last working day.

Prior to and early in the 1800s existence at Winton Hill we used this quasi-manual system. But then we decided that since we had a time-sharing system that we could develop an online charging system by adapting a system that was in use at a non-DPS data center that also had an 1800. We designed a job card into which we keypunched the charge number and job description and program to be executed.

When the computer read a job card we forced an interrupt to a charging routine, which read the system clock and closed out the prior job and calculated its cross charge and then initiated charging for the current job. The charges were accumulated on disk for each charge number. At the end of the month (not the fourth last day) we ran a job that punched one card for each charge number, which summarized its time, and costs. The cards were then sent to the corporate data center for consolidation.

It is interesting to note that, for some unknown reason, the existing system assigned new charge numbers to each department at the beginning of each charging month. Since we could not find out why, we stopped doing it and life became even simpler. This was part of the P&G mantra at the time: The IF question. "If it were not for what basic cause would we not be doing this?"

What would happen to our accounting data in the case of a disk crash or file corruption between backups? Being a belt and suspenders person, I had us develop a fallback redundant system to be used just in case of such an incident. As each job card went thru the system, the time of day and the elapsed time for the previous job was printed on the console typewriter along with the charge number and the charge for the job. In case of disk failure we could revert to the prior time sheet system by keypunching from the console log.

We were easily able to integrate cross charging for use of the terminal system into the online accounting system. Not only did we charge a higher hourly rate for the time-sharing terminal but also we felt it fair to charge the terminal user for the swap time. But how much time did a swap in and out actually take? Our early estimates were too high yielding an interesting situation, which confounded the online accounting system

Whenever the ending time of a job was less than the starting time, the time keeping portion of the accounting system believed that the job had run over midnight and that it was now in a new day. So it added 24 hours to the clock thus advancing the day. Over compensating for the swap time and crediting more time to the batch job than it took caused its stop time to be less than its start time and thus 24 hours were added to the end time and when the elapsed time was calculated and then multiplied by the nearly $100 hourly rate it caused an exorbitant charge even for small jobs as well as causing the date to be in error. Think of it, the smaller the job the more exorbitant the charge. With a little fiddling and adjustment we soon were able to obtain a reasonable increment to account for the program swap without confounding the accounting system.

What Does Our Income Tax Sound Like?

The computer used for Water in chapter 5 The Orange Juice Story was a Litton Industries 1700 desktop business machine computer, which was well suited for interactive computing.

An additional system for which we used the 1700 was a Federal Income Tax package for accountants—not individuals. Data for individual 1040 returns were keyed in the account's office into a program, which we developed, and stored on cassette tape. For additional testing, I did our personal income tax on the 1700 tax program and took the cassette home and played it on a tape player for our children who were then in junior high. I said to them, "Here is what our income tax sounds like." They were not impressed.

The income tax package was a modest success and we made a little profit off it but like the utility billing in chapter 5. Follow Stupid Rules Exactly; we made more on selling the specialized forms than we did selling the package.

As many software vendors of today are concerned with unauthorized copies, we at that time were also. So we invented a sort of copy protection for our income tax system. The normal tape format called for a beginning of tape mark, which actually marked the beginning of data – not the beginning of the physical tape. It was possible through low-level programming to access physical tape before this mark and actually write data on it, which could also be read by low-level programming.

We took advantage of this and wrote some of our program before this mark. The tape copy utility provided by the vendor would not copy data before this mark and thus our program copied using this utility would not run. So we did not think that any bootleg copies of our tax program were ever made. We used another unique tape operation at P&G. When we thought that console operators were not correctly handling our computer runs we would write a little routine in machine language that would initiated a tape rewind and then immediately issue a channel reset command. This would cause the tape to completely come off of the reel which was a real inconvenience to the operator.

Intercity Travel Desire Factor

The main theme of my studies for my MS in Civil Engineering was the application of the new tool – the digital computer to each sub-discipline of Civil Engineering: economics, structures, highways, hydraulics, sanitary, etc. During this time, the IBM 650 was replaced with an IBM 709.

My master's thesis project was a FORTRAN program on the IBM 709 to determine the Intercity Travel Desire Factor (ICTDF) for each segment of Washington State's highways. The ICTDF is a component of the rating system that was used at this time to guide the Washington State Legislature (politics, of course, was another) as to whether a road segment should be designated as a state highway or be left a country road or city street.

The ICTDF was based on the gravity model. It used the sum of the square root of the products of all pairs of cities between which a given segment of highway was on the shortest path divided by the square of the distance between them.

$$\text{Thus ICTDF} = \frac{i=1,n\ (PiPj)^{1/2}}{j=i,n\ Dij^2}$$

Washington State is bounded on the west by the ocean, the north by Canada, and the east by Idaho, a relatively sparsely populated state, and south by Oregon where the Columbia River forms most of the border. This geography means that the ICTDF correlated very highly with the minimum traffic volume on each segment of the state's roads. The minimum traffic was taken for through traffic that was the state's responsibility.

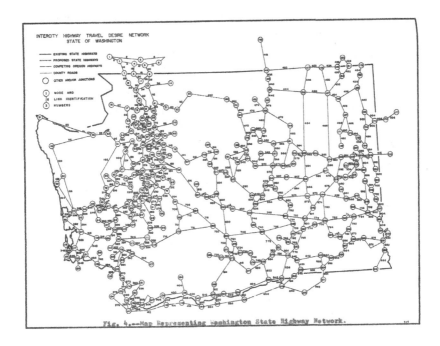

Fig. 4.—Map Representing Washington State Highway Network.

Washington, at that time had about 200 population centers and 600 segments of road connecting them. I had a draftsperson draw a map representing this layout and then numbered each point and highway segment. I then had cards punched representing each of these points and segments—some 800, to be used as input to my ICTDF program.

This was quite an effort (for which I, as a graduate student, had to pay) as was the development of the FORTRAN program, which I wrote—some 700 statements including comments.

Computer time, on WSU's IBM 709 was hard to get. So after the program had been developed and tested, I left the job at the computer center for the production run to be made when machine time was available.

On a Sunday afternoon, Dr. Rechard, the head of the computer center who was also on my thesis committee, put the job on the computer to run and then returned to his office. When he came out, some time later, to check the computer he found a pile of paper output from the console typewriter that said over and over and over ... "..route equal.., ...route equal..., ...route equal..." He called me at home and reported what was happening. I told him to terminate the job, set all the material aside, and I would come have a look at it.

What had happened was that in calculating the shortest distance between 200 x 199 (39,800) cities over all possible routes, some SMALL fraction—but still a large number, of the routes had equal distance, which I had not anticipated and thus not planned for. The console typewriter output was due to the way that I had coded FORTRAN's IF statement.

The FORTRAN IF statement of the day provided for a three-way branch. Taking one of the branches based upon a number being positive, negative, or zero as follows:

IF A+B (+, 0, -) or actually IF DIST1 – DIST2 (10,20,30)

10 C DIST2 is smaller than DIST1
20 C DIST2 is equal to DIST1
30 C DIST2 is larger than DIST1

Most programmers of the day tended to ignore the zero branch and treat it as follows:

IF DIST1 – DIST2 (10,10,30) or
IF DIST1 – DIST2 (10,30,30)

Had I done that I am not sure exactly what would have happened except that my answers would have been wrong (and I may not have known it) or I may have gotten inconsistent results from run to run.

But I always have been, and even more so after this, a very conservative programmer—often called a belt and suspenders programmer. Thus, even while not expecting the middle – 0 – branch, I had written the program to take a different path – one on which

I did not really know what to do so I just had it print out a console typewriter message.

What did I do then? I went back to the drawing board. I ended up rating each segment of highway starting with 90s for interstate, 80 for primary federal highways, 70 for secondary, etc. Then I had to make sure that no two segments that came into a node had the same value – so when two interstates met at a junction for example node 33 they had to be rated 91 and 92 as shown.

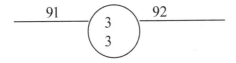

This, of course, meant that my segment data had to be recoded and re-keypunched (again at my expense). In the end, however, it added an additional richness to the output.

Today determining the shortest path though a network using a computer is very easy, GPS do it millions of times per day, but back in the early 1960s it was new. So finding and understanding the Moore Algorithm, an early algorithm for finding the shortest route through a network, well enough to write a computer program was a significant portion of the task. Having mastered the algorithm came in useful several times during my career. While at P&G I assisted the Engineering Division in developing The Electrical Design System (EDS) on the IBM 7080, and while with General Computer Services Corporation (GCSC) I worked on EDS II, an update of the original system for the IBM 360 and a total remake called System for Planning Electrical Construction (SPEC) and its offshoot which used SPEC's output, Construction Electrical Planning System (CEPS). Chapter 10. All of these projects used the Moore shortest path algorithm.

Computer Guru & Wire Sag

As I was working toward my Masters Degree in Civil Engineering, I became the computer guru of WSU's Division of Industrial Research. In this role I assisted the researchers in the division in their use of this new tool.

One of the largest projects involved sag curves for electrical transmission lines. Transmission lines are not at a constant height between supports—they sag. The amount of sag at each point can be calculated mathematically I developed a FORTRAN program that computed sag curves and then presented them as an array in memory, which when printed out resulted in graphical representations of the sag curves. Today this sounds simple, but given the technology of the time and my nascent computer programming knowledge, it was an accomplishment.

Relocation Without Index Registers

My first really big assignment with P&G was on a team of new programmer/analysts to replace the programming language system known as "sawing" MATRAN. MATRAN—Matrix Algebra TRANslator, was an assemble, load, and go language developed in-house by Dick, a senior programmer/analyst, to overcome the fact that the 705 was a commercial (not scientific computer) and, at the time, did not have a scientific language such as FORTRAN. Regardless of such limitations, P&G had a large, active group of scientists, engineers, and mathematicians who performed statistical, scientific, and engineering analysis of markets, brands, manufacturing plants, warehouse locations, and the like. Scientific computing, as it was called, was becoming increasingly important to the company. Assemble load and go means that each time a MATRAN program was run the MATRAN statements would be converted to machine language, loaded into memory, and then executed to accomplish the purpose for which the program was developed. The machine language code was not saved from run to run only the MATRAN code.

I learned the value of throwing away what turns out to be a bad start on the MATRAN project. In facet one of my favorite sayings is: "I am proudest of the code that I have thrown away. It is not around to haunt me." Our first design and first coding attempt for the new MATRAN would have been a nightmare to support. It was good that we had he sense to throw our first design and code away which lead to the very successful relocation described below. We all find it hard to throw out our hard work and start over again. Even now and in several cases on these reminisces I have spent longer trying to find or salvage "lost" documents when just doing it over would have been faster and easier. However, frequently, because the task has been done before, doing it over means that it is done better, more easily, and in less time than it originally took.

Due to limited internal memory, the "sawing" version of MATRAN that we were replacing for the 7080 kept processing subroutines, such as square root and matrix inversion, on a library tape and loaded them in to memory as needed. To do this, MATRAN had a subsystem that searched a portion of the library tape forward and backward for routines that were called for but were not currently in memory. This meant that the program library tape repeatedly went back and forth. This caused significant wear and tear on the tape and from time to time the tape was "sawed" in two. The 705III had 40 thousand six-bit positions of internal memory. (Remember this was before disk storage came into play.)

Even with the increased storage capacity of the 7080, we still were not able to load all the possible routines into memory at one time. But we certainly did not want to keep routines that were used in a given program on tape. To avoid the sawing, we wanted all routines used by a given program to be kept in memory while the program was executing. I was able to do this using "relocation."

In order to accomplish this each subroutine was made relocatable. A specific MATRAN program then only loaded those subroutines that it needed. Relocation was necessary since the subroutines could be at a different memory addresses in different MATRAN programs.

A relocatable subroutine is one that can be executed at a different memory location than one at which was assembled and can be executed in multiple locations from one program to the next. They were related to today's dynamic link library (DLLs)– except that they were not reentrant and thus could only be executed by one program at a time, which was all that the 7080 could run. (Note: many programs in a multi-processing environment can use reentrant routines asynchronously. This capability is due to the fact that reentrant routines do not make changes to any of their code or data. All changes are made to data in the calling programming.)

Sometime after the 7080 MATRAN system was operational, I told someone that it used relocated subroutines. They spoke in amazement and said, "The 7080 does not have index registers (the contents of which can be set and added to the instruction address at execution

time) and you cannot have a relocatable code without index registers."
I looked them straight in the eye and said, "I am sure glad that I did not
know that, because I have a working system that relocates 7080 code
and executes it."

This reminds me of the saying, "So much for the application! What
about the theory

How Relocation Was Done

Here is how relocation was done: After a subroutine
passed testing, it was assembled starting at memory
location 10,000. Thus when during actual operation,
the routine started at 33,333, 23,333 was added to
the address of each instruction as it was loaded
into memory. But this could only be done to the
instructional parts of the program and not to the
constants and the data. All the constant/non-instruction
portions of the program were forced to the end of
the executable code behind a marker (which was
called a lozenge or a pillow). When the marker was
encountered, relocation was stopped and then constants
and data were loaded unmodified into memory. One
more step was required for successful relocation. Since
routines called each other they had to know where
each routine was. Since reflecting the locations of
the routines in the relocated code would have been a
(almost) never-ending tail chase, a pivot table was used.

The actual entry point to each routine was at a
fixed address in lower memory below the start of the
main program or relocated code. The operation code of
the entry point in the pivot table was changed from a
no-operation to a transfer (branch) when the assembly
process recognized the need for the subroutine. As the
relocation occurred the loader checked for the entry
point for that subroutine and planted the address of
where the subroutine was (re)located for this program.

|_____□END□_____|

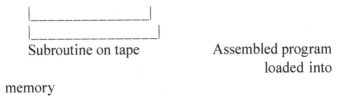

Subroutine on tape   Assembled program
                            loaded into

memory

Our main test vehicle was a gigantic program, which exercised all of MATRAN's whistles and bells and spun all of its wheels. However once this master test program worked and we placed the system into operation we found production programs that exposed bugs in the system. These bugs primarily dealt with the failure of a given operation to request a required subroutine.

The large test program masked these errors because if only one or two of the three features that used a certain routine, say square root, called for it to be relocated, it was there for all three. But if a production program just used that one feature, which due to our bug did not call for the relocation – it crashed. So we proceeded, post haste, to make many small, one feature, test programs and run them back-to-back.

Earlier I described how I was able to get the 705 III transportation program to run on the 7080. Several years later an analyst from the Industrial Engineering section and I took on a project to develop a new, modern version of the transportation program this time in MATRAN. It turned out to be quite a project, given my lack of Decision Science experience. Rewriting the transportation program in MATRAN together with my involvement in the development of the 7080 MATRAN compile load and go system brought these experiences together.

Years later, during my PhD quest, I took a course in decision sciences and learned the whys and how's of the transportation algorithm. And later on at Xavier I taught others how it worked.

Scatter Read

Probably my most significant accomplishment as a software programmer was while I was in the P&G's Computer Techniques Development Section (CTD). I was called upon to write a new locator/

librarian system. Today we might call it an operating system. The locator/librarian cataloged programs on magnetic tape and then loaded them into memory and initiated their execution under operator or control card request.

Normally, in order to load a program into memory, a portion of memory (a buffer) had to be set aside for a segment of the program. From this buffer, pieces of code would be moved to their proper memory location. The larger this buffer the fewer tape library accesses were required to load a given program. However, the larger this buffer the larger the amount of memory that would be unavailable for the program itself. Prior to scatter read the size of this buffer was 3,000 6-bit characters.

Al, one of the machine room shift supervisors, came up with an idea to eliminate the buffer and to make the entire memory available for programs. This became known as scatter read.

Input and output on the 7080 was to or from a memory address that was a multiple of 5 and had a multiple of 5 characters. The actual read from tape was through a register called Special Memory Access Counter or SMAC. When a tape read was initiated an address of where the data was to be read was given in the read instruction and that address was loaded into SMAC. Five characters were read one by one into a memory access buffer (MAB) and then placed in memory all at once and five was added to SMAC. That operation continued until an inter-record gap was encountered on the tape and the read operation was terminated. Al believed that SMAC could be programmed so that data coming in from the tape could be interrogated and SMAC could be modified during the read to redirect incoming data (program code in this case) to another location in memory, thus scattering the read without first having to go through a memory-consuming buffer.

If possible at all, this would be a time-dependent operation. So testing began to find a routine that would accomplish scatter read and could be executed in five machine cycles. The first few attempts failed miserably and data was strewn all over memory destroying the program and hanging the machine. But eventually we got the timing down and the scatter read routine worked. Now the job was to build a tape library that could use this feature.

To build or update a library a deck of cards was submitted to an update run. My librarian program ran in the upper half of memory and the lower half of memory was cleared and then all the instructions of the programming being libraried that were to be loaded into lower memory were loaded there. Then I scanned lower memory and created scatter read records for portions of memory that were program code or data. Once this was done, the rest of the program being libraried (that belong in upper memory during execution) was loaded into the lower memory space just vacated and cleared again (addresses being adjusted to cause this to happen). And then the process of creating a scatter read record for the rest of was performed – and the program was libraried and ready to run.

The record created for scatter read looked like this:

|Flag|Address|Program code to be loade
|Flag|Address|Prog code...|Flag|Address|...

The flag was a sequence of five characters that could not appear in a program. When this flag sequence was recognized, the next five characters were an address, which was loaded into SMAC. As the program code to be loaded was being read, scatter read checked each five-character block for the flag characters and when they were detected, SMAC was again loaded with the next five characters. This continued until the inter record gap was encountered and the read stopped. When an end of program flag was encountered, the program load was terminated and the librarian transferred to the first executable instruction in the program, otherwise another scatter read record was read and the operations described above were repeated.

Later on after I went to Winton Hill, I was called back to work on the adaptation of scatter read to the IBM S/360. The S/360 had a 7080 emulator but could not directly handle the time-dependent nature of the scatter. Fortunately the S/360 had more memory than the 7080 so in the S/360, again using a buffer, we could capture the scatter read instruction and direct the operation to the additional memory and then move the program to the location where it could be executed. This was a step backwards to where we were before scatter read as we were back to using a buffer. But the S/360 was faster, had more memory, and emulation was temporary.

Management At P&G

P&G, at least my bosses, had very good attitudes towards policies. Policies were guidelines to be followed unless there was a good reason not to. But that meant that, even if you did not follow the policy—you had to know what it was. Woe be to the P&G manager who violated a policy without knowing —but if you knew the policy and had a good reason for doing otherwise you were on solid ground.

One day when I was working on the scatter read locator/librarian, I was called into my boss Jack's office where he said, "Bruce, I have six programmers, in my group and a budget of $10,000 per month for cross charged data center expenses. Last month you spent over $10,000 all by your self. What do you have to say for yourself?" I calmly replied, "Jack, I am sorry but that was all the time I could get. I needed much more." His reply was, "Get out of here and get back to work." He just wanted to test the courage of my conviction. The scatter read/locator librarian saved the company $20,000 of "real" money per month for several years while we rented two 7080s and $10,000 per month after releasing the first 7080 and until we purchased the second one.

After I was transferred to Winton Hill Technical Center, I was asked by Jack, my prior boss to take a trip to Baltimore and help with testing of the conversion of scatter read to the S/360 using the Social Security Administration's computer. The S/360 while having a 7080 emulator could not directly handle the time-dependent scatter read. I filed an expense report on Jack's budget number.

Some time later Bob, my then current boss, said, "Didn't you take a trip for to Baltimore a while back? I have not seen or approved your expenses for the trip." I said, "But I have already been reimbursed." "How did you do it?" Bob responded. "Why I filled out the form and signed as traveler and as local manager, which was me. I then took it upstairs at Winton Hill to the treasury window and received my money."

Bob, with a horrified smile, said, "Bruce, don't do that again. You are the only person in P&G who approves his own expense account. The chairman of the board approves the president's and the president approves the chairman's. Don't do it again!" That ended the matter.

By mimicking the procedures leading to the successful conversion from the 7080 to the S/360 and helped by hard work by my staff we had a very successful conversion from our 1620 to 1800. Thus I gave everyone including myself who had worked on the project a day off with pay. After all of us had taken our day off I told my boss. His reaction was, "Mmm I have never heard of that but you are incharge out there and it was your decision to make."

Software Preventive Maintenance: Really a head of my time

I like to believe that I was forward thinking—ahead of my time. I consider relocation without index registers as an example of being "ahead of my time." Another is scheduled software maintenance. It was often impossible to test systems software with P&G's remote testing procedures, which worked reasonably well for commercial systems. I have reported cases where I painfully gained necessary access to the computer console. This is another case of management did not understanding the technology involved enough to make an informed decision – hence technical distance.

Scheduled hardware maintenance was an accepted phenomenon. At a specified time each week for a specified duration (or longer) the vendor, IBM in this case, would take the machine and test the hardware or install fixes and the like. I thought that the same should apply to system software as it became more and more complex and important in the operation of the equipment. I along with others wrote several of P&G's (in)famous one-pager reports recommending this and pushed very hard for system software maintenance—to no avail.

Some time later particularly with GCSC when I was a user of P&G's data center I was told, "Your job can not be run this morning as we are running system software maintenance." My idea, adopted later on, now came back to haunt me. Should I have been pleased that my idea was adopted—or annoyed that my job could not be run?

Spiral Curve

The summer before I graduated from college I worked in Alaska, first for the Bureau of Public Roads and then for the Alaska Rail Road (which paid much more). I worked as a surveyor and office "engineer." One of my tasks while in the office was to design spiral curves as we were relocating the railroad around a missile-tracking sight thus adding four curves to the longest straightest stretch of track on the line between Anchorage and Fairbanks. A "normal" highway curve is a "circular" curve where the arc of a circle meets the straight stretches. But a railroad requires a spiral curve, which gradually goes from an infinite radius (the straight stretch) to the radius of the circle and back out again. This is a tedious error prone calculation—when done by hand with a manual calculator and logarithms. But we did it.

Shortly after the Denver Regional Transit District's west light rail line opened up I took a tour, which include riding over the Indiana Avenue bridge which is a spiral curve—but done by computer. So was I ahead to my time? Not really because this was a bridge not just a level curve. But I was proud to have done part of it by hand.

Four To Zero DMIOCS

General Computer Service Corporation's (GCSC) first significant contract was to convert the IBM 1460 programs at Armco Steel's Washington Court House Plant to run on an IBM 1401. Armco acquired the 1401 from our sister company, the Halsey Corporation. Armco then engaged GCSC to have the 1460 shipped to London and perform the installation and training of their London personnel. While the 1460 had a higher model number, the 1401 was a more powerful computer and the 1401 being acquired had more internal memory than the 1460. The 1460 and the 1401 were compatible except for their Input/Output (I/O) instructions. The 1401's I/O was to and from fixed addresses in memory, whereas the 1460 I/O instructions designated the addresses to be read from or written to. The 1460 being replaced had 12,000 positions of memory; the 1401 replacement had 16,000.

But before Armco's Washington Court House Plant could take advantage of the increased power of the 1401 upwards of 200 existing 1460 Autocoder programs needed to be converted to run on the 1401. As their first major contract GCSC took on the job.

GCSC undertook the contract for $10,000 (in 1968 $) and we spent most of that before we had proven the technology used in our approach. This was a significant project that solidified our risk-taking nature, tested our *ingenuity*, and kept us up many a night both working and worrying. If this project failed our new venture would most likely fail.

Since we knew that we would literally be chasing out tails to plan to convert each of the 200 programs individually—we needed to come up with an automated solution. This solution turned out to be a two-part solution Dual Machine Input Output System (DMIOCS) and second was Four-to-Zero.

The Four-to-Zero program's input was 1460 Autocoder source program statements recorded on punch card decks, its output was Autocoder source decks with I/O instructions replaced with branches to DMIOCS. There were two versions of DMIOCS—one for the 1460 and one for the 1401. These source program statements were in a form that humans could write and understand. A program called an assembler converted these statements to object code that the computer used to actually execute the program

The 1460 programs after being run through Four-to-Zero were then run through the assembler program which produced object decks. The object decks could now run on either machine. When an I/O instruction was encountered it branched to DMIOCS. If DMIOCS was running on the 1460 it immediately returned to the next instruction to perform the original 1460 I/O. If, however, DMIOCS was running on a 1401 it immediately branched to the additional 4000 positions on the 1401 and performed 1401 I/O which was quite complicated.

When a program running on the 1401 requested an input operation the input area had to be saved, the operation performed, the data moved to the appropriate place in the program, and then the input area had to be restored.

When output operation was requested, a save was performed and the data was then moved to the output area. An additional complication was 1401/1460 word marks. Word marks were binary digits (bits) in memory that were used to delineate fields and to designate the beginning of a new instruction. Word marks had to be cleared and their placement recorded so that they could be restored after the I/O operation was completed. After the output operation was completed and the word marks restored then the data that was saved was restored to the output area.

Four-to-Zero and DMIOCS were developed on the 1460 at the Court House. George and I spent many a night there. We would leave the office late in the afternoon, drive the 70 or so miles from Middletown to Washington Court House, spend most of the night developing the programs, grab a few hours of sleep at a local motel, and be back in the office in time for business the next day. One night we had no sleep when, out of curiosity, I pushed one of the buttons on the computer console to see what happened. The program crashed and we had to start all over.

The final proof of our approach and our final hurdle came with the testing of DMIOCS at the 1401 to be acquired, which was at Longview Fiber Company in Longview, Washington. I flew to Seattle and then stayed with my folks at East Sequim Bay, Washington 175 miles from Longview. When I arrived at Longview, driving my Father's pick up truck, I encountered a challenge that we had overlooked – the bootstrap loader.

To start a program running on either machine, the object deck was placed in the card reader and the yellow "load" button was depressed. This caused the first card in the deck to be read into memory positions 1-80 and to execute the instruction at position 1. In these first 80 positions word marks had to be set and other program loading housekeeping had to be done before subsequent cards could be read to continue the loading of the program.

But now within these 80 positions I had an additional challenge, to decide upon which computer the program was being loaded. This stretched my programming abilities particularly since I did not have a great deal of experience on the 14xx family. But with long-distance phone-based help particularly from George I developed bootstrap loaders for both machines running DMIOCS.

We then hired George's high school aged son to staff the 1460 at the courthouse to run their programs though our Four-to-Zero program and then reassemble the output by passing them through the Autocoder assembly program.

The success of the DMIOCS Four to Zero project not only placed GCSC on solid footing with Armco but also gave us traction with other potential clients. What is more, it solidified our *risk-taking* and innovative nature—we had bet the farm on our first significant contract and won out. We would make similar technical bets in the future and would win most of them. Our *ingenuity* was tested, as it would be many times during the brief existence of GCSC. Our *ingenuity* would prove to be our strongest strength, but alas, it would not be enough to sustain our existence. More of the GCSC story is contained in chapters 8 & 9.

I was at it again —just ahead of my time!

Ingenuity/Insight In Other Chapters

7.8 Computer: chapter 7 Teaching Technology
Innovative Teaching: chapter 7 Teaching Technology
Demotivation: chapter 2 Curmudgeon
LITIO: chapter 5 Technical Distance
Orange Juice Story: chapter 5 Technical Distance
Early Email: chapter 10 SPEC

Chapter Bibliography

Bruce Johnson 1962 *Determination of Intercity Travel Desire Factor by the Digital Computer* Unpublished Master of Science thesis Washington State University, Pullman, Washington.

CHAPTER 2
CURMUDGEON

Setting The Stage

I am a CRUDmudgeon, which is a take off on curmudgeon—which I also am. The term curmudgeon is, of course, self—explanatory: a crusty, ill—tempered, and usually old man. I mean it more in the crusty sense not in the ill tempered, and early on in my career I was not old. Curmudgeons such as I are also outspoken and risk takers. Reviewers of this chapter have noted that I was/am a maverick. They further noted that while mavericks are quite well accepted and encouraged today, during the times that these events took place that was not necessarily so. I was fired twice generally for being an outspoken maverick.

The CRUD stands for Create, Read, Update, and Delete—the data life cycle. In this chapter I describe some representative curmudgeon issues and incidents and the centrality of data CRUD is presented in chapter 3.

My curmudgeonliness is inexorably tied to the technical distance, administrivia[12], and often just plain incompetence that I have encountered during my careers.

First Curmudgeonly Act In My Careers

My first curmudgeonly act occurred as I received my Masters Degree in Civil Engineering from Washington State University (WSU); in June 1962. I had finished and "defended" my thesis early in the 1961-62spring semester. Again I did not go through graduation. I have placed "defended" in quotes because unlike the "defense" of my PhD

---

[12] Dictionary definition: **administrivia** —the tiresome but essential details that must be taken care of and tasks that must be performed in running an organization; "he sets policy and leaves all the administrivia to his assistant" Only most cases that I was aware of the details were not essential.

thesis it was very collegial—not a defense in the traditional sense. I missed graduation for my first three degrees, as I was not on campus at the time of the ceremonies, but I went through three ceremonies for my fourth degree.

I had a good (but low paying) job with the Highway Research Section of WSU's Division of Industrial research. I enjoyed my position with Highway Research and with my role as computer guru helping members of the Division utilize the University's newly acquired IBM model 650 computer, I might have been willing to stay on —but. When my salary for the 1962-63 academic year was announced, my raise was $10 more than my raise the year before. This was a smaller percentage increase than I had ever received! I immediately submitted my letter of resignation. I told the director of the division that if my Master's Degree from his institution was worth, at the most, 83 cents per month, I felt obliged to resign.

By resigning without another (higher, better) offer, I immediately became person non-grate. No one ever resigned from the division without being lured away by a better offer. In the process, I was short changed—I had to give 90 days notice and with accrued vacation time this ran past the end of the academic/fiscal year—so I did not get all the pay or time off that was due me. I also was shunted around for the last few months, loosing my position in Highway Research. During this time I did my innovative graphical wire sag computer system described in chapter 1.

It was then time to get hopping; I only had a few months to find a job. By this time I had a pregnant wife and a year-old son to support. I interviewed for several possible jobs, eventually going with Procter & Gamble (P&G) in Cincinnati, Ohio for $750 per month. The story of how I obtained that job is contained in chapter 3.

While the P&G interview, site visit, and subsequent hiring experience was outstanding, I had other interview and site visit experience that was not productive. General Dynamics flew me, along with hundreds of others (at least it seemed that way), to San Diego for a recruiting visit. I was totally unimpressed—we were herded around like cattle and received no individual treatment. I did have time to drive around San Diego and check out the city and its housing. I felt that it was a place where I could enjoy living. I particularly remember that the houses did not have basements—everywhere I had lived up to then (and since) had basements or day lighted lower levels.

I had connections with the Washington State Highway department though my job with Highway Research and my Civil Engineering masters degree thesis and was offered a job in Olympia for $600 per month. This brought home to me that a good many professionals were willing to live in the Pacific Northwest for less than competitive wages. For example, at this time, the county engineer of Island County (The San Juan islands), a licensed professional engineer, was making, as I remember, about $400 per month.

During this period I also had my first interview with Boeing Aircraft in Seattle, where Frank my college roommate, an electrical engineer, went to work and rose to Chief Avionics Engineer before he retired. Boeing showed me a large wall-sized organization chart and pointed to a block in the middle and said that is the position that I would have. The thought of being stuck in such a position for the duration of my career made my skin crawl. They did not make me an offer at the time—but I eventually received an offer—after I was already at work at P&G.

However even before this, even in high school—I was a curmudgeon. In spite of my American History teachers insistence that the Civil War was fought over state's rights I knew and said so that the issue was really slavery. Which has been confirmed a number of times. I also insist on saying "sins" during the Lords Prayer instead of debts (which can be ok). Though trespasses is acceptable. I also say "universal church" instead of "catholic church." Maybe saying what you mean is a characteristic of a curmudgeon!

Short Sleeved Shirt

My curmudgeoness reared its head early on while I was with very conservative Procter & Gamble (P&G), which at that time had some unwritten rules that I ran afoul of.

Early on in my tenure at P&G the office manager, who had been very accommodating and helpful when I first arrived in Cincinnati, reprimanded me for wearing a short-sleeved shirt without a sport or suit coat when I was out of my office cubicle.

34

When the office manager saw me he requested that I come with him to his office. While there he informed me of the *unwritten* and *unsaid* rule that men were not to show their bare arms when outside their cubicle.

I later found out the lore behind this "rule." Way back when: Mr. Procter's, or was it Mr. Gamble's, female secretary was offended by men's bare arms. Hence the ruleit was unstated because, who would write down such a stupid rule? In fact, several years later, the rule went by the wayside when summer interns whom P&G was trying to impress to come to work full time, complained about the unwritten rule. They said, "If it's a rule fine, write it down, but don't sneak up on us with it and embarrass us." No one was willing to write it down and it stopped being enforced.

Don't Wearer A Vest Without A Sports Coat

A similar thing happened when I left my cubicle without putting my suit coat on over my vest. I was called into the same office manager's office and told that doing so that was unacceptable. I solved the problem by never wearing a vest again.

Lounge

The office manager again reprimanded me at one point when a fellow programmer/analyst and I shared an outside office with a window, which was unusual for our lowly stature. We both had jobs that involved helping other programmers, analysts, and engineers in their use of the computer. Today it would be called a help desk—except that they generally brought their questions to us in person.

Programmer A would come to me for help and analyst or engineer B would come to my officemate for help. And when finished, low and behold, they often would recognize each other and start a conversation. In this manner, we could have several of these conversions going on in our office at the same time. None of which involved either one of us.

This, of course, interfered with our helping others and our programmer-analyst tasks. So one day in desperation, I went to the hall outside our office and took down my nameplate, which said Bruce M. Johnson Jr.(as I was known then before my Father died) and turned it over to the backside and wrote "LOUNGE" on it with a felttipped pen. It was not long after that the same office manager who had chastised me about my bare arms and vest came by and saw the sign. He stepped into the office and asked me to come with him to his office. Again I was in hot water.

Programming (Non)Standards

P&G had published programming standards that all programmers and all systems were to follow. This was important because commercial systems, as they were developed, passed though several different groups: systems analysis, system design, programming, and then maintenance. Generally only one or two persons transferred from group to group as the system progressed. However, programming standards were often not adhered to. It was easier to develop new standards than to enforce existing standards. No one seemed to have the will for rigorous enforcement. As fate would have it I was assigned to one of the task forces instituted to revise the programming standards. As usual, I did not do this laying down. I wrote a memo questioning the process, for which I was reprimanded. The memo included the following, whose author is actually unknown but is often attributed to Petronius:

> "...we tend to meet any new situation by reorganizing; and what a wonderful method it can be for creating the illusion of progress while producing confusion, inefficiency, and demoralization."

The memo was otherwise ignored and we developed another set of "programming (non)standards."

"Where Were The Secretaries Last Night?"

Asking the question "Where were the secretaries last night?" was another of my curmudgeonly responses to issues at P&G. It was very difficulty to obtain the computer time necessary to test my programs. Our remotely submitted test jobs were generally run in the dark of the night in the computer center, which was isolated in the bowls of the building. In the beginning of my career I often said sarcastically that computers only ran at night. Actually during the daytime the computers were dedicated to running production, systems such as payroll, orders, shareholder records and the like. Thus from time to time I came in during the dark of the night to test my programs. But I was expected to be back at my desk by the normal starting time. When I tried to come in a little later on those mornings I was told, "What would the secretaries think?" This situation was exacerbated by the nature of the programming that I was doing. I was developing system softwareprecursors to today's operating systems that could not always be effectively tested remotely. Also I enjoyed watching my developed programs run. I would live with them often for a long time until they worked properly. When they past muster I turned them over to operations and work on another program until it worked. Thus I spent my time with not-yet working programs and for my satisfaction I liked to watch my working programs work.

Too Tense To Be A Curmudgeon

At General Computer Services Corporation (GCSC), chapters 8 & 9, I did not have many opportunities to be a crusty curmudgeon—the situation was often so tense that I all too often became ill tempered. Many times I considered my colleagues' actions dishonest, such as not disclosing our connections to the hardware vendor we were recommending, George's setting up our Brazil subsidiary in his name, not disclosing the role of our attorney in engineering the coup that displaced me as president and as an employee. These tensions weighed heavily on my marriage and negatively impacted my role as a father to my son and daughter. One of the characteristics of this time was that I only had bowl movements on Sundays

Dealing With Administrivia In Academia

Working freelance allowed me to teach adjunct during the day, which morphed into a full-time position at Xavier University. Xavier may have been no different from other universities—but it's where I was and the bureaucracy was rampant—from affirmative action EEOC meetings to sexual harassment workshops and in between. There also was excessive paper work and busy work. And I acted as a curmudgeonly maverick to it all.

Elsewhere in this work, I recount some of my problems with administration at Billboard and P&G. Not surprisingly, they continued at Xavier. For example, each semester we were required to turn in to the dean's office a copy our office hour schedule and a copy of the syllabus for each of our classes. I did this faithfully and on time. Frequently, however, I received subsequent requests from the dean's officeberating me for not submitting copies when it was actually their errors that caused them to be lost. I, of course, sent them another set and told them that I had already complied. At some point this request stopped. Our new and improved departmental secretaries were making additional copies for the dean when they reproduced our syllabi. How simple and efficient.

Fortunately our departmental secretaries were not in the same building as the dean's office and thus were somewhat isolated from the bureaucracy. When I asked our secretaries if we could do something they occasionally said, "We don't know. But it's easier to get forgiveness than it is to get permission." They were willing to be independent and work on the faculty's behalf.

Administrivia: An Element On The Periodic Chart Of The Elements

I once sent the Academic Vice President (AVP) and Provost, who was a physicist by training and should have known his elements, a tongue in cheek article about the element "administrivia." But while he acknowledged receiving it and thanked me, he did not get the message. This was the same AVP whom I met during half time at a Xavier basketball game on one of my trips back to Cincinnati after I retired. When I approached him in a group of faculty I asked, "How is the University?" He replied with a straight face, "It's a lot easier to run with you gone!" Internally I shook my fist and said "yippee!" Many of us diagnosed his blustering, anti faculty attitude as an effort to overcome his small physical stature. However as bad as he was he was better than the previous AVP who started her tenure with a statement to the effect, "I am new here and you must be tolerant of my mistakes, but I will not be tolerant with faculty mistakes!"

The Faculty Should Get Out Of Faculty Governance

While writing this, I read an article reporting that the number of non-teaching professional administrators in universities has doubled in the preceding decade. I experienced that phenomenon in spades at Xavier. One of the administrative farces was faculty governance the myth that the faculty had any saying in the operation of the university. One of my tennis playing colleagues, who was definitely a curmudgeon, made the statement, "The faculty should stop wasting their time participating in university governance—and insist that the administrators do their jobs right and hold their feet to the fire when they don't!" Another comment on this administrative bloat in academia, "...the growth of middle management in universities—the growing bureaucracy—and the increasingly top down nature of decision making. We must reverse these trends" ["Thinking about Washington State, 2005"].

Reducing Costs In Academia

Currently there is much hue and cry regarding the high cost of a university education. Just think of the reductions that could take place with the elimination of administrative bloat. To further decrease this cost let's reduce the amount of research and publishing required and have professors teach more classes. And thus fewer professors and less cost to factor into the tuition.[13]

On Fire For Good Teaching

Xavier's academic administration preached the need for good teaching, without ever defining it except as high marks on the student's instructor/course ratings? Beyond this we never received a good answer, however at least one effort was made. The college of business's professional development center had a course called "Train the trainer." And it was offered to (required of?) the faculty.

---

[13] Denver city council has just voted to place a small sales tax increase on the upcoming ballot to help fund higher education. While I support this, my solution is superior.

Frankly I don't remember much about it and did not receive much benefit from it. One reason, I think, was the vast difference between the classroom facilities in the professional development center and the classrooms where the university faculty actually taught. For example, one of the recommended techniques was to reduce distraction when view graphs[14] slides were used in the class but were not currently being discussed. The technique was to tape a piece of paper to the lens housing of the view graph projector. This could then be flipped over the lens to cut off the light when slides were not currently being shown. One of my colleagues and I tried this and—we each had a small fire. We only tried this once. The professional development center obviously had *cooler* view graph projectors. Converting to WordPerfect's Presentation and then to Microsoft's PowerPoint eventually solved this.

My Red Button

When Xavier installed one of their phone systems, there were at least two types of phones. Department chairs, deans and other big wigs received one type of phone and us faculty peons received another. Faculty phones had a little red light that the bigwigs could turn on when the faculty did not answer. But there was no way for we mere faculty member to turn on a big wig's red light.

When a faculty member came into their office and discovered that the red light was on they were to call the switchboard to see who had rattled their chain (turned on the red light). In my case, generally the red light being on meant that I was in some sort of hot water with one of the big wigs. This was not too too bad during business hours as I could determine who had called and resolve the issue. But when I came in at night or on weekends when the switchboard was closed, I could not determine who had called and all I could do is stew until business hours.

Being innovative, I solved my problem by placing a strip of opaque tape over my little red button and from there on I did not know whether my red light was on or not—but I suppose that it was permanently on.

---

[14] In the age of PowerPoint presentations and the like many readers will not identify with a View Graph Projector—a machine that shines a light through a transparent 8½ x 11 viewgraph slide onto a screen via a reflective mirror.

Interestingly enough, I never got into trouble for not answering my summons. Since I could not summon a big wig—they were not going to summon me.

If You Read This I Will Send $25+ To Your Favorite Charity

One vivid memory of Xavier was the multiple elaborate dossiers we had to turn in each year—supposedly as a part of the merit review process and/or for American Association of Collegiate Colleges of Business (AACSB) accreditation of the college. I spent a lot of time and was thorough and accurate. But...

After several years of carefully filling out these forms, I started putting in one of my favorite lines that I had used before—namely on System for Electrical Planning (SPEC) chapter 10,—"If you read this and call me I will give $25 to your favorite charity." Then it became $30, $35, $40 and up to $50[15]. No one ever responded and I still have my money! Prima facie evidence that it was never read.

Academic Year Versus Two Semesters

As the reader has no doubt guessed, there was a fair amount of tension between the administration and me particularly during my later years at Xavier. For example, I submitted a proposal for a research sabbatical, which while approved caused a great deal of hassle. I had clearly stated in my proposal that I intended to take a full year off at half pay. All four of our parents had just died in a period of eight and a half months shortly after all the stress, strain, and effort to finally achieve my PhD. I needed time to decompress and to invigorate my own line of research and publications.

But the college of business dean would have none of it. The business college was going for AACSB accreditation and the dean wanted all terminally qualified faculty (which I now was) actively teaching, so he reneged on the agreement. I appealed to the academic

---

[15] I just recently realized how dangerous this could have been. What if this was passed around and dozens, if not more, persons contacted me? But since no one read these things it turned out that I was spared.

vice president who had granted me the sabbatical. She refused to do anything saying it was between the dean and me. I appealed to the committee who recommended me for the sabbatical. They also refused to take any action saying that they had destroyed all the proposals once their recommendations had been forwarded. My associate dean and chair bowed to the dean and did not support me. All that I asked for help said, "It is too bad your dean is such an..." But none would help. I eventually had to give in and take two semesters off in different academic years. During this time, my waning years at Xavier, I was shunted from small office to smaller office. In fact so small that when I received a new book for review I had to get rid of another one in order to shelve it.

Uncommon Common Hour

My continual reporting that the "emperor has no clothes" got me in regular trouble. At one point the business college adapted a common hour period once a week on Wednesday when there were (supposed to be) no classes so that the faculty could attend seminars and such. This was adopted from Harvard where there were no classes on Wednesdays. Harvard faculty either taught Monday-Thursday or TuesdayFriday leaving Wednesday free for on-campus collaboration, and threeday weekends for consulting and research. Well guess who the dean assigned an introductory information systems class during Wednesday's Common Hour period? Yours truly. He subsequently used all those periods for AACSB accreditation work sessions. No enriching seminars to aid in faculty development ever occurred. So neither did I get to participate in enriching seminars nor the accreditation work sessions.

Thankfully during much of this time I was volunteering at Children's Hospital in Cincinnati. I would go in one afternoon a week and play with and/or hold the children. I would play pool, board games, run them around the floor in the cozy coup. The really young ones I would hold by their crib. Many were on oxygen lines and respirators. It was really rewarding and very therapeutic for me to be able to walk in with no baggage spend my time and leave without worry—just looking forward to coming back the next week.

Doing this was in response to our first grandson's time in intensive care in Children's Hospital in Denver with spinal meningitis and heurolitec anemia. He had well-off parents with flexible work schedules who lived nearby and two sets of grandparents (one grandmother was a nurse) who, while living long distances away, were able support him and his parents. But many of the children had no such robust support systems. For example, some were hard scrabble farmers who lived far away in Nebraska who had to spend long days in their children's room or be back home away from their child. So my stint at Children's in Cincinnati was meant to, in some small way, compensate for this.

Demotivation

During my PhD quest, I did not see eye-to-eye with the Organizational Behavior (OB) Faculty nor could I understand or mimic their way of thinking which eventually lead me to change my minor from OB to IT. When I took the Motivation course, from my experience I identified "demotivation" as the opposite of motivation, which was totally discounted by the professor. I viewed then and still do motivation as a force measured on a positive scale. But every now and then something comes along which totally destroys one. I called this phenomenon DEmotivation—which has a negative scale. Some time later, you guessed it, we began to read about—Demotivation in management and OB literature. I was just there too early! In fact as I was writing this I encountered the word "demotivation" in a comic strip.

Triskaidekaphobia

A recent favorite number was 7. I lived on the 17th floor at 1777, I am past 77 and check out and in a bike from dock 7 in the Denver bcycle bike sharing system when ever I can.

However at one time my favorite number was 13. When I defended my dissertation on Technical Distance I asked the assembled faculty, "Does anyone here know what Triskaidekaphobia means?" No one responded so I said, "It's the fear of the number 13, which I apparently do not have. It has been 13 months since I defended my dissertation proposal and 31 years since I obtained my first college degree."

I found that disarming the assembled faculty helped one get through the ordeal.

When I took my oral PhD exams the second time (only two times are allowed) the first question I was asked was to derive on the white board the Economic Order Quantity (EOQ) formula. Which, by the way, is an entirely useless academic construct—but I had it down cold and looked at the audience for their approval. All but one, including my committee, looked satisfied, but the one who did not look satisfied was the department chair—which did not bode well. But I recovered and said, "Jim you do not look pleased and I think I know why. I derived the way Jack does in his book. Let me go back and do it the way you do it in your book!" And I did and from there on it was smooth sailing and all that was left was the dissertation.

I have what I call an associative mind which means that I need time to come up with answers, connections, and the like. Thus the oral exams were very hard. Ask me anything and I can have an answer tomorrow.

This Is An Atom—This Is A Molecule

During my six-month army active duty stint I took a course for sanitary officers. The Colonel, who was the head of the Medical Service Corps, taught the chemistry portion. With a class consisting of engineers, physicians, entomologist, chemists and the like he started the class with, "This is an atom, and this is a molecule." And it went down hill from there. The course was just way too basic for the set of students attending. What a waste. Even as a second lieutenant I pointed this out in my signed evaluation. I never have or will turn in an unsigned evaluation.

"OK Bruce, I Will Change Your Grade To An A."

While the exact name of the managerial accounting course has faded from my mind, the incidents are still fresh. On the first exam I received a score of 300 out of a possible 300. On the very same day that the professor handed back the exams, we turned in a project also worth 300 points. When the project came back the following week, I received 120 out of the possible 300. The professor was puzzled as was I, and he asked me to pay close attention to how he scored the assignment. When he was through scoring I also had 120 points using his grading algorithm. I wrote him a letter and handed it to him the next week. In the letter, I said, "As a professor myself I understand the need for precise grading algorithms otherwise the students will nickel and dime you to death—but yours, in this case is wrong. I have run my own company and have handled such situations before. My answers were as good or better than yours." To no avail—at the time—I did fine in the rest of the course but because of the 120 I received a B.

Several years later I encountered the professor picking up a neighbor's daughter for a dance lesson. Immediately when he saw me he said "OK Bruce, I will change your grade to an A." And he did!

Isn't One Supposed To Go Back After A Sabbatical?

When I came up for retirement, I was given a semesterlong senior sabbatical after which I retired. I have been asked, "Isn't one supposed to come back for at least a year after a sabbatical?" I like to reply that, "I was given a sabbatical with the understanding that I would NOT return" I am one of the few Xavier faculty members who retired and left town and gave up their office. Most stayed, taught an adjunct course, and kept their office, which was brimming to the ceiling with books and paraphernalia, which they did not want to go to the trouble of disposing of.

Two Rights Make A Wrong

I have encountered several incidents where two rights make a wrong. The following two incidents are both from my time at P&G.

With P&G being conservative (and cheap) we ordered our IBM 1800 computer with only one disk drive. This was or turned out to be very short sighted—but then experience with disk drives was rare at that time.

With one disk drive (and no tape drive) how could one back up the disk? Even given the limited size of the disk in those days (I remember it as three megabytes (megs)—but it might have been ten!). But that still was a lot of cards[16]. Those of you reading this can figure how many 80-column cards it takes to back up even a half-full three-megabyte disk. And we had a very slow IBM 1442 card read punch, so backing up or restoring was a time-consuming activity. What is more, we occasionally ran into problems with the machine hanging up or not restoring the backup correctly—more about this later. So we soon ordered a second disk drive.

During the 1620 operations, object decks were kept in drawers. When a job card with accompanying data was received, the deck was retrieved, the data placed behind the deck and the stack of cards loaded into the card reader. The charge number indicated on the job request card was noted on a time sheet, as were the start and stop time. The 1620 did not have a printer—so the output was punched into cards, which were then listed on an IBM 407 accounting machine.

Now with the 1800, object programs were stored on the disk and the job card identified the program to be run, which was then called off of the disk into memory to be executed, using the data behind the job card. This was a much easier and more reliable operation than retrieving object decks. It also facilitated program segmentation as multiple program or program segments could evoke each other and data could be passed back and forth on the disk without operator intervention. It also facilitated the online accounting system described in chapter 1 remote terminal system.

It was soon apparent from both a storage point of view as well as from the requirement for faster more reliable backups that a second drive was necessary.

During this period, delivery times for IBM equipment and supplies from computers to disk drives to disk packs were inordinately long. So it was a long time between ordering the second drive and the time that it arrived. But eventually the second drive did show up and the long awaited installation day was at hand. But when the machine was powered up after the installation, it immediately crashed and went entirely dark.

---

[16] And remember, in addition to the data to be restored, the card must contain information as to where the data is to go. Thus all 80-columns are not available for data.

The 1800 now not only did not have a second disk drive but the first drive as well as the other peripherals and CPU did not function. After a long, laborious process with many phone calls to Poughkeepsie, a wiring error in the installation instructions was discovered and corrected and the blown electronics were replaced. The 1800 with two disk drives was finally functioning.

From there on we had smooth sailing with the 1800 operation but eventually a third disk was justified. The order time now was a little shorter than before and ultimately another disk drive installation day was at hand. Of course, everyone connected with the system remembered the earlier wiring error and carefully checked the installation instructions to assure that the error had been corrected. It had! Or had it?

But, again immediately after the installation, when the 1800 was powered up it went totally dark. Thus we were back to where we were when we installed the second disk drive, with calls to Poughkeepsie and many engineers hovering over the machine. However, it did not take as long this time to determine the problem. Not only had the wiring instructions been changed in the installation instructions—but the actual internal wiring had also been reversed so the same short circuit resulted. Apparently two conscientious—but uncoordinated and unsupervised persons had both corrected the problem. These two rights had created a wrong.

The dual correction of the disk drive wiring problem was one of many times in my career that this phenomenon (two rights making a wrong) occurred. Another was in the corporate computer center. When the day crew came in one morning they could not find the dividend checks that were to have been produced the night before. Being conscientious, they immediately initiated the job that produced the dividend checks. Then they listened to the tape recording prepared by the night shift, which reported on events from their shift. Low and behold an incident was reported on the recording. The night crew had produced the dividend checks—but thought that something might be wrong with them and set them aside to be checked with the treasury department before distributing. Thus now two sets had been printed. Ouch!

Additional IBM Hardware/Software Bugs

The IBM 1620 computer was an early scientific computer, which was installed at Winton Hill Technical Center Regional Data Center (WHTC RDC) and one or two other locations within P&G. It had a sibling the IBM 1710, which was used primarily for process control. FORTRAN was the main language and the 1620 (as it was on the 1800 later) was used mostly for engineering, scientific, and mathematical computing. P&G had a significant mathematics and statistical component to their computing.

While the 1620 was a scientific computer; it did not have arithmetic circuits. What it had instead was a dedicated area of core memory, which was an addition table. Mathematical calculations were directed to this table where addition was done directly, multiplication was done by repeated additions; subtraction was done via complementary arithmetic, and division, then by repeated subtractions.

The engineers determined that a repeated failure in the 1620 operation was due to a bad core position in the 1620 memory. The obvious way to fix this was to replace the bad core. However, this was very expensive, as an entire core module, not just the bad core position, would have to be replaced. A cheaper way, that was very acceptable, was found.

Given the dedicated use of the add table section of core, the engineers determined that by rewiring the existing core module, the bad core position could be placed in the add table in a position that was never used. A few wires were switched and the failure disappeared.

Our installation received the 17th IBM 1800 built and the first one shipped to a civilian installation. All previous machines had been shipped to defense-related operations. The IBM 1800 was a big sibling of the IBM 1130—or was the 1130 the little sibling of the 1800? Anyway they were related. And they both were related to the IBM 360 family.

We had issues with this early version of the 1800—but first our success(s). The 1800 replaced an IBM 1620. The computers were quite compatible but there were conversion issues, which we addressed long before scheduled delivery of the 1800. Two months prior to the 1800 delivery, the 1620 was shipped to another data center to make room for the 1800 and to enable us to do site preparation. The jobs were sent to the other data center, which in some cases slightly increased turn-around time. Not being able to see a computer in the computer center and the accompanying physical preparations for the 1800 installation had the added benefit of making the users of the 1620 aware of the impending conversion and the need for them to adhere to the conversion-oriented programming guidelines and schedule.

P&G procedures called for a report justifying the conversion on a rate of return (ROR) basis based on operating cost reductions offset by the conversion costs. This was called, in P&G parlance, a phase one report. We far exceeded the projected ROR—not based upon operating cost savings—but from a reduction in duplicate rental. The initial conversion went so successfully that we released the 1620 from the alternate location ahead of schedule. The phase two report indicated that our ROR was almost twice what we had estimated.

But! Soon after the 1620 was released all hell broke loose. The converted programs, which had initially run fine—soon began to fail on a regular basis and we could not go back to the 1620—it was gone!

The initial problem turned out to be splitting a disk sector boundary by overflowing a disk sector. As the program library expanded and data began to be stored on the disk (the 1620 had been strictly a card operation), the data and programs began to cross sector boundaries and the operating system in many cases could not handle this sector splitting phenomena.

We had frosty communications with IBM over repeated program failures, which turned out to be due to the sector splitting issue. A manager from the 1800 operating system group come to placate us. In one of our discussions he said that even though they tested thoroughly with extensive diagnostics, this was to be expected, as they could not test every eventuality. And I coined an expression, which IBM did not like, "You ran the test diagnostics with the power off—and, of course, they did not fail."

Does the splitting sector boundaries problem sound just like the problems with Microsoft's (and others) security vulnerabilities due to buffer overflow? It does to me! I know that I am an old curmudgeon, but I really don't believe that deep down under IT has really changed all that much.

After the sector splitting problem was solved, operation ran smoothly again, until… P&G being frugal (cheap), we had ordered the

1800 with only one disk drive which at the time sounded fine as we had had none before on the 1620.

Eventually our card-reading problem (which caused the machine hang ups mentioned above) became our overriding dilemma. All too often, while reading cards we would get a card read check and the job would abort and (as we found out later) this could cause a subsequent printing operation to fail. Until the card read problem was identified however, we did not know that the print failure and card reading failures were related.

Detecting the card read and print problem's cause was very difficult. But the eventual fix was simple and cheap. The problem became so bad that IBM had a special crew come in at 5 pm after we had quit for the day and work until we returned the next morning to try and determine the problem—and the fix. Each P&G data center (there were about a dozen at the time) published monthly performance reports showing a break down of the utilization of their computer(s). My report was questioned by many of my manager colleagues because we showed over 12 hours per day of IBM maintenance time, which they said had to be an error. It was not! It was due to the card read issues.

The IBM hardware maintenance engineers finally determined the cause of the problem and fixed it with a 25-cent capacitor. Electronic noise in the card read operation caused an occasional random column of the card to be skipped and thus the card was read into 81 positions of memory rather than 80. So not only was the data read wrong, but the memory word following the card read area belonged to the print buffer. It was the memory position that told the printer how long the print line was. Given the binary nature of the 1800 storage system, this often told the printer that the print line was 2048 characters long. This would cause the printer to hang up and the job to abort.

Eventually we did get all parts of the 1800 working and the WHTC RDC became P&G's model data center.

Curmudgeon Boss

At least in hindsight I would say that my boss Bob was a curmudgeon from whom I learned a great deal. Bob was not a techie and there was a great deal of technical distance between us, but he was an interesting manager. One of his favorite lines was: "You got the right answer for the wrong reason!" He appeared to favor the process over the answer. He was over the corporate data center, which did not always perform up to users needs or expectations—thus there were quite a few complaints about service. He had a great way of disarming complainants. Immediately when he felt a complaint coming on he would say: "I am refunding your cross charge!" This disarmed the complainants thus getting to heart of the purported problem leading to a more useful conversation. But, unfortunately, often the poor service continued.

There are many more such incidents but this is enough to give a flavor of my curmudegoning, now to CRUDmudgeoning.

Curmudgeon Incidents In Other Chapters
Billboard incidents: chapter 5
Spouse's Salary: chapter 9
Who is Responsible for the Financials?: chapter 9
Wage and Hour Laws: chapter 9
Bizrate Zimblast: chapter 9

Chapter Bibliography
"Thinking about Washington State" 2005 *Washington State Magazine* Fall.

CHAPTER 3
CRUDmudgeon:
LET THE DATA DO THE WORK

What Is A CRUDmudgeon?

I am a CRUDmudgeon, which is a takeoff on curmudgeon—which I also am. The term curmudgeon is, of course, self-explanatory: a crusty, ill-tempered, and usually old man. I mean it more in the crusty sense not in the ill tempered, and early on in my career I was not old. Curmudgeons such as me are also outspoken and risk takers.

The CRUD stands for **C**reate, **R**ead, **U**pdate, and **D**elete—the basic functions of the data life cycle. Over my careers I have become totally and irrevocably convinced of the over arching importance of data as the foundation of computer systems. All too often, particularly today, other facets of IT systems get in the way such as fancy GUI's (Graphical Users Interfaces), which we originally called formatted screens, as opposed to the character-oriented screens that debuted with cathode ray tubes (CRTs).

Curmudgeon stories are covered in chapter 2. Readers of which have noted that I was/am a maverick. And further noted that while mavericks are quite well accepted and encouraged today, during the times that those stories took place that was not so. I was fired twice, generally for being an outspoken maverick.

The centrality of data is expressed in the following incidents, systems, and their ramifications. Most of these incidents occurred while I was at General Computer Services Corporation (GCSC) and thus also give insights into the nature of GCSC's business presented in chapters 8 & 9. Remember again this is before disk, Internet, and the like.

If Only The Data Looked Like This

As I sat alone at my desk, I tried to concentrate on my programming project. Yet fear and worry continued to cross my mind. It was the spring of 1970 GCSC was in a slump; my project was crucial to meeting the payroll—and there was no one available to help me—all the other programmers were committed to their projects—mainly fighting fires. I had to get it done on my own.

As I studied the requirements, I was stymied—just plain stumped. I did not know how to proceed. After several false starts, I interrupted myself and got up to get a cup of coffee. While wandering around the office an idea dawned . . . I visualized a solution based upon a specific data arrangement—*if only the data looked like this* I could solve the problem. But unfortunately, the data did not look like *this*. No matter. I had no choice given the deadline so I sat down again and began to code the solution based upon the non-existent data arrangement.

Over the next few days as I developed code, I was still concerned about conditions within the company, my project in general, and the fact that the data did not look like this. But things might just be looking up according to one of our business measures—which side of the coding pad we were writing on. In those days computer code was written on forms specific to each programming language and then keypunched from those sheets. After keypunching we used the backside for drafting letters, proposals, and invoices. When we ran out of the backside of coding pads we turned to ruled yellow pads. We had been on yellow pads for some time due to lack of contracts. At least I was now writing on the "front" or coding side and soon we could use the backside for drafts of letters and hopefully, contracts.

As I approached the end of the development process I became more and more concerned about my imaginary data. But literally as I finished the last line of code a mental picture came to me. It was an algorithm by which the data could be made to look like this. Voila! With just a page or so of code, I programmed a front-end conversion routine that completed the system.

From this point things flowed smoothly. Testing and implementation must have gone well, as I barely remember them. But the lesson learned is real. Data constrains procedure. If I had waited to code the procedure until I understood how to do it in the original format, I would not have made the deadline.

Sales Reporting

In 1975 GCSC took over the entire computer processing for a Company across town. One of the applications was a sales reporting system, which included, among other information, a comparison of this year's year-to-date sales with last year's year-to-date sales. Some thought we needed to keep three years of sales data so as to be able to store and compare the appropriate data. I developed a record layout with 24 months of sales data and a index into the 24 fields based on months since some base date (like 1900) and then reduced to modulo 24 +1 to yield an index of 1-24. Then I developed processing routines that given the current month would store the sales data and then produce the year to date summaries and comparisons. Once this was done, I was able to turn the rest of the job over to junior programmers who used my record layout and my routines to produce the reports in record time. Basic function[17], of course, helped—but unique processing occurred in several of the blocks.

Here is how it worked.

What bucket is June 1973 in?

18=MOD((1973-1900)*12,24)+6

January 1975 is in bucket 13

13=MOD((1975-1900)*12,24)+1

IF YEAR=ODD THIS YEAR IS IN BUCKETS 13 TO 13-1 + MONTH #
LAST YEAR IS IN BUCKETS 1 TO MONTH #

To sum year-to-date in September 1975 and compare it to September year-to-date in 1974 as we have wrapped from our original starting point in 1973 we need to do the following.

1975 sales are in buckets 13-21; 1974 sales are in buckets 1-9.

---

[17]   Basic functions are described chapter 6 (In)Flexible Systems.

To sum year-to-date in July 1974

1974 sales are in buckets 1-7; 1973 sales are in buckets 13-19.

IF YEAR=EVEN THIS YEAR IS IN BUCKETS 1 TO MONTH #
                 LAST YEAR IS IN BUCKETS 13 TO 13-1 + MONTH #

| 1974 | | | | | | | | | | | | 1975 | | | | | | | | | | | 1973 still |

Month Number

1	2	3	4	5	6	7	8	9	10	11	12	1	2	3	4	5	6	7	8	9	10	11	12
1	2	3	4	5	6	7	8	9	10	11	12	13	14	15	16	17	18	19	20	21	22	23	24

Bucket Number

With this design we were able to produced year to date reports for this year and last year with only 24 buckets.

Time And Attendance System

Time (no pun intended) and time again and again, in the early 70s I was called in to finish systems that were "almost" done, when the original implementer had to leave the project. The Time and Attendance system saga described here is one of these systems. The labor contract at P&G's Ivorydale Plant had an elaborate set of very involved rules for calculating pay and bonuses. Among other things there was: regular time, over time, golden time, shift differential, payment based upon classification and/or task actually performed.

In the early 1970s GCSC was engaged to "finish" the system and I was assigned to the project. Given its nature as described below it was a tension-filled difficult project made even more so by the fact that the client's facilities were on an upper floor in a facility without elevators and I was recovering from an operation—which made it a painful experience physically as well as mentally.

Part of the complexity included three sets of nested IF statements (in PL/I) that were, respectively, 37 IF ENDIF statements deep, 34 IF ENDIF statements deep, and 29 IF ENDIF Statements deep.

When I came close to deciphering these rat's nests, I realized that the original author had completely missed a fundamental requirement.

55

He had not recorded actual start and stop times—just duration. Overtime and bonus were not calculated based solely on today's shift but on what happened over the last 24 hours. So if Joe clocked out yesterday at 4pm and came back to work today at 2pm, the two-hour overlap needed to be taken into consideration; it was golden time and received a pay premium. I could not see to how account for golden time without what I called a time map. Thus I had to add new data and a new record type.

Again data drives the system and given that a significant piece of data had been missed the implementation was severely delayed. The missed time map specification and others that I brought to the client's attention increased the cost of the system and delayed its installation over the original estimate and they were not happy. When one comes in at the tail end of a system implementation, which is really the middle, and, in some ways, the beginning, there is no way that a definitive estimate can be given.

Another missed data specification that I inherited was the machine adjuster who came into department X for 20 minutes on her way to department Y, her regular department, and then after seven hours and 20 minutes returned to department X for another 20 minutes to again check their machines. This was recorded as 0.33 hours plus 7.33 hours plus .33 hours, which gave the machine adjuster a total of 7.99 hours, which failed to qualify for the 8 hours required for vacation accrual and other purposes. The machine adjuster knew that she had worked 8 hours. The correct fix would have been to report input and store the time in hours and minutes. But the input formats were already fixed so I checked for 7.99 and made it 8 by adding .01 to the largest time —the 7 hours and twenty minutes.

As this example shows, without complete and correct understanding of data requirements, whether via studying the data itself or the processing called for, installation will be delayed and the project will need to be restarted one or more times.

Technical Recruiting System
P&G's recruiting procedures were of the highest professional stature, as I can vouch for given my own experience in being recruited in 1962 as shown in the sidebar.

P&G Recruits Bruce

I was not available when the P&G technical recruiter came to Washington State University, so I interviewed with another section of the company who knew nothing about positions in data processing. The interviewer took my credentials and recommended me to the data processing systems department (DPS).

Shortly thereafter I was contacted and invited to Cincinnati for a one-day visit. On the way I stopped for the weekend at my parents outside of Chicago. I was scheduled to take an early Sunday evening flight from Chicago to Cincinnati. The United Air Lines flight was delayed multiple times and I ended up getting to my hotel in Cincinnati at 2 am Monday morning, without my luggage.

After a very few hours of sleep I went shopping for a razor and some toiletries before the P&G representative met me for breakfast. Right after breakfast and with very little sleep, I was administered IBM's programmer's aptitude test (PAT). (The PAT had long been proven not to measure any aptitude, much less programming, but IBM pushed it—and P&G was an IBM shop.) During the test, my contact was informed that my luggage had arrived at the hotel. Right after I completed the test we went back (just a few blocks) and I changed clothes.

The visit went very well. I had lunch with a recent hire, just the two of us, so I could obtain a peer's outlook on the company. I interviewed with several department heads. When I asked what I would be doing if I came to work at P&G, I was given an enumeration of multiple interesting and challenging positions that new hires with my experience were likely to be assigned. This was so unlike my interview with Boeing where they just showed me the slot in the organization chart that I would likely be in my whole career. Or General Dynamics where I was herded around with several hundred recruits.

During my last interview, with the manager of system design, I was asked a really insightful question, "What might you not like about working here." Given that no job, no matter how good, is entirely a bed of roses this is an important consideration. I don't remember my answer—but my answer along with my PAT test results must have been acceptable as I was offered a job before I left to go back to my hotel. After returning home and talking over the offer with my wife, we agreed to accept the position. My pregnant wife, 18-month-old son and I moved from Pullman, Washington to Cincinnati, Ohio in time to start at P&G July 1, 1962.

In the mid 60s P&G consolidated the process of recruiting personnel (primarily college students) for the company's technical divisions: engineering, research and development, and mathematics and statistics. Then in the late 60s P&G decided to automate their technical recruiting procedures and GCSC, with me as project leader, was engaged to develop the computer system, which became known as Technical Recruiting System (TRS). This was one of the very first jobs that GCSC did for P&G—as P&G waited to be sure that we were viable before they gave work to the company formed by their ex-employees as explained in chapters 8 & 9.

Data for TRS came primarily from campus visits by recruiters from the technical divisions and the various follow up actions. More than one division could independently meet with the same recruit. TRS had to detect this occurrence. Also P&G did not want to treat recruits as numbers and thus did not want recruits identified externally via their social security number or other impersonal identification scheme. Once a recruit contact was established then various follow up actions could be initiated such as: P&G rejecting the recruit, sending the recruit an offer letter and, in turn, the recruit could accept or reject the offer, and these actions could occur for more than one division.

A file format and identification algorithms needed to be designed that would identify (as best possible) recruits based on their name, school, major and the like—with a computer-assigned identifier used only by the local maintainers of the system as a last resort. The identifier portion of the record design looked something like this:[18]

LastName | FirstName | MI | Suffix | School/Location | Major | Division |Action | Date | ID || other data ...

When data regarding a recruiting contact was submitted to the system it first tried to determine if the recruit had been seen before. If there was no match it was assumed that this was a new recruit.

The system was very successful and was utilized for many years by many technical divisions under control of the Division of Industrial Research. These successes lead to GCSC being chosen to develop P&G's Personal Records System described beow.

Contrasting Recruiting Results

It was interesting to contrast P&G's recruiting with GCSC's. P&G hired possibly hundreds of new employees each year, mostly recent college graduates. So that if a high percentage of them turned out to be productive in their jobs then they had accomplished their hiring goals. But at GCSC we only hired one at a time—sometimes college graduates but most often experienced programmers. So we were in a binary situation. Either they were a successful hire or they were not. Unlike P&G we could not play the percentages. And when a programmer did not work out in our organization it was generally after a considerable amount of unbillable time and effort spent working with him or her. When they had to be replaced a great deal of elapsed time was lost as well a considerable effort on the part of our prosessional staff.

We learned to check very thoroughly into the person's reasons for leaving their previous employers. We found that if a person was unsatisfied with their previous positions it was often due to dissatisfaction that they carried with them and thus they would

---

[18]   This is a standard record format convention: (key ||non key|).

eventually be dissatisfied at GCSC. We were not overly successful in hiring—batting about 50%.

Personnel Records System

In the early 70s P&G decided to develop a centraly consolidated personnel record system. GCSC was chosen to design and implement the Personnel Record System, which was called PRS. PRS had a very unique requirement. The idea was for PRS to rummage through existing systems such as Payroll; Company plans such as stock purchase, profit sharing; Medical; and the like and use data from these systems to build the PRS database rather than having its own unique data source.

This posed a distinctive challenge to file design—our overarching criterion was a file design that could be updated via rummaging. We developed a data file structure with essentially one (logical) record per field. The physical record was variable length and was transparent to the logical processing of the file.

|?|SSN||Data Element Name|Source|Date Acquired|Value....|Data Element Name|Source|Date Acquired|Value....|.....|?|....

A question mark (which was not allowed in any other portion of the data) indicated that a new person had been encountered and that the next nine digits were their social security number. From there on until the next question mark were fields/records pertaining to this person.

Each logical data element containing data about the person consisted of four fields. The first was the five-character data element name. The second was the source of the data element. The third was the eight-digit date (YYYYMMDD) associated with the data in the fourth field. The eight digit date gave us an almost 25 year jump on the Y2K problem of the year 2000 transition. The data itself was variable length depending upon the data name. For example gender was one digit, while last name was 30 digits. Thus each logical three-part data element was in itself variable length—13 digits plus the length of Value.

We developed programs to rummage through the various systems mentioned above and, for data elements chosen for PRS, extract them in PRS format for the monthly update run(s).

Depending upon its nature the data element could occur one, two, or many times following the general rule of data occurrence. For example a Person's birth date could appear only once, his or her salary an unlimited number of times. For some data only the earliest and latest value was desired. For data elements such as name, one occurrence was considered normal but multiples were allowed and reported for manual inspection.

Data values received extensive edit checks before becoming candidates for the master file. This created a situation reminiscent of the Y2K problem. In PRS the date of data acquisition was stored with a four-digit year and any two-year dates from the rummaged systems were quickly converted to four-digit format. Birth dates in the 1880 or 1890s, showed up as 80 or 90, which in the judgment of the system, was in the future, were entered manually in the eight-digit format.

Conflicts between sources and the data on the master file could and did occur. This was resolved by assigning a reliability value to each data source. In case of conflict with how a given data element was to be processed, the source with the highest value was used and the conflict was reported. The highest data source value was 90—manual input—which was entered by the staff responsible for the system based upon their analysis of a conflict report or other need that overrode the usual sources.

The replacement of data elements on the master file or the addition of new ones was controlled by decision tables within the update run that took into consideration combinations of data element name, source, date, and value. This decision table approach and this file format were ideal for this application. Decision tables allowed very fine-grained processing and the system was easily modified when new elements or new update rules were added or when rules where changed. While changes in processing required coding and compilation, the changes were localized and generally avoided side effects. This was an early form of flexibility, which is covered, in chapter 6.[19]

---

[19] Of course it would have been even more flexible to keep the tables on external files. In hindsight I wonder why we didn't do that. In truth, neither the update table nor the MARFILE tables changed very often.

This file format however, made it nearly impossible to produce reports using the master file—particularly ad hoc reports. The solution to this was relatively easy. During each monthly update run we also produced a series of MARFILES, which were normal flat files with specific subsets of the data appropriate for regular or ad hoc reports. The MARFILES were not updated; they were created anew each month. The name MARFILE came from the fact that generally reports were prepared from these files using a program called MARGEN (MAnagement Report GENerator) developed by an ex P&G programmer.

The production of MARFILEs was also driven by decision tables that controlled which field went where and which and how many occurrences of multi-occurring fields were to be produced. For example, one of the MARFILE included the last two salaries for analysis concerned with salary increments.

PRS was used extensively for producing ad hoc reports. For a number of years, GCSC maintained an office within P&G that received report requests in the morning and using the MARFILEs and piecing together various processing routines with some unique coding would produce the reports by early afternoon. Talk about reuse! Talk about modular programming. It was done daily using PRS. This also represents an early form of flexibility.

President Nixon announced his wage freeze on August 15, 1971. Within a week PRS was at work producing monitoring reports assuring that P&G was in compliance with the terms of the freeze. One of those terms was that salary increases could only occur with increases in responsibility. Thus a report showing the salary profile of those who did and did not receive an increase in responsibility gave the required information.

Currently there is much concern over the disclosure of personal and confidential information. In the 1970s, P&G's PRS was on top of this situation, particularly with salary data. Salary data at P&G was highly confidential and generally not disclosed, even to the person's manager. Salary data was doubly encrypted. One key was the individual's social security number and Ralph, our client, held the other. We had several close calls when Ralph forgot or lost the second key and/or used the wrong one. But, to my knowledge, no confidential data was ever disclosed to unauthorized persons. Nor was any data lost permanently.

Ralph: "Reverse your collar..."

Ralph was GCSC's very best client. He provided interesting, challenging projects such as TRS and PRS. He paid on time and often ahead (to beat the P&G budgeting system that zeroed out his account at the end of the fiscal year). He is responsible for our family joining the Sierra Club. He, like us, was often dragging on Tuesday mornings from watching the new phenomena—Monday night football.

Ralph was a P&Ger through and through, but he often was very frustrated with what he considered bureaucratic impediments to getting his job done yet he was generally very good at dealing with them. But occasionally he would call one of us into his office, close the door, and say, "Please turn your collar around (to resemble clergy) and listen to my woes—and keep the meter running. This is billable time for you."

Ralph participated in one of my courses at Xavier after he retired. Xavier allowed senior citizens to audit classes on a space available basis for $10 per credit hour. In one of my seminars where an important thrust of the class was presentations by student teams. Ralph and several traditional students made the first presentation and it was, of course, outstanding and, best of all, set a very high bar for the rest of the presentations.

When Ralph took an advanced Computer Science programming course from a colleague he was on a team with traditional students. They had a team programming assignment that was not going well, the traditional students wanted to blow it off. Ralph said, "No!' and they struggled and eventually got it right.

SuperRecord

GCSC's largest project, lasting from the early 70s to GCSC's demise in 1976, was System for Planning Electrical Construction called

SPEC[20], done for the P&G Engineering Division. I had participated in developing the first version of SPEC, called EDS (Electrical Design System) when I was with P&G in the 60s and GCSC had collaborated with the Engineering Division EDSII several years prior.[21]

SPEC was a large complex project, which was developmental in nature, which means the specifications were developed as we proceeded with the project. Today SPEC might well be called a design-build project. Engineers entered data regarding loads, wires, conduits, and other elements of electrical design directly from engineering drawings, using a special language which was then processed by a systems consisting of 36 program (including sorts) which sized the wires, conduits etc., and produced reports to direct wire pulling and connections and lists of materials to obtain.

Given our lack of understanding of the nature of the data and the need for simultaneous activities, we initially developed an all-inclusive file format—called SuperRecord. SuperRecord included all known fields, such as size, color, beginning and ending nodes, for all types of electrical and hydraulic components (wires, raceways, conduits, devices, loads, etc.) regardless of whether the data would be needed in one of the specific 36 program steps, which we did not yet know. This provided several levels of flexibility during development. First, it allowed a central, machine processable, place to collect and record our then current understanding of data fields needed anywhere in the system and to adjust data field characteristics as we gained understanding.

Second, when it was time to develop specific records such as for wires, devices, or conduits, we used this central declaration by conditionally selecting a given field when it was required in the record being generated. In this way wherever a field occurred in a SPEC program it was presented in the exact same format.

Third, SuperRecord allowed us, with relative ease and flexibility, to shift emphasis from effectiveness to efficiency as we progressed through the development stages. Early in the implementation, when

---

[20]   SPEC is covered in chapter 10.

[21]   P&G had an extensive engineering division, which managed manufacturing plant construction, modification as well as production line installation and the like.

our understanding of the data requirements was low, the tendency was to include all fields in all intermediate records. While, admittedly, this was not very efficient as we were passing excess data—it was effective because it gave high assurance that the fields needed at any stage of processing would be available. As we proceeded through the development and learned more about the nature of the data, we gradually dropped fields from specific records where they were not needed.

The availability of tools has a major effect on the choice of and use of implementation techniques. In the SuperRecord example, two features of our development environment materially aided our implementation efforts and we relied heavily upon them. The first tool was a computer library in which we stored copies of our record declarations to be included in the programs when they were compiled from PL/I to machine language. As mention before, we automated the process of creating record declarations by writing a program to produce the library files for the specific records from the machine-readable SuperRecord itself.

The second, an extremely valuable tool, was the PL/I language feature called LIKE. We declared fields to be LIKE another field called the base field. In our case the base fields came from the specific records, which were in turn derived from SuperRecord. We used LIKE to declare program hold areas, temporary files, tables, etc. So when the attributes or makeup of a field were modified, only SuperRecord had to be modified and the modification was automatically propagated through the specific records to the work areas declared within each program. To readers who understand Object Oriented Programming Systems (OOPS) this may sound like OOPS inheritance. And how about views?[22] This was another example of being ahead of our time.

With our reliance on the OS/360 PL/I LIKE feature, I found it fascinating to note that much later (when I was at Xavier) P&G's engineering division shut down their electrical engineering section and transferred SPEC to a local engineering firm that used a Digital

---

[22]   Inheritance: Certain data may inherit some or all of its attributes from other data higher up in a hierarchy. Views: A data structure can be viewed in several ways. For instance, a view of a accounts receivable system may exclude data about the goods sold which in turn could be shown in a different view.

Equipment Corporation (DEC) version of PL/I that did not have the LIKE feature. Hours and hours of work were required and hundreds and hundreds of lines of PL/I code had to be added by brute force. I offered to consult with them to find an easier way—but they were unwilling to pay.

Eventually the client's specifications and our understanding of SPEC and its data was refined to unique formats that efficiently and effectively represented the data that needed to be transported between processing steps. But the point remains that SuperRecord itself could have provided this communication for the life of the system— but of course, not as efficiently since superfluous data would have been read and written between programs. Also before modifications to SuperRecord could take effect, individual records needed to be regenerated and affected programs recompiled. Still, SuperRecord was an early form of flexibility and prefigured later data dictionary systems as it provided consistency, ease of system modification, and the reduction of side effects.

Conclusion

I trust that these examples have convinced the reader that I am, with good reason, a CRUDmudgeon. Let the data do the work, Amen. But Technical Distance, which is covered in chapter 5, can undo all this. But first lets me get a PhD so that I can keep my professorship with Xavier.

CHAPTER 4
BRUCE HAS A PhD

A left-hander's flexibility, along with an innate ability to adjust more easily to change in the environment and to perform tasks with either hand, can be seen as a gift. [2006 Left-Hander's Calendar: Wednesday 13 December.]

It was not December 13, as mentioned above, nor was it Friday the 13th, nor was my tenure deadline very flexible, and it may not have been because I was left handed—but I made it by the skin of my teeth. Friday the 13th however, does play an important role in making it. I was wearing my cap and gown and ready to receive my PhD— my forth degree. I was actually attending my very first university graduation ceremonies as a graduate. These ceremonies included: my PhD hooding, the college of business administration (CBA) graduation ceremonies, and the all-University of Cincinnati (UC) graduation convocation.

It was June 10, 1990 when my PhD was officially conferred. In June of 1985 I had been awarded my Master of Business Administration (MBA); in June of 1962 I had received my Masters Degree in Civil Engineering (MSCE). And in February of 1959, thirty-one years earlier, I had earned my first degree —a Bachelors Degree in Civil Engineering (BSCE). I had attended none of the first three graduation ceremonies.

The number 13, and specifically Friday the 13th plays an important role thus I must back up to my PhD dissertation defense. After my opening statement, I knew I had passed.

I defended my dissertation on Monday, April 16, 1990. The Xavier University College of Business annual banquet had been held the Friday night before—on Friday the 13th. The mistress of ceremonies had asked the crowd, "Does any one here know what triskaidekaphobia means?" No one did. So she responded, "It's fear of the number 13!"

When I opened my defense I asked my doctoral committee, "Do any of you know what triskaidekaphobia means?" After a few moments of blank stares I announced. "It's the fear of the number 13—which apparently I do not have. It was just 13 months ago that I defended my dissertation proposal—and 31 years ago that I received my first degree—a BS in Civil engineering in 1959!" This totally disarmed the reviewers and at that point, I knew I had passed.

When I presented my dissertation proposal, I was told that I was to have very specific hypotheses, which could either be supported or rejected, and that I was not to fish for meaning in the data that I collected. However, during my defense almost all the faculty present saw the value of my data and were openly fishing through it for meaning in their own research. The data was rich indeed.

The rest of my dissertation defense consisted of presenting my hypothesis and how the collected data caused my hypothesis to be accepted or rejected. There were very few questions. A few minor changes to the dissertation itself were requested. These changes were easily made. I then accomplished the final stepsubmitting the required copies my dissertation to be microfilmed.

I was now a Doctor, a Doctor of Philosophy, a PhD, but not a real doctor as the old joke goes:

On the phone to a restaurant, "May I please have a reservation for two for dinner tonight at nine?" "Yes," replied the person at the restaurant. "In whose name shall I record the reservation?" "Dr. Johnson," I replied, when back came the retort, "Is that a real doctor? Or just a PhD?"

I also am unable to convince my 6-year old grandsons and 4-year old grandniece and nephew that I am a doctor. Six-year old Andy says "Grandpa you are not a doctor!" even after I show him my diploma.

In anticipation of a successful defense, I had arranged with my physician (a real doctor! who, by the way, had been closely monitoring my health during the stressful quest for the PhD) to obtain a stethoscope and an eyepiece.

I had not told my long-suffering wife that I was defending my dissertation this Monday morning. I say long-suffering because, in some ways, my eight-year long struggle was as hard or harder on her than it was on me. After all, I was in the fray and had control, even if very limited, which she did not have. All she could do is watch and agonize with me. So I chose to spare her the added tension of that day.

She had wondered why I was so dressed up when I usually dressed quite casually on days when I did not meet classes. But I deflected her curiosity with some excuse and went on to UC. Now I was a doctor and had the official equipment. So right from UC, I went to the school where she was teaching and found her in a prep bell. I surprised her with my cap and gown and stethoscope and eyepiece and stunned her with the fact that I had finally successfully accomplished the last step required for my PhD. She said that she could take the rest of the day off and we could celebrate. Not knowing that she could take the time off, I had already called a colleague, the associate dean, Marcia, and said, "Would you like to take Dr. Johnson out for lunch?" Marcia had known that I was defending because I was missing an important meeting at Xavier and she was covering for me.

After lunch I went to the department offices and paraded around in my doctor's gear—but my colleagues were too distracted by their own work to even notice my getup and get the joke. That evening my wife and I went out to celebrate at a five-star restaurant.

I immediately contacted our son Russell, who had received his PhD before I did. In the summer of 1989 he called me from Washington State University in Pullman, Washington and said, "Dad, I am tired of waiting for you to obtain your PhD and I am going to go ahead and defend my dissertation so that I can get my PhD." He did, successfully, and became a PhD almost a year before his dad. I subsequently read his dissertation in the field of Plant Physiology. I hardly understood a word. But I could tell from the before and after graphs and charts what ever he did caused something to react differently. He had proved or disproved his hypothesis.

Russell and I have different takes on our PhDs. He has been Doctor Johnson virtually all of his professional life and has been recognized as such and called Doctor Johnson, whereas I became a PhD very late—almost at the end of my career. Thus I was known for 30 years as Mister Johnson. Therefore it is very important to me that I be called Doctor Johnson—not Mister Johnson. Shortly after I received my PhD I received an offer to join from the UC alumni office addressed to

Mr. Johnson. I promptly sent it back without my membership telling them, in no uncertain terms, that I reason I was eligible to join was because—I was a Doctor!

The next summer, our extended family and friends were at Washington State University (WSU) in Pullman, Washington to attend Russell's wedding. The day after the wedding we held a picnic and celebrated both of our PhDs. Everett, my father in law, called it the "pair-a-docs" (paradox) picnic. WSU is where Russell had completed his PhD studies and where he did his first post-doc. I had completed my MS and BS in Civil Engineering studies 30 years before at WSU.

Since Everett had only a peripheral view of my life during my PhD quest, little did he realize what a true paradox my actually receiving the terminal PhD degree was?

To gain an appreciation of this paradox, I will chronicle my journey to obtain the PhD.

The period of my PhD studies overlaps with my time at Xavier starting in 1982 until 1990. I will treat it here as it started while I was an self-employed IT professional teaching as an adjunct at the University of Cincinnati.

As a self-employed—independent—IT professional, I was available during the day to teach classes at local colleges and proprietary schools and thus was in great demand. These schools included: Betts Business College, Southern Ohio College, the Raymond Walters Branch of the University of Cincinnati (UC), and Xavier University. As an adjunct at the Raymond Walters Branch, I was eligible to take one class per quarter, tuition free, at UC. So never one to turn down a freebee, I took several courses while teaching at Raymond Walters: one in computer science, and several in education (since after all I was teaching), including classes about community and junior colleges.

When I started at Xavier all I had was a BS and MS[23] in Civil Engineering. I did not have the terminal degree required for tenure—a PhD. Since I was switching careers from doing to teaching, I thought that a degree in education would be appropriate. But—it would not be. Education as a field of study is looked down on in some other parts

[23] Though the MS was very important because generally a masters degree is required for even adjunct and/or part time teaching.

of academia. I would have to obtain a PhD in a related field. Thus I chose Operations Management and Organizational behavioreventually adding Information Systems.

When I started at Xavier I was not a PhD, I was however, a professor—an assistant professor. But the placard on my office door read Mr. Johnson—not Professor Johnson. I felt, and still feel, that this reflects some of the arrogance of PhDs at least in academia. Ron, a Jesuit Brother, who ran the computer center called me Professor— he was the first one to do so. And I still remember and respect Ron for that, although from time to time we had our differences. I was saddened when I read about Ron's death in a Jesuit magazine.

When I started back to school I decided to take the Graduate Record Exam (GRE), which consisted of two parts: a general knowledge and aptitude in a specific discipline. I took the general in the morning and the specific in the afternoon. None of the specific disciplines addressed the work that I was doing, but since I was in computers I signed up for what appeared to be the closest thing: computer science.

I scored in the 90th percentile in the general—and in the 20th percentile in the computer science portion. My son, Russell, who had studied and worked in biology, also got in the 90th percentile on the general—but he also scored in the 90th percentile on the specific in biology. I, of course, had a time living that down.

After all that when I applied for admission to the UC Business College PhD program they would not accept the GRE and I had to take the GMAT (Graduate Management Aptitude Test). I passed and was admitted to the PhD program at the University of Cincinnati.

Thus in 1982, at the age of 46, I went back to school, this time at the nearby University of Cincinnati, to earn a PhD—which was necessary to obtain tenure and keep my Xavier. Professorship. I had seven years to obtain my PhD in order to have a chance of obtaining tenure.

Thus I was in a hurry, which was difficult because I was teaching full time and was required to be a full time PhD student—to prove that I was serious. Full time meant taking a full course load (12 quarter hours) for three quarters out of five and two consecutively. I buckled down and took full loads in the spring of 1983 and the summers of 1983 and 1984. In the five quarters bounded by those summers I took a total of 61 hours of the required 120 hours (45 was scheduled for my dissertation). I ended up taking 107 hours of course work and 52 hours of dissertation for a total of 159 hours. I also received an MBA along the way—in 1985.

Given this hurry, I did not always have the luxury of taking prerequisites or courses in their designated sequence. So, for example, I took my five statistics courses (15 quarter hours) in almost reverse order, multiple regression, forecasting (time series), and the introductory courses in statistics—statistics I, statistics II, and sample survey/experimental design. I received A's in the introductory courses and B's in the other three. I had taken one statistics class, Mathematical Statistics, as an undergraduate, at WSU (Washington State University). It was too long ago and too theoretical to be of much help. In fact, I had asked the WSU professor, "What if I had this bunch of data and wanted to derive meaning from it?" He, being a theoretical mathematician, had no idea. The WSU course had been all about deriving formulas for different distributions etc., which was totally backwards from my way of thinking.

While at P&G I had helped developed multiple regression programs—but had never really studied the topic. So I really buckled down to slip through without having to wait to take the prerequisites first. But there were several bumps along the way. First, the textbooks for the class did not arrive until several weeks into the 10-week class. When I found this out, I went to the engineering library right after the first class and checked out the only copy of the text. Thus I had a text before the rest of the class. This, of course, helped me perform, as did the instructor's guide I obtained by writing the publisher on Xavier stationary. The other bump was when the department chair called the instructor and me into his office and confronted us with the fact that I had not taken the prerequisites. I was saved when the instructor said, "Bruce is doing just fine. He is mastering the material." That was that and I stayed in the course.

During the first class of a quantitative methods course another instructor asked, "Would those who have not taken course such-and-such—the prerequisite—please raise your hands?" Even though I did not have the prerequisite, I did not raise my hand. I obtained the text for the prior course and with side study received an A in the course.

The same instructor was later to give me my only B, (hotly disputed) in my major. The rest of my major subject grades were A's.

This is not to say that prerequisites are not important. At Xavier many students were not prepared, often due to lack of prerequisites, for the course that they were taking from me. But the students and administration often blamed me for their difficulties and lack of performance.

In my experience, statistics is one of the most frightening courses at all levels. This may be due partly to math phobia, but there is more to it than that. When I taught the subject, I called it variation. I would line the students up by height, age, or some other attribute and then show how they varied and that statistics was just a study of that variation. Nothing else.

During my last several years in Cincinnati before we retired, I volunteered at Children's Hospital. Early on my supervisor had a degree in child development and was studying to become a nurse. She was taking a statistics course, which had her freaked out. When she found out that I taught statistics she asked for help, which I gladly gave —but only after we both agreed to call the subject variation—not statistics. Just this name change considerably eased her anxiety.

One of the statistics courses that I took out of sequence was time series. It was a very difficult course with a very demanding professor—the same one from whom I had taken regression. It was a small class held in a small classroom with black boards on all four walls. He would make a least two complete trips around the room writing formulas, calculations, graphs, and the like on the board. There was no way to take complete notes with this approach—and not all the material covered was in the textbook. I wished then that I had had a Polaroid camera. Of course, today a digital camera would be ideal. Two specific incidents stand out.

The first was our take home mid-term exam. The instructor entered a set of a dozen or so time series on the computer and told us what series were in the data set and how many of each—but not which ones were which. That was the exam. We were to identify the type of series for each one and record our thinking process. It was a tough exam and I struggled with it. I struggled so hard, in fact, that I forgot to keep track of my process. I had been too focused on overcoming the pressure of the exam. And when I turned the exam in I had all the series correct—but was graded down for not reporting my thinking process.

The final exam was even worse. It was a sit down in the same little classroom where the class had been held. The instructor was giving our time series exam plus an exam for an undergraduate statistics class. When I looked at the exam my first thought was, "Was I in this class?" Almost all the problems were unfathomable—I just stared for the longest time. I thought, "My instructor wants to pass me. But I have to give him reason." So I tackled each problem answering what ever I could and then going on to the next one. One by one the undergraduates left. I was still going from problem to problem making a mark or two here and there. Then the other time series graduate students began to leave one by one. By this time I was sweating profusely and the floor under my seat had drops of sweat on it. Then time was up—only the instructor and I were still there. He did not move— I kept pecking away at the problems—finding a little bit here and there that I could add to the answers. I was not in a hurry to leave. I was going out of town and would head directly to the airport after the exam. But, how long would he let me continue this pecking away. Finally an hour and a half after the exam was supposed to be over, he got up and so did I—soaking wet and totally drained I gave him my paper and we walked out.

I got a B on the exam and in the class. This incident became a symbol of the difference between true diligence, tenacity to get though, as opposed to what I often saw in my students at Xavier who gave up and dropped the course at the first sign of adversity.

Xavier's easy drop policies made it difficult for students to learn commitment to a task. Graduate students could drop right before the final exam and undergraduates could drop within five weeks of the end of the semester. Much effort went to support students who eventually dropped classes, which could have been much better spent on other endeavors. I had to obtain a PhD degree to keep my job—I just buckled down and did what was necessary.

Business faculty are often what I call straight through PhDs[24]. That is they have gone straight though school and obtained their PhD and then went straight into academia. Nowhere was this more evident than

---

[24]   I mean this in a derogatory way.

in the handling of case studies. In my judgment, good case studies are supposedly designed to facilitate multiple interpretations and, possibly, heated discussion. Butmost professors I encountered did not subscribe to this view. They thought that the school solution given by their professor was the only answer. This view seemed to get passed on from generation to generation.

I had had significant business, professional, and technical experience, plus I was an active participant in the classes where the cases were assigned. Thus I had a great deal of experience and knowledge to bear on the case—but generally to no avail. I specifically remember an accounting class. In one of the early meetings I volunteered to present my solution, I went up to the front of the class and started my analysis—as soon as one figure deviated from the professor's solution, which was his professor's, professor's, etc. solution, I was interrupted and not permitted to continue. Needless to say, I did not volunteer again—and did not spend much time analyzing the cases from there on.

I wrote several cases during my PhD years as class projects. But I never wrote the one I really wanted to about the (lack of) ethics of one of the General Computer Systems (GCSC) clients. But my professors said, "We only write positive cases. We don't write negative cases." This I felt was wrong—but they were in charge.

When I used cases in my teaching, I bent over backwards not to develop a pre-conceived notion of how the case should turn out. Maybe it was an over reaction, but I did not develop a school solution. I analyzed the pros and cons of my students' analysis.

When I started my PhD studies, UC was far behind Xavier in information technology. Most of assignments, which involved use of the computer, required punched cards and there was generally a long line at the limited number of keypunches in the UC input/output center.

While Xavier's system did not use punched cards, I stumbled upon a lone keypunch in an out of the way location and thus, to some degree, solved the problem of the keypunch line. I would do my card punching at Xavier and then drive the 3.5 miles over to UC and submit the job. If, when the job came back, it required additional keypunching I would drive back to Xavier—do the punching—and return to UC. The only real problem was parking at UC—but still this was much quicker than waiting in the UC keypunch line. When a particular job required multiple runs, I would punch all the data ahead of time and then replace data and/or control cards and submit the job multiple times—thus saving trips between schools.

Speaking of parking—I received three tickets at one time. Since I was teaching a class at the UC Raymond Walters branch campus I was able to take a course for free and I was also given a parking pass. So for several weeks I drove on campus, waved at the person at the gate, drove in front of the classroom building and parked.

On night several weeks into the quarter, which I came out to my car I had three tickets. One for running the gateapparently a different person was on duty and their wave had meant for me to stop. The second ticket was for parking on the main campus when my permit was for a remote lot, and the third ticket was for not parking between the lines. I immediately tried to find the officer who had served the tickets but he was off duty. After several appeals I got one of the tickets canceled and paid the fines for the other two. We all know that we cannot receive our degree with outstanding tickets or library fines.

There was a serious mismatch between my background, my personality, the UC PhD program, its faculty, its requirements, and me. I was over 46 years old when I started serious work on my PhD. I was older than all but one of the faculty in my program. I was extremely successful in my field. I had a nice house and a nice life. I was not a starving graduate student. I had a large ego. I thought the degree was about learning. I was naïve and just plain wrong!

This mismatch did not really show up until I took my written qualifying exams. They were in no way related to the 107 hours of course work that I had taken. I received word of failing just as I headed to my daughters wedding in Colorado. What a bummer!

When I saw my program chair, in the hall shortly afterwards, he said, "You really look down." Of course I was and told him so. His reply was, "At least you are not starving." As it turned out this was a large bone of contention with the all male faculty and particularly their wives. I had made, what turned out to be, a serious mistake early in the program.

Helped by the fact that I had gone to two years of high school in India, I became friends with a number of my fellow PhD students who were from India. We held a khana (Indian meal) at my house for the PhD students and faculty. The Indian students and their wives prepared the meal. The spouses of the faculty were very pointed in their comments to their husbands "We did not live like this when you were a PhD student!" That kind of petty statement came to haunt me and other students in a similar situation. (A successful career before entering the PhD program was particularly hard on my first department chairman at Xavier.)

After flunking my first written exams, I was placed on an accelerated schedule reading and studying and being tutored by the senior professor, in the operations management (OM) literature that had somehow been left out of my classes.

I also had to study the organizational behavior literature and the convoluted way the practitioners wrote about it—as I had also flunked that part. In doing this I was given a very small chance of being able to pass it even with the additional study. A candidate gets only two chances. So I switched minors to Information Systems and took additional course work.

I somehow mastered and passed the OM written retake—but the IS faculty was not happy with the results of my take home exam. But rather than outright flunking me, they kept sending me back for more work—until I finally passed or they just plain got tired of me.

Almost the same thing happened with my oral exams. I was flunked the first time around and I was back to the drawing board studying material not covered in class. When the day came for my second (and last attempt) the entire department faculty were assembled. Normally only three to five would be present: my committee and a college and department representative. But academics are conservative and they wanted strength in numbers. If I was to be put out of the program by failing my second oral they wanted support by their colleagues.

However, I aced my second oral. One of the early questions was to derive (on the blackboard) the economic order quantity (EOQ) formula. Which, by the way, is a theoretical, useless, entirely academic construct. I swept though it in blazing colors. Then I noticed a puzzled stare on the face of the department chair—the same one who had given me my only B in my major. I was terrified as I addressed him, "You seemed puzzled. What have I done wrong?" Then it hit me and I said, "I know. I derived the EOQ formula the way my major professor does in his book. Let me derive the EOQ formula the way that you do in your book." Voila. I did and the chair was pleased as punch and the rest of the exam was a breeze.

But I reflected then and still do about how wasteful it is to require the memorization of the derivation of a useless formula—and from two different viewpoints no less. But that is what was required at UC at that time to progress toward a PhD. Apparently this phenomena still exists as Cindy, my daughter, says that the Project Management Professional (PMP) exam that she took required the memorization of formulas and "junk."

While the name of the course has faded from my mind, the incidents are still fresh. On the first exam I received a score of 300 out of a possible 300. On the very same day that the professor handed back the exams, we turned in a project also worth 300 points. When the project came back the following week, I received 120 out of the possible 300. The professor was puzzled as was I, and he asked me to pay close attention to how he scored the assignment. When he was through scoring I also had 120 points using his grading algorithm. I wrote him a letter and handed it to him the next week. In the letter, I said, "As a professor myself I understand the need for precise grading algorithms otherwise the students will nickel and dime you to death—but yours, in this case is wrong. I have run my own company and have handled such situations before. My answers were as good or better than yours." To no avail—at the time—I did fine in the rest of the course but because of the 120 I received a B.

Over a year later I encountered the professor in my neighborhood. He was across the street picking up a neighbor's daughter for a dance lesson. Immediately when he saw me he said "OK Bruce, I will change your grade to an A." And he did!

Here is another grading scenario. I went into academia to share my experiences in industry to try to help the next generation of managers to do better by technology and to help the next generation of programmers to be more professional. That is to overcome technical distance. One of the unfortunate things about my PhD quest was that for a very long time I was unable to do this—I had to write about what my professors wanted. In one of my classes I saw an opportunity to deviate slightly and think about and research a topic of interest to me. When I got the final paper back it had a B, with the comment, "Bruce if this had been the subject that I had assigned this would be an A paper and you would have gotten an A in the class. But it is not on the topic I assigned—you are lucky to have gotten a B on the paper and a B in the class." I found that a small price to pay for picking my own topic. I guess this also shows how willing I am to take risks—I could have done worse for not sticking to the topic.

Already having engineering degrees and being technically experienced, I felt that a good minor area of study would be management, specifically organizational behavior (OB). This turned out to be a bad idea. I just could not follow the thinking of the OB types. I guess being an engineer and IT person, their OB thinking was just too, too obtuse for me. An interesting anecdote that drives this home was an exam. OB's essay-type exams were supposed to be anonymous—we only wrote down our student number (SSN). However on at least one exam when I was arguing counter to the department line the professor scribbled a note in the corner, "Bruce, is that you?" It was.

In one OB class we were told that a goal of the class was to flunk half the class, as the university allocation from the state would not handle the number of students that were enrolled. I passed receiving a B in the course. I took the course in the summer. I studied hard —even at the neighborhood pool.

I took a course called Motivation. And wrote a paper on De-Motivation. I had many discussions with the professor regarding negative motivation or de-motivation. He never acknowledged its existence. Now many years later I read articles about de-motivation. Again, I guess I was just ahead of my time.

I'd had a successful career, was older, and already knew a great deal, yet the UC faculty did not treat me respectfully. I was able with some difficulty to maneuver around this—but how was I going to obtain the necessary dissertation advisor?

Conventional wisdom says pick an advisor who has already had several candidates successfully become PhDs. But of course an advisor has to have one before he or she can have many. I made it through by choosing an advisor for whom I was the first candidate. Since the faculty wanted him to succeed and to achieve tenure—I would be able to succeed in the process. It was not easy or fair—but I did it. Coincidently my advisor was from India. His wife was also working on her PhD. He had heard of Woodstock and met students from Woodstock.

I often found my PhD dissertation advisor hard to understand or work with. As I presented a chapter of my dissertation to him, he would often read it and then point to a specific section and say, "I don't like this." And I would say, "What is wrong with it?" His reply was often, "I don't know, I just don't like it. Rewrite it!" This, of course, gave no real guidance on how or what to change and was very frustrating.

When I was near completing the development of my dissertation questionnaire, my advisor suggested that I contact Wickham Skinner as an additional means of validating it.

Dr. Skinner, who was retired from the Operations Management faculty at Harvard Business School, was one of the foremost professionals in the field with several main line textbooks and many journal articles. He was to be in Columbus, Ohio within a few weeks.

My advisor thought that I could arrange to meet him there. He had Dr. Skinner's phone number at his residence on Cape Cod and I called him. Dr. Skinner answered his own phone and was very receptive to the idea. We arranged to have breakfast on the second day of the conference. I got up early that morning and drove the two hours to Columbus to meet with him.

When he came out of the elevator from his room he greeted me with, "Are you on an expense account?" I said, "No." So he offered to pay for my breakfast. Just an early indication of what a genuine human being this guru of the Operations Management field was. I had a bit of difficulty to get him to talk about my research and my questionnaire. He was most interested in my "adventures" in pursuing a PhD at my age (early 50s). As it turned out, his wife had recently received her PhD late in life, and had experienced many of the same hurdles that I was facing—even being the wife of a famous professor. Incidentally my advisor's wife was also working toward a PhD. I do not know the outcome of her quest.

Once I received my degree I sent him a summary of my results and suggested that we co-author a paper using my data and outcomes. That would have been a sure way to get a publication out of my dissertation. But Dr. Skinner did not need publications and regretfully for me declined my offer.

My successful dissertation defense was on April 16, 1990. My terminal contract was to expire on May 30th. On that date my professorship would end and I would be without a job. Thus I had six weeks to appeal my denial of tenure and lack of promotion to associate professor. With some difficulty and added stress I was awarded tenure —however I was denied a promotion. The dean[25] said that since I was on a terminal contract I had not even been up for promotion. I did not consider this fair treatment. I was promoted to associate professor the next year. Again I was short changed by Xavier. At the time a promotion to associate professor was supposed to carry a $1000 increase in pay. I received the $1000 but my merit raise was reduced by a like amount.

At this time Xavier's tenure procedures were such that only those who thought that they were eligible for tenure or promotion needed to apply. When I first arrived at Xavier, one had to submit their dossier every year—even though denial of tenure for lack of terminal degree was automatic. This took a lot of time and effort as one did not wish to be remembered for a sloppy or incomplete dossier when the time came that one was actually eligible. Thus having submitted a dossier every year, I was well prepared and was able to immediately submit my dossier with my appeal.

It was sort of a miracle that I actually got tenure. A beginning assistant professor has seven years to obtain tenure. But it took me eight. I had to take a leave of absence from full-time teaching to stall the tenure calendar. Also, I was outspoken, continually telling the emperors that they had no clothes. Through a colleague on the rank and tenure committee I determined that I actually received tenure as follows. Not expecting me to really obtain a PhD after the way I was treated at UC, and the lack of respect by Xavier Faculty for UC, a Xavier academic vice president promised the department chair that I would get tenure when I received my PhD. This appeared to be a safe bet for not granting me tenure. Thus, when I actually did receive my PhD—they had no choice but to grant me tenure.

---

[25] This was the same dean that denied my yearlong research sabbatical that I had been awarded see "Year Versus Two Semesters" in chapter 2. As an aside his mother lived next door to good friends of ours and I was told that she would have nothing to do with him.

No publications relating to technical distance or operations management actually came out of my dissertation. My advisor had been very interested in extracting papers from the dissertation research—but I kept telling him that I was under the gun to get the dissertation finished and defended, and that afterwards we could work together diligently on publications. This was not to be. Once I had my degree he did not show up for appointments or return my phone calls. One of my committee members from marketing and I produced several papers regarding attitudes toward technical marketing.

In 1984 my program advisor, the editor of *Operations Management Review* published a paper I had written for his class titled "Data Processing—Out of Control." One of my management (organizational behavior) professors and I tried to get my paper "Technical Distance—Bridging the Gulf," published. But to no avail! We received several rejections and it finally died. I still think that the reason it was not published was because of, what else, technical distance. Technical distance causes the problem of technical distance not to be recognized.

I also wrote several papers regarding my experiences with the System for Electrical Planning (SPEC) and Billboard Publications. Unfortunately due to the pressures of obtaining the PhD none of these were even submitted for publication. Of course it did not help that while under the gun to obtain the PhD while teaching fulltime, I did not have the time or means to develop relationships with editors of appropriate publications.

At the time I was at UC, and I think almost universally, the PhD is about jumping through hoops and memorization. Both of these attributes worked against me.

I have what I call an associative mind. I do not memorize well—but I associate things and when given time to process I can solve a wide range of problems and have good recall. Thus the concentrated oral stand up and written sit down exams are not my forte. This is in opposition to the fact that in normal writing I probably have my best relative performance on the first draft rather than on the polished document.

Also being in the midst of a successful career with a reasonable income and a comfortable life style I did not act like a straight though PhD student groveling at the feet of their faculty. This really worked against me.

The breakthrough on progress toward my degree came when 1) I stopped asking, "Why?" and instead said, "How high?" when I was asked to jump. And 2) I accepted the fact that the world would not end if I did not obtain a PhD. As bad as I wanted to be a professor and profess, I had a successful career that I could continue.

One of the saving graces toward accomplishing the PhD requirements was the difference in academic calendars between UC and Xavier. Xavier was on a semester system and started before Labor Day. UC was on quarters and started late in September. Given the different Christmas and spring breaks it turns out that only about half of the time from Labor Day till late June both schools were in session at the same time. So quite a bit of time I just had one or the other: teaching at Xavier or taking courses at UC.

What did I learn along the way? Well frankly, not much. Except maybe how to jump though hoops. Oh I also learned the difference between among and between. One of my dissertation committee members—the only one I think who took the exercise as more than hoop jumping—made a really, really big deal of my misuse of among and between in early drafts of my dissertation. You better believe I know the difference now.

My skills at research were honed and I learned academic writing, citing, and documenting. But was that worth the quarter of a million in expenses and lost earnings? You bet—we had our summers off for many years, as my wife was also a teacher.

I have somewhere between few and no pleasant memories of my PhD quest. As I agonized my way toward the degree, I saw others around me obtaining their PhDs and I was just unable to celebrate with them—I hurt too much.

Since my GCSC days I have been a fan of Peter Drucker and his writings. His 1974 book *Management, Tasks, Responsibilities, Practices* sustained me then and together with several of his other books have a prominent place in my library. Yet in eight years as a PhD student at UC and 17 years as a faculty member at Xavier, I never heard his name mentioned by business professors. On the occasion of his passing, I wrote a letter to the editor of the *Wall Street Journal* regarding this fact, which was published on November 22, 2005. As a result I received several phone calls from as far away as Chicago and New York from others who echoed my feelings that most management professors are jealous of Drucker and/or rejected him because he did not have a PhD. Just one more example of the arrogance of many PhDs and university professors. Another example was the treatment of Will Durant and his history of the world—since he was not a PhD or academic, academics and historians dismissed his monumental work. In the process I learned that Peter Drucker often summered at the Estes Park YMCA center, which was within view of our home at that time.

My PhD cost me over $13,000 in cash (a lot of it for parking), nearly a quarter of a million dollars in lost earnings, eight years of stress and strain, and detrimental health effects for both my wife and I. But now I was a tenured professor with summers off. All in all it was worth it. But, in reality, it should have been a lot less hassle and pressure.

But now I was free to teach and pursue my scholarship and research desires without having the lack of a PhD hanging over my head.

Chapter Bibliography

Drucker, Peter 1974 *Management, Tasks, Responsibilities, Practices* Harper & Row, Publishers.

Johnson, Bruce 2005 "On Drucker" *Wall Street Journal* November 22.

Johnson, Bruce 1990 *The Interaction of Equipment and Process Technology Knowledge and Decision-Making Methodology,* Unpublished PhD dissertation, University of Cincinnati, Cincinnati, Ohio.

Johnson, Bruce 1984 "Data Processing—Out of Control." *Operations Management Review* Volume 2 Number 2 winter.

CHAPTER 5
TECHNICAL DISTANCE

Introduction
Technical distance: the gulf between decision-making managers without appropriate technical knowledge and technologists who possess the technical knowledge necessary to made an informed technological decision but do not have the authority.

Technical distance, managerial ineffectiveness, unnecessary bureaucracy, administrivia—all have the same undesirable result, bad technical decisions. The technologist, the manager, or both can cause technical distance. The ills of managerial inadequacies and unnecessary bureaucracy lie squarely with the manager—as do the cures.

Technical distance is a major cause of inflexible systems. Thus many of the stories in this chapter also have a foot in chapter 6 (In) Flexible systems.

The incidents included in this chapter cover the gamut of ills caused by this gulf between the technologist and the manager.

Washington State University Car/Expense Account
I had some early contacts with bureaucracy administrivia, while working in the Highway Research Section of the Division of Industrial Research of Washington State University (WSU). Was this early evidence of technical distance?

When I started, the Section had just begun the Highways Streets and Bridges Need Study for the Washington State Legislature's Interim Committee on Highways, Streets, and Bridges. Reid, the section head, had a full-time car from the college motor pool, as did the man who was contacting the cities and counties in Western Washington that did not have highway/street departments. I also needed a full-time car to handle the east side. But Reid was told that we already had all the cars that they could allocate to the section. He then asked, "What do we need to do to get another car?" He was told, "We have to go to the president of the university." He then replied, "OK when can we go?" He was told that they would check into it.

A few days later a call came for me from the motor pool. When I answered I was told, "Mr. Johnson, your car is ready for you to pick up." Reid had called their bluff—we never did go to the president. Was this bureaucracy, administrivia, or technical distance? You call it.

After traveling for several months, I began to run out of money having to pay my expenses prior to being reimbursed. In fact, I had to borrow money and I fudged the interest into my expense account—with Reid's knowledge. Our expense accounts were turned in monthly and took six or more weeks to process. So on my small salary I could be out my expense money for up to three months. When Reid complained about this, he was told that that was the best that could be done. Reid then told the expense account office that we would be submitting our expense accounts every two weeks. And we did. But soon thereafter they agreed that if we would go back to monthly expense reporting our expense accounts would be processed in only two weeks. They did not want twice as much work. (Was this bureaucracy, administrivia, or technical distance? You call it.)

TECHNICAL DISTANCE AND (IN)FLEXBLE SYSTEMS

Technical distance and inflexible systems often go hand in hand—technical distance causing inflexible systems. This was nowhere more prevalent than at Billboard Publications' computer operations in Cincinnati—both before and after I was Systems and Programming (S&P) Manager.

Billboard

After my ouster from GCSC (chapter 8) my next stint was with Thoman Software and then with Billboard Publications as major client of Thoman Software with intermediate stints as a self employed IT professional. At Billboard my curmudgeonly side was honed to perfection. Bill the vice president of marketing and sales in New York was ostensibly over the computer operation in Cincinnati. He was my bosses' boss. But Bill was the swashbuckling sales type who was anathema to the discipline necessary for successful data processing. His herky-jerky requests and constantly changing "priorities" made the reengineering necessary to bring Billboard's data processing into the current century nigh unto impossible. While Bill's office was at Billboard's New York City headquarters he all-too-often came to Cincinnati. And, of course there was the all-to-present telephone and my occasional trip to New York City. The bulk of the Billboards production facilities were in Cincinnati where the centerpiece magazine, *Billboard*, was published, where the many book clubs were processed, and where the computer operation was housed. I vividly remember Bill as a formidable figure and how hard he was to work with. My boss worked diligently but unsuccessfully to act as a buffer between Bill and the day-to-day computer operations.

Sales Reporting System Design Meeting

Billboard Publications was interested in having Thoman Software develop a sales reporting system including commission calculation. My boss Dick Thoman and I were in Billboard's Cincinnati conference room with Bill, Billboard's vice president of sales, to get a handle on initial systems requirements. But we, particularly Dick, could not get Bill to come up with any specifications that we could work with. Bill kept saying that he wanted to keep his options open and, I guess in today's terms—flexible. But there are limits to flexibility. A computer system must exist for it to be flexible. No computer system may have the ultimate inflexibility of a manual system. On the other hand IBM can stand for "It's Better Manually."

Dick, who was not a patient man, finally got up and handed a COBOL coding pad to Bill and said, "Here is a COBOL coding pad. You must write your own program. Until you come up with some specifics of how you want things handled—we can't help you!" And as Dick walked out the room—so did I. The idea of a sales reporting system was dropped and never came up again. Today we could likely handle these ambiguities with our Dynamic Condition Search as presented in our book, *Flexible Software Design*.

Inflexible Accounting System

My first priority as Billboard's new Systems and Programming (S&P) manager was to tackle the monthly business disruption caused by Billboard's outdated and quirky accounting system. First I took the many un-integrated pieces and tried to rationalize them and at least make common understandable procedures that could be used each month. But still during the first 10 days or so of each month, it was one panic after another until the month-end financials were published. Not only was the system not flexible, it was barely even a system.

In order to develop an up to date flexible accounting system, I attempted to form a team to determine the required capabilities. Unfortunately, the accounting personnel were unavailable for this. When they were not absorbed by the month-end panic, they were traveling around the country attending demonstrations of packaged accounting systems. All too soon a feature-rich best of breed accounting package was purchased over my strenuous objections. Once installed and in operation it was apparent that many functions vital to the company were missing or deficient. Several other functions were superfluous to the business but required significant hardware resources to operate and personnel time to maintain.

So the new accounting system did not elevate the panic and kept my staff and me continually in firefighting panic mode. This led my colleagues and me to the myth of comparative evaluation.

The Myth of Comparative Evaluation

Take care not to fall prey to *the myth of comparative evaluation.* If a packaged system is to be purchased, don't compare apples to apples; compare them to a description of the apple you need.

Myth: To choose the best product, compare candidate products to each other.

Reality: The best product is chosen by comparing candidate products to *requirements.*

Do not go on a wild goose chase finding six candidate systems and then choose the "best." The "best" may be less than, more than, or not even close to what you need. If you must go on such a chase compare the candidate to your requirements—not to each other.

It seems obvious, but the myth persists, so it's worth a reminder. Don't compare apples to apples; compare them to a description of the apple you need. Also, having the requirements specification first will go a long way to assuring flexibility.

Billboard: Strategic Plan

As Systems and Programming manager for Billboard's IT operation my staff and I were continually bombarded with conflicting and overlapping requests from Billboard's schizophrenic management in New York, especially Bill the vice president of sales. Fire fighting was rampant, my group's morale and effectiveness were going downhill fast, and it had been a long time since the job was fun.

With considerable effort, I prevailed on Bill to grant a multi-day strategic planning session, which was held off-site at a downtown Cincinnati hotel. Bill and other key executives from New York were there so that a strategic direction and schedule could be established, thus eliminating the conflicting interruptions to the staff. When the meeting ended, I left with my list of priorities and a great sense of relief. The next day, back in the office, I called my staff together to plan our schedule and to show them that our jobs should now be more professional and rewarding. As I was speaking to them, the departmental secretary interrupted and said that Bill was on the phone. I picked up the phone and was informed that influential individuals (squeaky wheels) had gotten priorities changed. We were back to fire fighting. Eventually, as reported below, I protested once too often and was fired.

Unfortunately none of these executives had the requisite technical knowledge and understanding required to oversee an IT operation—thus creating technical distance that prevented me and my staff from providing a quality IT operation.

A Double Dose Of Technical Distance

Billboard in connection with their book clubs and other merchandising, had a warehouse in Kentucky across the Ohio River from the Cincinnati office. The mission of this warehouse was to ship books and related items for Billboard's many book clubs. This was quite a sophisticated operation with many, many small shipments.

The manager of that warehouse was considered to be one of the foremost warehouse managers in the area, if not the country. In typical Billboard fashion they hired a consultant to study the warehousing operation. After nosing around for the appropriate length of time the consultant made a series of recommendations that were totally at odds with the successful way that the warehouse was being operated.

Billboard followed the warehouse consultant's recommendations. As the recommendations were implemented the warehouse operation in Kentucky ran into problems and became unable to fulfill its mission. The manager left, and the Kentucky warehouse was soon shut down and the operation was moved to the New York area near Billboard's headquarters. I can only imagine how the relocated warehouse functioned knowing the abilities of the now nearby executives.

At about the same time Billboard's management hired another consultant to study the computer operations. What about the computer consultant's recommendations? He supported Cincinnati computer operations whole-heartedly. My boss, my staff, and I agreed fully with his recommendations—but Billboard management in New York chose not to accept the recommendations. And the computer operation was also moved to the New York area. Again, I can only imagine how the relocated computer operation functioned.

This certainly was a double dose of Technical Distance. The warehouse manager knew his business, was on sight, and managed a successful operation. Management in New York, did not understand warehousing, had most likely never been to the site, and in my judgment could not manage anything but marketing and sales (if that?). For the computer operation, they did not follow the consultant's recommendation, which meshed totally with the staff. So Billboard's management made the wrong decision TWICE!

Let Us Integrate

We received a memo from Bill in early October 1978 that Billboard had purchased another publisher and that their data processing would be integrated with ours by the end of the year. I shot back a short memo saying, "Bill, that is impossible, how can we integrate something that itself is most likely not integrated into something that is not integrated, namely our system which is not integrated and can never be as long as you micro mange us." I was immediately fired as Manager of Systems and Programming. But soon thereafter I was hired back as a consultant (actually maintenance programmer) at a considerably higher hourly rate of pay. In this role I just did what was right and stayed out of the politics and out of Bill's way.

So as you can see Billboard's management style was anathema to the development of flexible systems or any other rational or effective execution of their information technology operations.

LITIO

A prime example of needing to be at the computer and the difficulty of obtaining access was the saga of LITle Input/Output package (LITIO). For commercial production with heavy Input/Output (I/O), Procter & Gamble (P&G) had an in-house written I/O package that handled record blocking and unblocking, automatic overlapping reading and writing the next data with processing, and other important aspects of used for commercial application systems with heavy I/O. It required 7,500 positions of memory that were not available to be used by application programs. Since scientific, engineering, and mathematical computing is not generally heavy on I/O. P&G also had a smaller (at 2,500 positions of memory) I/O package, called LITIO for such systems. After Dick, the original author left P&G we discovered a bug in LITIO. Both I/O packages allowed tape mount ahead so that in the case of a multi-reel file, if necessary, the second reel could be mounted on a second drive and then the third reel back on the original drive and so on. LITIO crashed when a third reel was encountered.

We studied the problem and believed that we had found the cause and a fix that would fit in the limited memory available. But I had to be at the computer to test what we thought was the solution. Trying to get machine time at the console from the operations supervisor was nigh unto impossible. But several times over an hour was lost without any results when LITIO encountered the third reel. But I could not get the shift supervisors to understand that if, that is if, I had a true fix, then for one hour of testing with me at the console he could gain back the lost machine time and enable the runs to be successful. Finally after I had hounded one of the shift supervisors beyond his tolerance, rather than requesting that I be fired he said to his lead operator, "Stop everything, and give Bruce the damn system until he gives it back!" I took over the machine and with a test program and three short reels of input data. I anxiously watched to see what happened when the program called for the third reel back on the original tape drive. Voila! The revised LITIO switched to the third reel perfectly. I was correct. Our fix worked. Thus, no longer was an hour or more of machine time wasted without producing results. I have no idea of how much time was wasted previously due to this ill-advised policy. See my concept of system software preventive maintenance in chapter 1. System software maintenance time would have made this much more satisfactory.

Following Stupid Rules—Exactly!

While I was not initially involved with General Computer Services Corporation's (GCSC) Utility Billing system, I became intimately involved with it after George went to Brazil. George supervised the development of a sophisticated system with estimated billing and a number of other bells and whistles. Unfortunately, while the system was sophisticated, it was not very well written. It was of poor quality and required constant maintenance and hand holding, which became a real albatross, taking away from billable time for other projects. In a word it was very inflexible.

While operation of the system, keypunching from meter books and receipts, running the bills and reports, was marginally profitable, we actually made our money on the forms. We purchased and stored the forms and marked up their price. So like Gillette, we literally gave away the razor and made money on the blades. Today's analogy would be essentially giving away ink jet printers and charging an arm and a leg for the cartridges.

Case in point. Recently I purchased a new printer for $129.63 (using a $10 coupon), which included a full set of ink cartridges that lasted for several months. The first set of replacement cartridges cost $105.48. So did the printer really cost between $25 and $35? Many years ago I purchased a really cheap black and white printer for $29.95 whose replacement cartridge cost $31.95, I could have save two bucks by buying anther printer saving the cartridge and throwing away a printer.

Our first and main customer was a utility from a nearby city. The head of the utility and his second in charge did not get along very well and their disputes intruded upon our interaction with the agency. They experienced technical distance. There appeared to be an aggressive contest to see which one picked up the output from our monthly run of their utility bills. To supposedly put an end to this the agency head said, "Please do not give our output to anyone but me." After erroneously not following his request a time or two he really laid down the law: "No one, but no one, but me is ever to receive the output from our runs!" We got the message. The result was not pleasant. The head of the agency went on an extended vacation and the bills did not get picked up. The bills did not get mailed. And the payments did not come in. When he got back he was livid—until he realized that the situation was caused by his instructions, which were quickly rescinded.

Incidents like this are behind one of my mantras "Follow stupid rules exactly!" So often while well meaning—not following stupid rules enables them to become institutionalized because the consequences are not realized. Conscientious people knowing that the rules are stupid do not follow them so they never get changed. I champion following such rules exactly to expose their stupidity to the light of day where they may hopefully be changed.

Markets

One of GCSC's clients Markets, a wholesale grocery distributor, had a sizable installation with IBM hardware that was not very well operated by a manger who personified technical distance. This manager frequently contacted us to help them out of a problem, for which we charged reasonable fees. But more frequently Markets turned to IBM whose solution to almost every situation was, "Buy More Hardware." Or IBM—I Buy More." Markets' monthly rental to IBM was in the range of $20,000. Time and time again we offered to do all of their processing on our 1401 computer for a little over half of that. It would have been a very lucrative contract for us. But IBM, at least at that time, had great salespersons and a great sales approach. We could not break their hold except for comparatively minor maintenance programming.

Industry mantra at that time was, "If you choose IBM and fail you will keep your job. But if you chose another vendor and fail—you will loose your job." Few chose to take the risk and Markets data processing manager certainly did not, even at the cost of nearly $10,000 extra per month. To me this is a shining example of IBM's hegemony, which subsequently was replaced by Microsoft's hegemony. Now Google? This is also an example of how costly technical distance can be.

A problem that Markets hired GCSC to solve was a classic in its day. Since physically starting and stopping a segment of computer magnetic tape is much slower than the actual electronic reading thereof, often data on tape is blocked. That is, many logical records such as for a customer are combined into one physical tape record. If each customer had a record consisting of 100 characters and we blocked 10 logical customers per physical tape record, the physical record would be 1000-characters. Thus 9 start/stop operations would be avoided for the small price of a larger buffer and the computer code to unblock the logical records. This code, being a part of the Input-Output Control System (IOCS) was transparent to the programmer and took no extra work. Except...

It would be highly unlikely that the firm would have a number of customers that was an exact multiple of the blocking factor, say 10. So the last physical record would have to be padded with some non-data characters to fill it out. In the case of output, the IOCS would block the records as records 1 through 9 came in and the 10th record would be placed at the end of the block forcing out the current block and preparing to start a new block.

But when the firm had say 1005 customers the job would end with 5 customers in the output block buffer and a specific "file close" would need to be issued to force the last partial block out since there was no 10th customer to do the force. This was/is called flushing the buffer.

In Markets' case this last close was missing from their program and each time they ran the program adding and deleting customers the last 0 to 9 customers would be lost. They could not figure out why and called us in to the fix the problem—which did not take us long. We just added an end of job file close operation.

This was a classic system bug in the early days of computing. While modern computing systems still block records even on disk, today languages automatically flush the buffer when the program terminates—avoiding this problem. But belt and suspenders programmers such as myself still include this final close.

The Orange Juice Story

The following orange juice story gives a strong flavor of the nature of the General Computer Services Corporation's (GCSC) business. While this scenario shows clearly that we were not good salespersons it does, however, show that we were good technically and that we were good order takers. It may also show that I was not immune to the ills of technical distance.

Desperate to obtain new work to meet the upcoming payroll and other expenses, George, the President and I, the Executive Vice President, had been out on a sales call to a local company we shall call Water on a Friday afternoon. We did not get back to the office until after 5 pm. Everyone else had gone home for the weekend.

In our judgment, the sales call had gone poorly. We were both very discouraged. To pump up our courage we pulled a bottle of scotch from my desk and poured ourselves a stiff drink. Midway through the second sip the phone rang and I answered it. It was, Pete, the President of Water, calling from across town. Pete said, "Can you come back over and meet with us some more?" I responded, "This late on Friday afternoon?" The answer was, "Yes, if you can?" "OK we will be right over," I replied.

When we got to Water's offices they also had a bottle of scotch on the conference room table and they poured each of us a glass. After we had taken a sip they came right out and said, "You have the contract! How soon can you start?" We were flabbergasted! This was so counter to our assessment when we left earlier that afternoon. In fact we were so flabbergasted that we shared our initial assessment and asked them, "What had caused you to choose us?"

Then Pete said, "It's like the orange juice story." George and I both starred at him and repeated, "The orange juice story?" "Yes," Pete replied and then told us the following story.

"A while back, a colleague of ours was arranging for an upcoming conference in a nearby city. They were expecting somewhere near 800 persons at this three-day conference. At the first hotel he checked with he told them that all 800 persons wanted freshly squeezed orange juice for breakfast. The hotel's immediate response was, 'We can't do that.' So he went to the second hotel with the same request. Their response was, 'No problem.' So he went to the third hotel and again said, 'I have upwards of 800 people who wish to have freshly-squeezed orange juice for breakfast.' Their response was, 'Wow! We can do that. But it's going to cost you!' You have already guessed that the third hotel hosted the convention."

Pete then said, "Your firm was the third hotel. You said, 'Wow! We can do that. But it's going to cost you.' You were the only vendor that understood our needs and were willing to tackle them. Your price is high, but our requirements are significant and complex—and we recognize that they will come with a high price tag. But the cost of going with a firm who does not understand our business and our needs and who does not have your expertise would be much costlier in the long run."

The system GCSC developed for Water had no internal paper trail at all. All paper stopped at the loading dock and started again at the shipping dock. All internal transactions were done with an online interactive paperless system utilizing a Litton 1700 business machine computer. In the early 70s this was revolutionary—and expensive. But the payout for both GCSC and Water was very, very significant. We were again, ahead of the times.

This scenario taught us that we were better order takers than salespersons. We learned again that our technical prowess exceed our pomp and pizzazz. Our "sales pitch" was honest and strait forward and dealt with the difficult technical realities of Water's requirements. It was geared to the actual nature of their situation. It was not fluff; we did not minimize the job to get our feet in the door. When we made our straightforward, technically-oriented presentation and went away discouraged we had misjudged the folks at Water. They had in fact understood our approach to be in concert with their needs and desires.

Unfortunately, many other potential clients did not react that way and we never learned how to overcome these potential clients lack of appreciation of our approach. Our experience with Water may have been an example of Technical Distance manifested as our not being sensitive to body language that may have been transmitted during the meting.

The Water system was one of the few systems that we did for small businesses as most of our contracts were with divisions of large company's such as Armco Steel, or Procter & Gamble.

APPALLING AUTOMATED APPAREL

Automated entrepreneurial founders were, as is so often the case; much better at starting a business than keeping it going, better at obtaining business than at executing it. One of Automated's largest systems was Apparel a uniform rental system that produced documents and postings for a franchiser of uniform routes. The next several incidents have to do with this system.

A Beer In My Right Hand

A prime example of my interaction with Automated's management and systems was a Fourth of July weekend in downtown Cincinnati. The long weekend, with the Fourth falling on Saturday, celebrated on Friday had required that an extra amount of data be processed. A combination of antiquated cheap mainframe hardware and their slap-dash approach to programming had caused a large file on the disk to wrap and the beginning of the file had been overlaid by, what should have been, the end. Their bread and butter system was down!

I was called in late Sunday afternoon to fix the problem(s) and to get them up and running again. I was in the terminal room with the two helpless entrepreneurs and a case of beer. It was Hudepohl not even Christian Moerlein. While their operation was primarily batch, they had a character-by-character online terminal, which I literally operated with my left hand; I am left handed, while I drank a beer with my right hand.

My ego was floating so high (surely helped by the beer) while I wrote programs to print out various portions of the disk and then write one time programs to say—change the 17th character of the 626,367th record from a 7 to a 1 and to delete the records on either side. Needless to say, these were truly one-time programs—because after each run—the layout of the disk file changed. After several hours I had them up and running again—but they had to reprocess all the data. They ran all night so as to mail the results to their customers on Monday. In spite of the beer, the tension, and my ego—I made no errors that evening. Given the situation an error could have been catastrophic.

While working on the Apparel system, I encountered a particularly frustrating problem. Each Thursday their system would produce inconsistent results that I was requested to track down and correct. I studied the program listings, watched the operation, and checked the input transmitted from the field, yet I could find nothing and the problem continued. One lucky Thursday while in the data control room I saw a data clerk take a small deck of cards out of her desk and place it in the input to the Apparel program. When I asked her what she was doing she said, "Jack (who had long ago left the company) told me to enter these cards into the Apparel run every Thursday."

These cards were apparently the solution to some long ago problem—but at this time they *were* the problem. I removed the cards from the Apparel input, placing them in my brief case, and the problem no longer occurred.

Appalling Apparel Parallel

One of the most consistent technical distance scenarios had to do with parallels. It seems logical when converting to a new system to run the old and the new side-by-side and compare the results. This sounds like a belt and suspenders approach. But it neither tests the belt nor the suspenders. There seldom are sufficient resources to truly do this effectively, much less run two complete systems for any length of time, and certainly not enough resources to fully compare the results of two runs. We will discuss the nature of the problem and the solution at the end of this little scenario.

As Automated's management headaches exceeded the entrepreneur's ability to handle them the business slowly began to slide and the owners started selling off their systems.

The apparel rental application system was sold to Service just outside of Minneapolis. For a about a year during and after the transfer

I spent a week each month at Service's installation. Work was required to transfer the programs from Automated to Service given slightly difference hardware, software, and operations.

Based up my experience, I pleaded with the management both in Cincinnati and Minneapolis not to run a parallel and was overruled. So we ran both systems for a week—one in Cincinnati and one a thousand miles away in Minneapolis and compared the output—but it was the output from the old system in Cincinnati that was actually used and mailed to the routes. The route system processing was done four days per week Monday through Thursday, with slightly different processing done each day.

Given the success of the parallel, the cutover took place the following Monday. The processing in Minneapolis went fine without an apparent hitch—the first week. Whew! But the next week "fit hit the schan." Many transactions dropped out and some output was in error. I was Johnny-on-the-spot in Minneapolis to rectify the problems. After much searching through current and past results (printouts which had been boxed and saved) and comparing them, I found that during the previous Wednesday's parallel run in Minneapolis, a large number realignment transactions had dropped out and not been processed. I went back to the output from the parallel run from two weeks ago and, low and behold, the same thing had happened. This was a delayed glitch that do to lack of diligence was not detected and laid in wait to trap us.

I asked the trembling data clerk why this had not been brought to our attention. She said hesitatingly that during the intensity of the parallel this output had been set aside—and when the results mailed last week checked out they were either forgotten or not considered important. The errors in the realignment operation being mostly internal to the system with their delayed results had been completely overlooked in the heat of the moment—which typically happens during parallels.

Here is what had transpired. As routes grew and shrunk, they would be consolidated or split. This process is called realignment and was processed on Wednesdays to take effect the following Monday so as to allow for mail delay—as this was before serious data transmission was economical. Since the realignment had not happened, data for the realigned routes and stops mailed in by the uniform suppliers did not match and could not be processed.

This further solidified my belief, which I still hold; that parallels are most often a bad idea. What is much better is a full and complete testing of the new system to assure that it does what it is supposed to do when it is supposed to do it.

Much earlier during the GCSC days running parallels really bit me. When we took over payroll processing for one of our customers. The parallel was our second mistake. Our first mistake was cutting over during the calendar year when we had to pick up year-to-date data. So once we thought that we had the payroll system checked out, we loaded their year-to-date data and ran a weekly payroll and compared to the output from the system being replaced. The two systems did not agree! So we had to determine the reason and then try another cutover, which required again loading year-to-date data. This happened several times and was very time consuming and expensive for our little outfit. In the final analysis our system was right and their existing system was in error. But we had to reflect these errors in the year to date figures and eat the extra costs. We should have had more confidence in our system and not done the parallels.

As I have often said, "Many systems are accidents of history." In this case so was the output from the payroll system that we were replacing.

WASP EEOC Officer

Have you ever seen a white, Anglo Saxon, Protestant Equal Employment Opportunity Commission Officer? Well I was once one.

Thoman Software was developing financial and sales systems for a cosmetic factory. I was asked to perform a very un IT task. The factory apparently was under the gun from the Equal Employment Opportunity Commission (EEOC) with some question regarding the diversity of their work force. Thus I was set up with an official looking office and came dressed in a suit and tie. Each employee came into the office and sat across from me while I interviewed them about their background determining their name, maiden name, mother's maiden name, and ethnicity. I assigned them EEOC points from one to four depending upon their nationality, color, name, or maiden name, etc. I, of course, was not necessarily qualified—but who would be? Was this again bureaucracy, technical distance, or incompetence? You judge. Luckily I did not have to ask them if they were gay, straight, lesbian, or transgendered (LGBT). This was before sexual orientation was such a big deal.

Another similar instance had to do with restrooms in GCSC's Middletown, Ohio offices. We had a three-floor building with a restroom on both the first and second floors. Both men and women worked on each floor and one of the workers on the second floor had a physical handicap. But the Occupational Safety and Health Administration insisted that we segregate restrooms. So we labeled the first floor restroom Men and the Second floor restroom Women. Then we used whichever restroom was near by when we had a need. This was a case where we did not follow a stupid rule exactly. But we had to when we remodeled the second floor of the building next door as two restrooms were required and they both were on the same floor.

What Is COBOL For?

At Billboard our application systems were written in COBOL. We experienced a number of problems with the Hewlett Packard 3000 (HP3000) COBOL compiler, which converted our human-readable code into machine-readable code. Some COBOL statements were not implemented and compiled incorrect code

Coincidently, when I sent two of my Billboard programmers to a HP conference where they met the woman who headed the team that developed the HP3000 COBOL compiler. She asked the programmers, "What do you use COBOL for?" She was a computer science graduate and had no understanding of business processing. I felt this explained many of the problems that we had. This was an early example of technical distance even between techies.

IBM Hegemony

In the 1960s P&G, was an entirely IBM shop with a national account status and having nearly 20 IBM computers and a large amount of peripheral gear. However, we occasionally looked elsewhere for computing equipment. A team of four of us was formed to investigate hardware for a data transmission application, which, by this time was being done computer-to-computer utilizing a model of the IBM S/360.

The S/360 was rather expensive. Several cheaper potential alternative machines became available and our team studied them—each of us representing a different vendor, including IBM. I was assigned the Univac 1004 card processor, which was a clever little plug board wired machine with 961 positions of memory. I thought that it was ideal for the application. I do not remember who the other vendors were or what their machines were. But I do remember the final presentation on a Friday afternoon and one of the vendors other than IBM or Univac was initially chosen.

As it was late Friday afternoon IBM asked, "Can you give us the week end to rethink our proposal? You are not going to really do anything until Monday." It was agreed that that would be OK. The entire Cincinnati IBM branch office worked all weekend. Monday morning they presented a proposal utilizing different hardware that P&G ended up accepting.

I am sure the reward for making a sale was great—but the penalty for losing the sale was even greater—that was what IBMers feared the most. And this is just one case in point.

Holey Punched Card

One of the engineers with whom I had frequent contact used our equipment at Winton Hill to develop an application utilizing aperture cards which, as shown here, had a piece of photographic film embedded in its center.

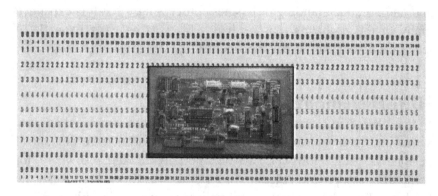

I am not sure what kind of testing he didbut as it turned out, it was not with aperture cards. Our card reader/punch—an IBM 1442—was photoelectric. Rather than using brushes and electronic contacts the reader used light. So when the light shown through a hole position, a punch was sensed. The machine had two stations, a read station and a write (punch) station thus enabling punching into the card just read. So, I guess for a production run, he ran his aperture cards through his application, reading the data on the cards doing some calculation and sending the read data along with the results of the processing to the punch. OOPS, the apertures, being translucent, were read as holes in the incoming card and when combined with the calculated data were sent to the punch. And his apertures were neatly laced with holes.

P&G IT Progression

P&G's Data Processing Systems Department (DPS) organization and culture was built correctly at its inception. Its uniqueness was documented in a *Fortune Magazine* article in the early 60s. In most firms, data processing was an adjunct to accounting/finance and thereby was several levels removed from the CEO and the boardroom.

At P&G not only did the Data Processing Systems (DPS) department report directly to a VP but also the department existed, with Chet a very strong manger, for some time before acquiring its first computer—an IBM 705. During this time it developed a corporate-wide charter and thus DPS never became captive to any one segment of the company. The early systems were: shareholder records; company plans; order, shipping, and billing (OSB), and the like. This overwhelming early success with company-wide commercial production systems may have lead to Chet and the department's subsequent failure to listen to and respond to the technical community which had entirely different computing needs. This failure led to its DPS's eventual demise through reorganization shortly after I left.

All systems were justified through a vigorous rate of return analysis called the phase one (estimated return) and phase two (actual return) approach. The hurdle rate, as I remember, was 20%. Since many foundation systems were justified on this basis, many subsequent systems that built on these foundations had very attractive returns due to their piggyback effect.

One of the early large systems was Order, Shipping, and Billing. (According to stories that I heard later, many persons in P&G thought that OSB could not be done. For example, each field office, etc. had a slightly different way of handling the pre-computer processing. KS the VP in charge of the project was a famous P&G curmudgeon who spawned many stories about his doings. One of these had to do with OSB. He was initially told, "There is no way that all the variety of processing can be incorporated into one system." His reply reportedly was, "That's OK because we are going to process all orders, shipments, and billings in just one way—MY way!" And P&G implemented OSB—his way. And to my knowledge, the system is still spitting out orders, shipments, and billings and has paid for itself many times over.

No Shared Time FORTRAN Class
I taught or actually started to teach at least one more class while with P&G. I was approached by a group of my peers who desired to upgrade their skills buy learning FORTRAN. We established a FORTRAN class at the Winton Hill Technical Center Regional Data Center where I was manager. We met from 4:00 pm to 5:00 pm one night a week. As 4:30 was quitting time this was half on company time and half on our own time. We felt that this was fair since they had no immediate need for FORTAN. But when management got wind of the class they asked us to stop using P&G time and equipment for a class that had no immediate application. So the class was cancelled. As I continued my careers I encountered many other incidents, which were decried in the management literature, where organization were unwilling to invest in employee training. This is an another form of technical distance.

Amazed At Lack Of Redundancy
Having always designed redundancy, like that in the accounting system part of the remote terminal system described in chapter 1, into my systems I find it truly amazing that others would not do the same. For example, to delay, at the cost of millions of dollars, the opening of Denver International Airport (DIA) because there was no alternate way to deliver baggage is inconceivable to me. DIA's (actually United Air Lines) automated luggage system never worked reliably and after many years of malfunctioning it was shut down, dismantled, and removed! Also to cause passengers to miss their flights because there

is no alternative way to get to and from the gates when the trains at DIA are down is also totally unacceptable. In fact, it is just plain dead wrong! At P&G these were called Emergency Alternate Procedures (EAP). EAPs were carefully thought out and rigorously tested and enforced.

I am appalled today that anyone is even considering much less using an electronic election system without a voter-verified paper ballot audit trail.

IT Department Has No IT

We are all aware of the story about the shoemaker who was so busy making shoes for others that neither he nor his family had shoes. There is also the story of the builder, who built my parent's house in a Chicago suburb (and there are many other builders to whom this applies). He kept selling the houses that were intended for his family such that, after many disappointments, his family never had their dream house and eventually his wife divorced him.

IT is often the same way. The Information Technology (IT) department or what ever it is called generally has immediate and unlimited access to IT technology—but often does not take advantage of it for their own operation—while pitching it to other departments. The P&G cross charging system (chapter 1) that used punched cards is an example of an IT department at the time not using technology to the fullest to do their job. I must admit that at Winton Hill we had a distinct advantage of being a mixed operations and technical group, having some slack, much technical knowledge and interest, and an ambitious staff; whereas the operations staff down town was pretty much swamped with operations and the software group was not directly involved with operations.

Even today there is many examples in the trade press where IT fails to take full advantage of the technology at their doorstep.

How Many Pairs?

This happened long before I taught statistics—but the lesson stuck with me when I did and still sticks with me. Management suffered from technical distance but the statistician did not.

P&G had a world-renowned statistician in their Mexican operations. He occasionally came to Cincinnati and to my data center to run calculations. He told us about the time P&G de Mexico was planning a lottery to give away the million-dollar equivalent in pesos based upon matching two halves of a ticket included in each box of a high volumeseveral million cases per yearproduct. The statistician was asked to calculate statistically how many pairs of winning tickets should be included to assure that only one million-dollar prize would be awarded.

After careful calculations, he came up with 3.5 pairs. When management asked him, "Well, how many should be include? Three or four?" He replied, "One!"

Technical Distance In Other Chapters
Professional Programming in COBOL (PPIC) book review process: chapter 7 Teaching Technology.
Lack of Adequate Key Punch support at P&G: chapter 1 InsightIngenuity.
Failure to Accept Incremental Install of Computer Systems: chapter 10 System for Planning Electrical Construction (SPEC).

Chapter Bibliography
Johnson, Bruce, Walter W. Woolfolk, Robert Miller, Cindy Johnson 2005: *Flexible Software Design: Systems Development for Changing Requirements,* Auerbach Publications.

CHAPTER 6
(IN)FLEXIBLE SYSTEMS

Introduction

Late in my careers I identified a phenomenon that had been with me the whole way: computer system inflexibility. "Why are computer systems so hard to modify?" "Why does modifying computer systems cause so many undesirable side effects, often including system outages?" It is because computer systems most often are not designed to be flexible: to be easily modified without undesirable side effects. It's obvious organizations change!

As organizations **change** computer systems designed to support them must be **modified**. Organizations *change*, computers systems are *modified*.

Some of what follows is hindsight. I did not always recognize that what we were doing contributed to computer systems flexibility or that the problems I was having were due to computer system inflexibility. Late in my careers and into retirement, computer system flexibility became my primary research interest, cumulating in the publication, with two colleagues in Cincinnati and my daughter in Denver: *Flexible Computer Systems: Systems Development for Changing Requirements*.

My colleagues and I define flexibility as the ability of a computer system to track organizational changes with little or no program or data structure modification. And, more importantly, with little or no involvement of the IT staff—the users should be able to make the necessary modifications via data values. While not all of the following examples meet that criterion precisely, I believe that many are early examples of the search for computer system flexibility—or at least extensibility, which is the ability to add additional capabilities.

The Third Best System

A Procter & Gamble (P&G) mantra was, "We build the third best system." P&G was aware that we were not smart enough to build the first best system, which would require knowing all future requirements. And we were not rich enough to build the second best system, which would require knowing how all our competitor's systems were going to work. Possibly today with a flexible system mind-set one would not have to settle for third best—a subject to be debated with a glass of red wine in hand.

MATRAN

The first example, MATRAN, deals with easy-to-modify programs; the next two examples IEBGENER and multiple regression actually have to do with replacing control cards with programming. In some ways examples of reverse flexibility, but still making it easier to track changing organizational requirements.

The actual development of MATRAN in the early 1960s, my first big project with P&G, is presented in chapter 1 Insight/Ingenuity. P&G brand managers were prominent users of MATRAN. Rather than developing one system, with or without multiple parameters, to report brand movement data to brand managers, MATRAN allowed each brand manager to tailor his (don't think there were any hers at that time) brand's reports to his particular management style. Their desires for information ran from simple displays to sophisticated statistical analysis with and without comparison to past periods or other brands, including those of competitors. Brand managers either understood MATRAN and did their own programming or used analysts from the industrial engineering department to provide the needed support. So while the reports were actually tailored via programming in MATRAN this flexible approach enabled multiple ways of converting brand data into brand information. The programming was at such a high level that it was easy to understand, easy to develop and, most important, easy to modify.

Over the years P&G developed a very powerful, sophisticated and option-rich stepwise multiple regression program written in the 705/7080 Autocoder language. While I lacked specific knowledge of the multiple regression application, I was still able to play a significant role in its continuing development—including its phasing out via MATRAN.

Elaborate control cards set the many options. These operations were described in a thick loose-leaf typed manual that was continually being updated. Given the complexity of the regression applications and the non-intuitive nature of the control card options, quite a few errors were made in setting up regression runs. For example, instead of punching a 1 in column 28, a 1 would be punched in column 38. Rather than an X in column 36, a Y would be punched erroneously— and on and on.

As MATRAN became more powerful and as analysts increased their ability with the language, they began tailoring their own multiple regression programs.

With the ease of program writing and reading due to the mnemonic nature of MATRAN and its powerful instructions such as, Eigen value, matrix transpose, and matrix inverse, which could process a tall matrix in single bound (instruction).

The analysts often found it easier and more flexible and reliable to directly write what they intended without the 1 and X punches. As a result, the use of the stepwise multiple regression program itself declined significantly over time and was eventually phased out.

Years later, when I was working toward my PhD, I was required to take five statistics courses. Being in a hurry to obtain my degree and, given my teaching schedule at Xavier, I had limited time available. I ended up taking the statistics courses in reverse order. Multiple regression was supposed to be the last course in the sequence, but it was the first course that I was able to take. When the course was over I finally understood what we had been doing in the stepwise multiple regression program and its MATRAN derivatives. The multiple regression course presented several obstacles, which are covered in the side bar.

Prerequisites And Related Incidents

When I started working for Xavier University, I had seven years to obtain my PhD in order to have a chance of obtaining tenure. Thus I was in a hurry which was difficult because I was teaching full time and was required to be a full time PhD student —to prove that I was serious. Full time meant taking a full course load (12 quarter hours) for three quarters out of five and two consecutively. I buckled down and took full loads in the spring of 1983 and the summers of 1983 and 1984.

In the five quarters bounded by those summers I took a total of 61 hours of the required 120 hours (45 was scheduled for my dissertation). I ended up taking 107 hours of course work and 52 hours of dissertation for a total of 159 hours. I also received an MBA along the way—in 1985.

I did not always have the luxury of taking courses and their prerequisites in their designated sequence. So, for example, I took my five statistics courses (15 quarter hours) in almost reverse order, multiple regression, forecasting (time series), and the introductory courses in statistics—statistics I, statistics II, and sample survey/experimental design. I received A's in the introductory courses and B's in the other three. I had taken one statistics class, Mathematical Statistics, as an undergraduate, at Washington State University (WSU). It was too long ago and too theoretical to be of much help. In fact, I had asked Dr. Rechard the WSU professor, "What if I had this bunch of data and wanted to derive meaning from it?" He, being a theoretical mathematician, had no idea. The WSU course had been all about deriving formulas for different distributions etc.—totally backwards from my way of thinking.

While at P&G I had developed multiple regression programs—but had never really studied the topic. I buckled down to slip through the higher-level courses without taking the prerequisites first. There were several bumps along the way.

First, the textbooks for the multiple regression class did not arrive until several weeks into the 10-week quarter. I found this out during the first class and as soon as it was over I went to the engineering library and checked out the University's only copy of the text. Thus I had a text before the rest of the class. This, of course, helped me perform, as did the instructor's guide I obtained by writing the publisher on Xavier stationery. The other bump occurred when the department chair called the instructor and me into his office and confronted us with the fact that I had not taken the prerequisites. I was saved when Al, the instructor, said, "Bruce is doing just fine. He is mastering the material." That was that and I stayed in the course.

During the first class of a quantitative methods course another instructor asked, "Would those who have not taken course such-and-such—the prerequisite—please raise your hands?" Even though I did not have the prerequisite, I did not raise my hand. I obtained the text for the prior course and with side study received an A in the course. The same instructor was later to give me my only B, (hotly disputed) in my major. The rest of my major subject grades were A's.

This is not to say that prerequisites are not important. At Xavier many students were not prepared-for courses I taught, often because they had not completed the prerequisites. The students and administration often blamed me for their difficulties and poor performance.

In my experience, statistics is one of the most frightening courses at all levels. There is more to this fright than mere math phobia. When I taught the subject, I called it "variation." I would line the students up by height, age, or some other attribute and then show how they varied and that "statistics" was just a study of that variation. Nothing else.

During my last several years in Cincinnati before we retired, I volunteered at Children's Hospital. Early on my supervisor had a degree in child development and was studying to become a nurse. She was taking a statistics course, which had her freaked out. When she found out that I taught statistics she asked for help, which I gladly gave—but only after we both agreed to call the subject variation—not statistics. Just this name change considerably eased her anxiety.

Another statistics course that I took out of sequence was Time Series. It was a very difficult course with a very demanding professor —the same one from whom I had taken regression. It was a small class held in a small classroom with black boards on all four sides. He would make a least two complete trips around the room writing formulas, calculations, graphs, and the like on the board. There was no way to take complete notes with this approach—and not all the material covered was in the textbook. I wished then that I had had a Polaroid camera. Of course, today a digital camera would be ideal. Two specific incidents stand out.

The first was our take-home mid-term exam. The instructors entered a set of a dozen or so time series on the computer and told us which series were represented and how many of each —but not which ones were which. That was the exam. We were to identify the type of series for each one and record our thinking process. It was a tough exam and I struggled with it. I struggled so hard, in fact, that I forgot to keep track of my process. I had been too focused on overcoming the pressure of the exam. And when I turned the exam in I had all the series correctbut was graded down for not reporting my thinking process.

The final exam was even worse.

It was held in the same little classroom where the class had been held. The instructor was giving our time series exam plus an exam for an undergraduate statistics class. When I looked at the exam my first thought was, "Was I in this class?" Almost all the problems were unfathomable—I just stared for the longest time. I thought, "Al wants to pass me. But I have to give him reason." So I tackled each problem answering what ever I could and then going on to the next one. One by one the undergraduates left. I was still going from problem to problem making a mark or two here and there. Then the other time series graduate students began to leave one by one. By this time I was sweating profusely and the floor under my seat had drops of sweat on it. Then time was up—only the instructor and I were still there. He did not move—I kept pecking away at the problems – finding a little bit here and there that I could add to the answers. I was not in a hurry to leave. I was going out of town and would head directly to the airport after the exam. But, how long would he let me continue this pecking away? Finally an hour and a half after the exam was supposed to be over, he got up and so did I—soaking wet and totally drained I gave him my paper and we walked out.

I got a B on the exam and in the class. This incident became a symbol of the difference between true diligence, tenacity to get though, as opposed to what I often saw in my students at Xavier who gave up and dropped the course at the first sign of adversity. Xavier's easy drop policies made it difficult for students to learn commitment to a task. Graduate students could drop right before the final exam and undergraduates could drop within five weeks of the end of the 16-week semester. Much effort went to support students who eventually dropped classes, which could have been much better spent on other endeavors. I "had" to obtain a PhD degree to keep my job —I just buckled down and did what was necessary.

I have encountered other cases where programming was easier than filling out control cards. For example the IBM 360 Operating System had a utility called IEBGENER, which could be used to copy files, reformat files, make test data, and the like. But, again, it required mastery of many esoteric, non-intuitive control cards. I did not use IEBGENER. I accomplished such tasks by writing simple one-feature PL/1 programs having two or three statements.

Symbolic High speed InterpreTer

Make no mistake; code reuse is a good thing. That is probably why so much has been written about it. But it seems to me that, in some ways at least, code reuse was better in the early days of my career. In the 1960s when I was in the Computer Techniques Development side of P&G's Research Group (today it would be called the Systems Software Group), our programming language was 7080 Autocoder, which had an extremely powerful macro capability[26]. We learned to write our own macros. As a result, our group agreed that whenever we wrote similar code for the third time we would encapsulate it into a macroinstruction. The new macroinstruction was then written up in a standard format and distributed to the group for filing in loose-leaf notebooks.

These macros could be very powerful. Each had a varying number of operands, which could be checked for data-type (numeric, alphabetic, floating point, etc.) and other attributes. Elaborate decision scenarios could be developed at macro generation time based on this and other metadata (data about data). These macros could generate many, often dozens, of machine instructions (talk about reuse!) and it could be tailored to many variations of a specific situation (talk about polymorphism![27]) If an error was found it could easily be corrected in the macro and take effect after the next assembly. In fact we built our own Research Group autocoder assembler tape that we called the Symbolic High speed InterpreTer, contrary to the fact that it was not symbolic, not high speed, and definitely not an interpreter. But we, being young techies, liked the acronym and we were big into acronyms. In fact, we even had a system whose acronym was ACRONYM, but for the life of me I cannot remember what our acronym ACRONYM stood for.

What this approach did not have was machine independence. This became an overriding consideration within the industry, leading to

---

[26] A macroinstruction is a high level instruction often with operands (parameters) that can generate a large number of machine level instructions, which vary according to the nature of the operands.

[27] Polymorphism is a term from Object Oriented Programming—a relatively modern development, long after I was at P&G. It means the ability to take many forms —or in this case for programs to accomplish many tasks.

development of machine-independent languages such as, COBOL and, to some extent, PL/I. COBOL did not have a macro (code generation) facility though it did have an include and copylib capability which enabled prewritten code to be included from a library just prior to compilation. PL/I went a little further with its preprocessor, which IBM called a macro capability but these features never came close to providing the power and the flexibility that we had in the 7080 and 1401 autocoders with their macro capabilities.

P&G/GCSC[28] Basic Functions

While the advent of direct processing via disk has tended to cause the demise of basic functions, the discipline and logic of basic functions is just as applicable to direct processing, though the benefits are not as apparent as they are with serial devices. Nevertheless, basic functions served both P&G and GCSC in their quest for improved system development and maintenance. They provided early flexibility tools and techniques.

The seven basic functions were developed in the late 1960s and early 1970s at P&G. Their aid to productivity, in my mind, is unparalleled by any other system design and development technique.

Basic Functions are particularly valuable in processing controlled by serial devices such as tape. By serial, I mean one; generally record, after another, each one having essentially the same processing. This often characterizes the middle of the beginning, middle, and end program model. Most basic functions also require or assume that the file is in sequence. That is, each record related to its predecessor (generally equal to or higher) based upon one or more designated control fields. This I call serial sequential.

Generally each basic function is limited to one or two input file(s). There are two exceptions: 1) the sort and/or merge which, at least logically, can have an unlimited number of inputs, and 2) linked basic functions. In linked basic function the output of one function can serve as (one of) the input(s) to another and that the output of that basic function can serve as (one of) the input(s) to another and so on. The data transfer between basic functions can be external via input/output

---

[28] Procter & Gamble/General Computer Services Corporation.

operations or internal via data areas in memory. This has the added benefit of enabling two programs to be easily combined into one or one program with multiple basic functions to be split into two programs should the need arise after the system is in production.

All serial processing that we encountered fit the pattern of one or more (linked) basic functions. In pre-disk days and given our basic function orientation, all processing was serial. For example, the SPEC system, though on a machine with disk drives, was a combination of 36 basic functions in over 30 programs that often took over an hour to execute on a S/360 model 65.

The Seven Basic Functions And A Brief Discussion Of Each

Extract: One input with no sequence assumed. Each record is processed independent of any other. Often use to "extract" or pull out selected data. Is essentially the select and frequently the project from the relational select, project, join.

Sort: Form data (records) into a sequence based on one or more control fields. Generally a utility sort provided by the hardware vendor is utilized. If there is more than one input file to the sort a merge is accomplished in the process.

Merge: Combines two or more files that are in the same sequence by the same control field(s).

Summarize: Processes groups of in-sequence records with the same control field(s) values. Often used for report roll up, such as summing all orders for a customer.

Match: A "master" file is matched against a "table" file in the same sequence. A common use is to run an order file via an item price file to extend the prices.

Find: Similar to a match except that the table file is kept in memory.

Update: A "master" file is updated with data from a "detail" or "transaction" file so as to add, change, or delete data (records) on the master file. The update is often accomplished by the combination of two basic functions—the merge followed by a summarize.

Most tasks can be accomplished by more than one basic function or combination of functions.

The logic of each basic function consists of five (extract) to eight (update) blocks depending upon the basic function. Processing blocks exist within a logical control structure whose flow is determined by the input data stream(s). Each block has a definite task and a definite place in the control structure. The first and last block in each basic function performs, respectively, initial housekeeping and end of job processing. The remainder of the blocks handle input, record comparison, various forms of processing, and output. While the logic of the basic functions is not what is important for this presentation, a smattering of their operation is presented below. The important is that they exist(ed) and the stories of their value.

HSKP – Housekeeping: One time logic executed at the beginning

GET 1 – Only file for Extract, Summarize, detail file for Update, Match, Find, and first file for Merge

GET 2 – Second file for Merge, Match, Find, master for Update etc

COMPARE: For Merge, Match, Update, Find, Summarize

PROCESS (up to three blocks depending upon function): hi, low, equal for Merge, master with or without detail, detail without master for Update, record for Extract, equal records and control breaks for summarize, etc.

EOJ: End of Job: One time logic executed at the end of processing—the opposite of Housekeeping

There were obvious opportunities to capitalize on the fact that each program was a combination of one or more of these basic functions. We did this in several ways.

The earliest capitalization on basic functions was utilizing 1401 Autocoder macroinstructions. George developed a macro for each basic function block. The operands of the macros included such information as: file names, which basic function the block was being executed in, labels of routines to be executed under specific circumstances. Thus writing a program in 1401 Autocoder involved filling in the operands for the macros for each block and then writing the actual code for the five to eight processing blocks many of which had designated labels or labels declared via macro operands.

Programs written using these macroinstructions were often free of logic errors once a clean assembly was achieved. In fact, I remember significant programs of George's that ran correctly on the first clean assembly.

Since COBOL and PL/1 did not have the macro power of the 1401 Autocoder, we designed partially pre-written coding sheets in each language for each of the seven basic functions. Once the basic function structure of the program was determined, all the programmer had to do was to fill in the blanks and write the processing code for the appropriate blocks. We eventually took this one step further and made master card decks for each function in each language that we used. When a system was to be developed we ordered the appropriate number of decks for each of the functions and they were duplicated and interpreted for our use. This significantly reduced the keypunching required reducing both cost and elapsed time.

To a degree, P&G considered basic functions proprietary and thus did not publicize them widely. There was a presentation at a conference and a chapter in an unpublished manuscript. Some internal manuals and instruction booklets were written and GCSC was allowed unrestricted use of them as GCSC had three ex P&Gers who thoroughly understood basic functions, and much of our use was on P&G projects.

I feel that the loss of basic functions along with the loss of macroinstruction in favor of direct processing and higher level languages has not been completely beneficial to the IT field.

In some ways, the in-memory transfer of data between basic function predated the virtual I/O feature of Operating System 360 (OS 360). In OS 360 you could, via Job Control Language (JCL), designate a work file that passed data from one program to another in the same job.

OS/360 supported multiple memory partitions, which could be of different sizes. Each partition ran a separate job using time slicing. The operator set the number of partitions, their sizes, the types of job, and priority of jobs that could run in each partition. When the machine was lightly loaded and not all partitions were in use, considerable efficiencies could be gained utilizing virtual I/O because data would be kept in core rather than written to disk. If core was not available, then the data was written to an external disk file. This required no changes to programs or to job control statements.

This is somewhat like the way linked basic functions worked. If there was room in memory for two or more basic functions, they could be linked via data passed in memory. If there was not room in memory then the data could be written to an external device, generally tape, and read by a subsequent basic function implemented in a separate program. In this case minor modifications requiring a recompile needed to be made to the passing and receiving basic function programs when they needed to be split or recombined. My two most outstanding memories of the value and power of the 1401 basic function macros follow.

Jack and I were collaborating on a large complex program, which had to run yesterday. The results of our first test run were a disaster. We struggled to discern a pattern in the erroneous results in order to find a place to start our debugging. But there did not appear to be any pattern at all. So we went back to the drawing board and reviewed our design logic and began to desk check our code again when Jack shouted "Eureka!" He had found the problem. We had written the correct code but in two cases we had inserted the code in the wrong basic function block. We switched 800 cards between blocks, reassembled, and voila the program executed perfectly. It is hard to imagine any other technique or technology that could yield such results on significant programs.

Over time GCSC developed systems for Armco Steel subsidiaries in England, France, Italy, Germany, and Mexico. One GCSC employee and several locals who were being trained staffed most of these locations. In all cases basic functions were used. There was more than one incident where the GCSC analyst at the client's location in a foreign country would call long distance to the home office in Middletown, Ohio for help in debugging a program. The caller would generally start with something like, "I have an update linked to a summarize and the following is supposed to happen in block six of the update. Immediately the listener understood the logic of the program and without much more explanation could help the caller solve the problem. Again, I am unable to imagine any other technique where this would be so easily done.

A story is told that after some GCSC indoctrination and training the local programmers in England were skeptical and wanted to take a class from the reigning geniuses in the field—IBM. So George signed them up and the local programmers attended a systems and programming class where the IBM instructor told them that one could not modify master file records in the same run in which they were added or deleted. That was enough for the programmers; they had already programmed the GCSC (P&G) update basic function in which all three functions—add, delete, and update, are easily accomplished in a single program!

Thoman/Independent

After General Computer Services' demise in 1976 I spent the next six years as a consultant. My assignments included work with Thoman Software and Billboard Publications. Thoman Software performed system development work ranging from gathering the initial requirements through programming, coding, and operation. One of our goals was to be able to specify a system in a machine-readable form and then on a Friday night turn loose our system generator and come in Monday with a generated-operational system.

While we did not reach this utopia, we did—or Dick did—develop several tools, which facilitated bridging the gulf between design and implementation. These included a text editor, which handled text a page at a time rather than, like most editors of the day, a character or a line at a time. This facilitated both program writing and the development of documentation.

The most useful tool was a system that generated formatted screens (which today would be called GUIs—or graphical user interfaces). At this time online interaction with a computer system was in its infancy and formatted screens were quite a breakthrough as were page editors. The input to this program was a screen specification language, which included the size, type, and placement of fields upon the Cathode Ray Tube (CRT) screen. The output was COBOL code, which described the screen fields in the data division as well as procedural code to manipulate the fields. This code would then be combined with hand-coded procedures to make up the program.

A similar generator was developed to produce reports. The input was the report layout in terms of field sizes, placement, and rules for processing (totals, etc.) and the output was COBOL code to place the fields and processing code to manipulate them. Most of this work was done in COBOL on the Hewlett Packard HP3000, but some portions were written in Software Programming Language (SPL) for the HP3000. SPL was much like PL/I and writing in one then switching to the other, as I did regularly, caused numerous small syntax errors. For example, one ended a statement with a semi colon—the other did not.

While Thoman Software was strong on implementation and program coding, the firm's forte was system design—specifically data base design.

We never really considered our designs done. One checkpoint was when we seemed to be ready to implement—we asked ourselves "What are the next three change requests likely to be? How would we incorporate them into our design?" If we could not come up with at least three potential changes and visualize how they would be incorporated into our design, we knew we were not ready for implementation and we went back to the design drawing board. This seems like an early form of what I now call designing for flexibility.

Thoman Software obtained a contract to design a replacement system for KT, a multi-line appliance and floor covering wholesaler. While we were designing the system, I was assigned as manager of KT's day-to-day computer operations, which were in dismal shape. Thus I was on sight most of the time. Once a week or so Dick would come over and for several hours we would sketch out a design for KT's proposed new system. After he left I carefully copied our blackboard design onto large sheets of paper—as a place to start when Dick came the next week. But when Dick came the next week he was not interested in the diagram developed from our work the week before. We started all over again from scratch. He said that when we had the same design two weeks in a row we had it right. Unfortunately, before we could finish, KT went bankrupt.

As operations manager for KT I fought many fires. One was what I call the three/four/N customer number problem. When I first arrived the sales manager said, "We have no sales statistics from which to calculate sales commission." I checked their order, billing, and shipping system (OSB) and, sure enough, no record was kept of the customer whose salesperson that was to get the commission credit (referred to as the statistics to customer). I modified the system to include the statistics to customer. No sooner had I done that and the warehouse manager said, "All of a sudden there is no information on where to ship the goods." Oops I had overlaid the ship to customer with the stat to customer. So I fixed that and the next complaint came from the accountant, "Recently we lost information on who owns the goods we ship—who takes title to them." Yes, I thought, I had overlaid the sold to customer." And so it went.

KT's existing system had provision for only three customer numbers—not the four or unlimited number that they really needed[29]. They needed, at the minimum: an ordered by customer (who actually made the order), a sold to customer (who took title to the merchandise), a ship to customer (where the merchandise was to be delivered) and a stat to customer (whose salesperson received commission credit). For example, one of KT's customers was a national hotel chain. The regional office in Columbus, Ohio would order TVs. The TV's would be sold to the regional franchise owner in Cincinnati who took title to the TVs. The TVs were delivered to several different hotels in the Cincinnati-Northern Kentucky area. The sales commission went to the national sales representative out of headquarters in Chicago. So with the three customer numbers that had been provided in the existing system one of the customer facts was missing on such an order. I could move the problem around to satisfy the latest squeaky wheel but I could not make the sales manager, the warehouse manager, the accountants, and the shipping dock happy all at the same time. I could, and did, of course, add an additional field for stat to customer, but that approach only works until next need for another customer type arises.

---

[29] In database design entities occur either 0, 1, or unlimited (N) times. Any other count will cause the system to be inflexible.

This is an example of the type of systems maintenance problem that started my research into computer system flexibility. Were I designing such a system today I would allow for a variable number of customer types or even better use a Generic Entity Cloud, our ultimately flexible data structure from our book *Flexible Software Design*.

Inflexible Access

One of our projects at Thoman Software involved the integration of data processing systems of a company in Cincinnati with their new parent in Milwaukee. I spent considerable time in at the parent company's data center in Milwaukee. Access to specific parts of their operation was gained by keying a code into a pad whose keys were shielded. Initially I had an escort to accompany me and to enter the codes required to access various areas of the facility. But frequently when I needed access my, escort was off somewhere else tending to his real job—thus impeding my progress.

By paying close attention, I was able to divine the codes and soon I was wandering around freely making good progress on my assignment. At one point one of the client's top managers came up to me and said, "Bruce, I noticed that you are freely wandering around our facility without an escort." I acknowledged that fact and his response was, "Good! As we really can't afford to take someone away from their responsibilities to follow you around and we recognize that you need relatively unfettered access to our systems to accomplish the integration." We smiled and parted.

This is only one incident where I found that security doors, codes, and the like got in the way of a person doing their job. At a client's installation in Minneapolis where I spent one week a month for almost a year, I had a badge, but the badge-reading system often failed on my badge as well as others and a loud alarm would go off and need to be reset. Also from time to time one of us would forget our badge and

thus have to have others to let us in on their badge—
which somewhat defeated the purpose of the system.

Another incident involves Jim, the SPEC
champion. He was head of P&G's electrical
engineering section, which occupied several floors in
one of the building at the Winton Hill Technical Center
in Cincinnati. When he was denied weekend access
to the building, he was undeterred. He broke into the
building, setting off the alarm and causing security to
come running. Fortunately he was well known and was
let into the building. He was not reprimanded for his
forced entry and by early Monday morning the access
system was updated to include his badge number.

Cincinnati Health Department

In the late 60s a firm whose president was a friend of ours had a
contract with the Cincinnati Health Department (CHD) to develop a
health care system to handle the operation of their 12 public health
clinics. This would require a large sophisticated database and their
firm did not have database expertise. Thoman Software did and I was
assigned to work with CHD.

At the first meeting I attended, Andy, the health commissioner,
under whose auspices the project fell, was very reluctant to have
Thoman Software (me) aboard. "We already have a large team! Why
do we need more people?" The president worked hard to convince
Andy that they needed to have database expertise on the project. Andy
reluctantly allowed the meeting to proceed. While he was addressing
me the question came up, "What is health care?" I immediately
extracted from my brief case a paperback dictionary and looked up the
definitions of "health" and "care." I was immediately accepted in to the
team to work on the project as Andy said, "Can you imagine a techie
with a dictionary in his brief case?"

Over time we determined the requirements for the Health Care
System and began to write a request for proposal (RFP) for a vendor
to implement the system. This was a large and complicated document.
The Cincinnati Health Department was a quasi-city department that
was independent of the City of Cincinnati in some ways; dependent

upon it in others. One of the dependencies was that the city had to be the contracting agency and the system, for political reasons, had to run on hardware from the city's vendor.

Thoman Software had the expertise to develop the database and subsequently the entire system, but the Health Department was not willing or able to pay for the development of a system from scratch and was looking to use or modify an existing system. As it turns out this may well have been a mistake.

Even with the city's insistence on using their hardware, we still investigated other hardware vendors. This was very instructive and benefited me immensely. On a visit to Prime Computer I became very impressed with their hardware and operating systems and shortly thereafter purchased their stock, which did quite well—while I owned it.

The original RFP was slanted in the direction of the city's vendor. Toward the end of finalizing this document, one of the team members became aware of a system that appeared to meet our needs that was in operation at a health clinic in New York City.

Our team made a quick in and out trip to New York City on a Friday and took a good hard look at that system. We could not believe our eyes or our good fortune—here was an existing operational system that appeared to completely meet our needs, it ran on hardware from Cincinnati's preferred vendor, and the software was developed by a subsidiary of the same vendor. The fact that this trip took place on a Friday was significant as many of the people we were trying to interact with had to leave quite early to get back to the suburbs before the Sabbath started at sundown. This may have limited our interaction and affected our ultimately erroneous decision—I will never know.

We scurried back to Cincinnati, revised the RFP and sent it out to multiple vendors. The subsidiary of the Cincinnati's vendor responded satisfactorily and the city was ready to proceed. But before the contract could be executed the subsidiary's parent company got into the act and refused to have the contract signed. Signing would have required them to rewrite the underlying data storage structure of the system—making it highly unprofitable.

What we had missed—and I still wonder how we could have known—was that the system that we had observed was developed for health screening. Companies would send employees or applicants for a series of tests and medical record reporting. This produced a screening report, which would then go back to the company. The data for that person would then be deleted. We did not realize that the system's tailor-made database did not have the capability to store long-term data from Cincinnati's twelve health clinics. The address portion of the data management software would have to be increased; the data management software would have to be rewritten. Clearly a grossly inflexible system, which the New York clinic may have regretted buying in the long run.

This was a tremendous setback to the project. I strongly recommended that the City sue the vendor for breach of contract. But they did not. After this I was not involved much longer and lost track of what happened. But as I recollect they accepted a second-rate system, which did not measure up to what we had proposed.

Automated's Editing Program

I was frequently called in to straighten out problems with Automated's systems. Often I was there so much (and so expensively) that I billed them every three weeks instead of monthly so it did not appear to be such a large amount. Automated's management was sensitive to the charges though because just as I would get the system straightened out, they returned it to Automated's staff and shortly thereafter the cycle would repeat and I again would have to straighten it out.

In such a role, one is not popular with management or the staff. Management is aware of how much you are costing them. The staff is jealous of the fact that you are making more money than they are. What is more, you are there because of their screw-ups, which may be due to their incompetence or their manager's incompetence. You are a constant reminder of the firm's inadequacies and the technical distance between the programmers and the managers.

It is often better to write a program—that can be read and understood—than to use a utility. Automated had a parameter-driven interpretative utility that was used to edit/validate incoming data. But like the X's and Y's in P&G multiple regression program or IEBGENER, there was no way to intuitively follow what was happening or to validate new fields—so on the sly I bypassed this utility and substituted a simple editing programs with intuitive COBOL statements such as: IF ACCOUNT-ID NUMERIC THEN ... etc.

Calling Answering Listening And Linking

During part of my time as an independent contractor, I had a large contract with a United Way Agency in Columbus, Ohio. Again, I inherited a large, unwieldy, incompletely developed system that was to keep track of their activities and provide both online support for phone inquiries and produce a directory of services.

This system was written in COBOL for the Hewlett Packard (HP) 3000. I had had experience with both. As I worked with the program and the agency, I found that the program as conceived by their previous analyst-programmer would not do the job. A great deal of additional analysis and programming were required. After the original allocation for investigation was used up, I gave Agency a very high estimate of the cost of completion. I did not expect them to go ahead with the project but they did and I was awarded a fixed price contract to cover time, materials, (except for computer resources), and travel expenses.

IRS Audit Of Independent Data Processor

It is almost inevitable that a self employed Schedule C person will get audited by the IRS sooner or later. And I did. Due to various adjunct teaching positions and programming assignments, I postponed the face-to-face meeting for several months. But eventually the day came, in Columbus the state capital.

The auditor looked over my records and very soon said, "You have a lucrative contract and you are eating at Wendy's and staying at Motel 8. You are too cheap to cheat on your income tax. Get out of here." He did however find a discrepancy. I had to re-file tax returns for two previous years to correct mishandled options on IBM stock. I had reported the income in the wrong year. The resulting switch had no material effect upon my taxes—but allowed him to find something.

For most Sunday afternoons for more than a year, I drove the 100 miles from Cincinnati to Columbus and worked on the Agency's computer until the wee hours of Monday morning. Then I went to a motel or hotel to catch a few hours of shuteye. During the business day on Monday, I would meet with various client personnel to update them on progress and to continue the analysis as more holes in the original design were encountered. Then on Monday night I would go back and use the HP3000 again until the wee hours of the morning and then, after a few hours of shuteye, I would drive back to Cincinnati bright and alert on Tuesday morning to deal with my other clients. This way I could accomplish a great deal of work in Columbus and be absent from other clients' sites just one day.

I could do some testing remotely via phone through my Texas Instruments knockoff terminal. I had used this as my first printer on my Heathkit Z80 PC. I often did testing from the hotel/motel room right there in Columbus where it was a local call. Or from Cincinnati paying long-distance charges. Sometimes these charges were on Billboard's nickel as I was on often on sight at their data center supposedly consulting with them which what they actually needed was maintenance programming.

The Agency HP3000 was heavily used and machine time was hard to get. That is why I was able to do my compiles and tests only at night. The program was in the neighborhood of 6000 cards, which took over an hour to compile. When testing revealed a flaw, the compile had to be done over again, and again, etc.

I thought, "Why not break the program up into more than one module?" So I did, splitting it roughly in two halves. But now I had 9000 cards. The program had a tremendous number of statements/cards declaring database definitions what we then called formatted screens (Graphical User Interfaces—GUIs that were needed in both modules, as were common routines that accessed these screens and the database.

When the problem was in one of the screen or database declarations or their associated processing routines, both modules had to be changed and both modules had to be recompiled. The HP3000 COBOL compiler that we used did not have a COPYLIB or object code linkage capability. In my judgment, this was another example of the over-hyping of modularity. It certainly was not flexible.

Incidents In Columbus With CALL
One of the United Way agencies that used the HP3000 hired Ed, a blind programmer, a really nice guy from whom I learned a great deal. Ed had a device which

would read the CRT screen and convert it into sounds. It was really fascinating to listen to the computer "talk." One particularly interesting sound output that I remember was "C I Error," followed by a number, in a really high-pitched voice. C I stood for Command Interpreter—so this was a command interpreter—operating system—error. It sounded really neat, just like, "CIERR."

At the time I knew Ed my wife was teaching GED and she had a blind student. I would bring questions to Ed about how a blind person could learn a specific task and then take the answer back to my wife. It was very useful.

The HP 3000 was designed for multi-processing, interactive computing, which allowed batch and online processing to run side by side. This was handled quite brilliantly by a sophisticated priority scheme. A priority was assigned to each job/task running in the computer. The highest priority task would get the most time slices. Each priority was assigned a range of values—say from 0 to 999 with 0 being the highest.

Only tasks associated with the operating system would have the first 100, and then online interactive the next couple of hundred, then the batch jobs the rest.

To make sure a job would eventually run, after each slice of time each task would have its priority value decremented so that it eventually would get high enough to get a time slice. Then after its slice it would go back to its initial value and start on its way up again, and again, until the task was completed or the machine was shut down.

Each user was given certain privileges, which he/she could assign to a job. To enable multiple customer engineers (CEs) to service a given system, the password for the customer engineering account, an account with the highest priority, was a consistent derivative of the primary CE's name. So once one learned the name of the CE at a given installation and the system for deriving passwords, one could log onto the CE account at any HP3000 and set and alter priorities.

One time when testing remotely over the phone from my hotel room, I noticed that someone else was on the machine with a much higher priority than his type of job would allow. This slowed my response considerably—in fact, it was unacceptable. So I logged on the CE's account and upped my priority above his. That did not last long. He did the same thing and got an even higher priority. After a few rounds of this, our jobs were of such high priority that we locked out other processes and brought the machine to it knees.

Since he was in the computer room, I logged off and called him on the phone and we negotiated a truce and both went back to work at normal priorities and got our jobs done.

Modularity And Its Myth

Modularity can be a good technique when applied properly. But the most important thing is to have the proper definition of a module and to recognize that a module does not have to be a subroutine and that is does not have to be performed out-of-line. A program should, wherever possible, read like the body of a book—not like the index of a book. The main line should contain the substance of the processing—not an index to it. This is one of the phenomena that have led me to the myth of modularity.

The Myth of Modularity must be overcome. It is not that I am against modularity. It is a necessary technique for both understanding and conquering complex problems and for isolating portions of systems from each other. But often modularity is miss-applied or over-applied, creating burdensome communication problems with their attendant explosion in code volume, documentation requirements, and the like.

Myth: A program should be organized as a series of callable modules called from the main line.

Reality: The overuse of out-of-line modules can obscure understanding of a program or system.

Modularity and reuse are highly interrelated. Properly modularized models facilitate reuse. Also, to a point and within certain bounds, reusability is enhanced as the size of the task performed by the module decreases. This makes it more likely that an exact fit without extra baggage can be found. You don't want to pay the price for a complete math function module when all you need is the square root. This does, however, increase the number of modules/objects that must be managed. Of course, if we were to go completely to atomic modules we would be back at machine code or maybe, more properly, micro code —or a Turing Machine. As with most things, there is a happy medium—a trade off.

Modules require communications, arguments, and documentation. Modules have their own bureaucracy. Also multiple modules—parts can make problems very difficult to diagnose and fix when something goes wrong with the whole. Remember, changes to customer's business requirements do not necessarily neatly map to specific modules or objects.

There is a hierarchy of modules. We assume that these forms are stored in a repository.

In-line
    Source code
Out-of-line (subroutine)
    Source code
    Compiled code (pre linkage (OBJ) or not linked DLL)
    Object (linked) (EXE)

Thus, it can be observed that modules do not have to be separately callable, or even separately code generated. In fact, in-line source code is the most readable and therefore the easiest to understand, to diagnose, and to modify. Out of line source code is next—at least the main program source listing contains the code. Separately complied code modules, including the object (an old use of the term object) code form, are necessarily out of line and are not included in the main program source code listing. Thus they are much harder to diagnose—you can't see their code without looking somewhere else—or you cannot see it at all.

Yourdon [1992 p. 222] calls his classification of modules "levels of reuse." His levels are source code cut and paste, source-level includes, and binary links. As stated, this classification has more to do with reuse than modules. The importance of this classification is that it recognizes various degrees of configuration control.

Some sources believe that only subroutines can be modules. However there is a difference: modules have one entrance and one exit and should be no more than a page of code. Subroutines can be called from multiples places in a program. Subroutines are modules, but not all modules need to be or are subroutines. This often leads to programs that are very difficult to read, understand, and diagnose when the inevitable problems occur. Nothing is done in line—it is like reading a book using an index—one has to page back and forth. This form of modularization passes the actual processing off to somewhere else, rather than doing the processing in line and so often obscures what the program is doing and how it does it.

When done right, modules have several potential advantages including reuse and independence. Under any circumstances, they generate overhead and can impede communication—specifically in the area of program readability.

Weinberg [1992 p. 238] describes what he calls the *modular dynamic*. The more modular you make a system, the fewer the side effects. But this is traded for *modularity faults*, faults in the interfaces between modules. You never get something for nothing. This is related to the overhead just mentioned and reminds us that programming and maintenance still must be managed.

Modules must be properly modularized. Reduced task size is desirable to a point and within certain limits. The discussion above gives some good examples of when and when not to create separate modules as to what form those modules should take. A module should be in line unless there is an overriding reason otherwise. If a procedure is used often (three times?), it should be made into a reusable module, documented, packaged, and distributed. This is what we did at P&G with our Symbolic High Speed InterpreTer. The bottom line is that dividing something into pieces should save work in the long run. These are guidelines and, of course, like most design issues are subject to interpretation.

An important question is—where do (reusable) modules come from? Should they be created from the bottom up? Or should it be done top down, as design needs are recognized? Yourdon [1992 p. 122], in asking the question "Where do new modules come from?" stresses the need to recognize generic patterns—metamodels. He gives a good example of the supposed 255 generic architectural patterns from which any house can be assembled. He also stresses the importance of a separate group of programmers for creating reusable components [p. 35].

A valuable benefit of modularization (including Object Orientation) is in the development of bottom-up modules, objects, or whatever you chose to call them. These, in essence, create a meta-machine which can be much closer to the application, thus vastly reducing the transformation. This is somewhat counter to our argument, but not totally. The myth still exists. We just need to correctly identify modules and to work with them. Again the question is "What really should be reused?" After all the blue prints of screws and mechanical components can be reused/standardized but the blue prints of cars are SECRET!

IBM's Report Program Generator Is Not Flexible—Is COBOL?

Many of the small shops at which I consulted used IBM's Report Program Generator (RPG). RPG was easy to program in and thus was suited for such shops and it pumped up IBM hardware sales. While RPG programs were relatively easy to write—once written they were almost impossible to read, understand, or modify. When a "small" modification or variation to an existing program was required, it was easier to write an entirely new program than it was to adjust or modify the old one. The number of programs tended to increase exponentially—until the number reached 600. At which point the RPG shop became unmanageable and they switched to COBOL Hence I coined the "Six-hundred RPG programs—switch to COBOL" rule.

Writings about the status of COBOL state that languages like JAVA and C+ are write only languages, which means that since they are difficult to read and understand, when a modification is desired often an entirely new program is written rather than modifying and existing program, which does almost the same processing. I agree and RPG is/was also a "write only" language. Computer programming languages such as COBOL and PL/I can be self-documenting and thus better facilitate modifications. Natural the language used to develop UniverSIS, discussed below is self documenting. Can we then say that they are "more flexible?" No we cannot! Flexibility is about reducing or eliminating the need for modification.

Y2K And Flexibility

Since I wrote many programs affected by the Y2K crisis, I felt that I could be of valuable service to alleviate some of the problems. In retirement I offered myself to work up to 12 hours on Wednesdays to help firms that needed to deal with the Y2K situation—but to no avail. Every one that contacted me wanted full time—meaning 100-hour weeks, and I had had enough of 100 weeks and did not care for any more. Remember "bugs" did not cause the Y2K situation. Early on in computer history both internal memory and external storage were limited and expensive this years were stored as 2-digits instead of 4 and sometimes the days of the year as 3-digits instead of 4.

As early as the 1980s a few of us were aware of the need for 4-digit years in dates. As increased and cheaper memory and storage became available, the need to save memory and storage space by processing dates as the 6-digit YYMMDD or the even more frugal 5-digit YYDDD became unnecessary and we quickly went to 4-digit years in all new development. But some systems last almost forever (at least in computer terms) and most data processors were not as conscientious.

Flexible Software Design: Systems Development for Changing Requirements

Computer system flexibility had been an interest of mine for most of my career. However it became a serious part of my scholarship and writing while I was at Xavier. It came to fruition with the publication in 2005 of our book, *Flexible Software Design: Systems Development for Changing Requirements* [Johnson et al 2005]. Here's how it all started and how the team of four authors came to be.

I was tapped by Xavier to join the ADRM (Association of Data Resource Management) —where I met Walt Woolfolk. Shortly thereafter Walt went to England for several years. When he returned he contacted me and we began our multi-year collaboration dealing with various aspects of computer system flexibility—the ability to modify and adapt computer systems to changing organizational needs and opportunities without a long wait in the IT maintenance queue.

Walt and I struggled with the material and its presentation. We argued, studied and wrote. We outlined books—but could not fully agree on presentation of the material. Sometimes our disagreements were serious and we exchanged heated words. Walt is a slow, careful, deliberate thinker and I am more impulsive, quick to come to conclusions. In the long run, this was a good balance—but it often was not easy to handle the disagreements. It was frequently frustrating to not see eye-to-eye. But as a result our ideas got better and better and we came closer and closer to a product that might actually see the light-of-day.

The time was becoming imminent when I would be retiring from Xavier and moving to Colorado. Our final push is what I chose to call "The Manifesto" (a public declaration of principles or intent). But Walt never really bought the title. Many more strong disagreements came about as we tried to encapsulate our best current thinking before I left.

The Manifesto was never published as such (it was placed on the web)—but served as base material for several journal articles published after I retired. One of the major outcomes of the collaboration with Walt was the GEC—The Generic Entity Cloud, a stable and flexible data structure. The GEC became a centerpiece of our book where it is presented in Chapter 10. The GEC was also the subject of our paper "Generic Entity Clouds: A Stable Information Structure for Flexible Computer Systems" published in the *Systems Development Management* [October 2001].

Bo was Manager of Application Development at Xavier and attended our church. I actually met him at church and after a few conversations we discovered our mutual interest in flexible computer systems and particularly in database design.

I invited Bo to make a presentation to my database class. I had no idea what exactly he would say—and even whether our views were compatible. If Bo's views were compatible with mine, great—if they weren't then I could use it as a teachable moment. Bo's ideas, philosophy, approach so closely matched mine that I was unable to convince the students that I had not written Bo's script.

After what Bo (and I) considered unfortunate decisions by the college administration regarding administrative data processing at Xavier, Bo left and went to the University of Cincinnati. Before coming to Xavier, Bo had developed a flexible system at Boston University. At UC he subsequently developed UniverSIS, the University of Cincinnati's Student Information System. UniverSIS was the basis of the paper "UniverSIS: Flexible System, Easy to Change" published in the *Educause Quarterly,* Number 3 in the fall of 2002. UniverSIS subsequently was used extensively as an example of a flexible system in our book *Flexible Software Design.*

Often while Walt and I were writing on flexibility, my daughter Cindy would review our material and help us along the way. She became the fourth author along with Bo, Walt, and me. Her contribution is covered below.

In retirement I kept up my collaboration with Walt and Bo on flexible computer systems and we managed to get several papers published: "Counterintuitive Management of Information Systems Technology," in 1999. In 2001 we had three papers published: "Information Free Identifiers—A Key to Flexible Information Systems Parts I and II," and "Generic Entity Clouds: A Stable Information Structure for Flexible Computer Systems." And then in 2002, "UniverSIS: A Flexible System: Easy to Change."

These papers were a good start on getting our flexible computer systems ideas published but, given that the Generic Entity Cloud (GEC) is the centerpiece of our approach, I felt that for the sake of credibility we had to have at least a prototype computer system that built and operated GEC-based systems. I had started this while at Xavier using COBOL on the PC—but soon realized that while COBOL was then and still is the most used computer language, it lacked/lacks the modern pizzazz required to make us credible. So I set out to learn Java.

As anyone who has tried Java knows, it has a long, hard learning curve. I obtained several books, a Java development environment for the PC, even books on Java for COBOL programmers, and database structures and Java. These got me a little ways—but it was still a struggle.

It is interesting to note that many of the sample programs included via CD with the books did not work, even after contacting authors and receiving updated sets. A fact that blows my mind is that of all the many books I have encountered dealing with Java and data structures—databases, etc., none—that is none—had persistent storage. Structures are built and manipulated in memory—and just disappear when the program terminates. Thus there was no model to follow for keeping a Java database on disk.

I eventually overcame some of these problems—but not all. Even a weeklong proprietary course in Java was not sufficient. However it did build my confidence somewhat and the manual that was handed out became my primary reference. But it was a consultant in Boulder, Colorado that provided the needed breakthrough.

The GEC-based system needed to operate with a much better Graphical User Interface (GUI) than I was able to produce with my knowledge. A local community college offered a class in Java GUI—but that I would be out of town for about half of the classes. When I called the instructor he said that the class has been cancelled for lack of enrollment. When I expressed my disappointment he offered me a friendly rate for a personalized session. After only one afternoon session with him I had what I needed.

I still am not a proficient Java programmerbut I developed a reasonable prototype system to produce and manipulate GEC-based systems. And several are demonstrated in our book.

Auerbach's CRC Press published our book, *Flexible Software Design: System Development for Changing Requirements* in June 2005. While we had studied and written about flexibility for almost 20 years we had never really allowed ourselves to dream that we would ever get a hardcover book published on the subject. I had frequently thought of vanity publishing our material—in fact that was going to be my last hurrah before I "retired again."

Some of the papers mentioned above appeared in journals produced by Auerbach Publications—publishers of scientific and technical journals and books. As a result of this we were on their email list. In early 2003 I received a RFP for books that Auerbach would consider publishing. I immediately forwarded the RFP via email to my daughter, Cindy, who was in charge of new business development for her company that did IT work primarily for utilities and government agencies, asking, "Must we fill out this entire document? Can't we just send them a chapter or two?" She immediately sent back the curt message, "Dad! I am in charge of proposals for my company. You either submit exactly what they request or don't bother at all!" Attached were two files containing PowerPoint presentations on how to do proposals.

Some time later we I sat down at her dining room table with the proposal template and our laptops and came up with the first draft. We circulated the draft to Walt and Bo, and in another month after passing the draft proposal around multiple times we submitted it to Auerbach. Within a month after their receiving it Auerbach offered us a contract. By this time it was fall of 2003. We committed to producing the manuscript in a year—by September 2004.

Cindy continued to contribute. As a non-technical professional in the field she could often present a higher-level view than us techies in the trenches. She also was (and is) an outstanding editor and helped make sure that the book is readable by ordinary technologists.

In spite of having had several drafts of proposed books on the subject before—all of a sudden this was real—and we realized that we had to entirely rethink the book's organization and content. A full year of writing, studying, researching, revising, and negotiating followed the contract signing. Of course I was retired, but Walt, Bo, and Cindy had real jobs. I was project leader, contact author, but all of us did yeoman work. The manuscript was submitted to Auerbach on time on September 19th 2004.

I do not know how we would have produced the book without email. With the two-hour time difference between Cincinnati and Denver, it was often possible for each of us to comment twice in one day on a section of the manuscript and proposal.

Given that there are four authors many readers expect the work to have multiple voices, but when they read it they say that there appears to be only one voice. But, interestingly enough, for each section I can read it and tell who is the primary author.

Here is a graphic of the book's cover.

My Next (Third) Publication

Even before the flexibility book manuscript was submitted, I began work on these reminisces—*My Years in the Information Technology Trenches: From Data Processing to Information Technology: Reminisces of a CRUDmudgeon.*

As a part of my Reminisces project I cleaned out some of my old files from teaching and earlier work on flexible computer systems that did not make it into the book. Over the years for both teaching and research (primarily on technical distance and computer system flexibility) I amassed a large amount of literature, presentations, and other material. Since it has been many years since I taught and our computer systems flexibility book (First Edition?) has gone to press I decided that it is time to purge these files.

Flexibility Topics Covered In Other Chapters

SuperRecord: chapter 3 CRUDmudgeon.

Sales Reporting Design Meeting (Ultimate Flexibility?): chapter 5 Technical Distance.

Inflexible Accounting System: chapter 5 Technical Distance.

Side Bar: The Myth of Comparative Evaluation: chapter 5 Technical Distance

A Beer in My Right Hand: chapter 5 Technical Distance.

Chapter Bibliography

Johnson, Bruce, Walter W. Woolfolk, Robert Miller, Cindy Johnson 2005: *Flexible Software Design: Systems Development for Changing Requirements,* Auerbach Publications.

Johnson, Bruce, Walter W. Woolfolk 2001: "Generic Entity Clouds: A Stable Information Structure for Flexible Computer Systems" *Systems Development Management* October.

Johnson, Bruce, Walter W. Woolfolk, Peter Ligezinsky 1999: "Counterintuitive Management of Information Systems Technology," *Business Horizons* March-April.

Miller, Robert W, Bruce Johnson, Walter W. Woolfolk 2002: "UniverSIS: Flexible System, Easy to Change", *Educause Quarterly,* Number 3, Fall.

Weinberg, Gerald 1992: *Quality Software Management:* Vol. 1, Systems Thinking Dorset House.

Woolfolk, Walter W., Bruce Johnson 2001: "Information Free Identifiers—A Key to Flexible Information Systems Parts I and II," *Data Base Management* July, August.

Yourdon, Edward 1992: *Decline and Fall of the American Programmer,* Prentice Hall.

CHAPTER 7
TEACHING TECHNOLOGY

Teaching As Creativity

Teaching, to my mind, is an ultimate form of creativity. There is an almost infinite number of ways to present a given set of material. For example, before each new class begins one has a clean slate as how to approach the subject matter. One would think that when teaching on the semester system the (re)-design would occur for the fall semester when there is more time over the summer to think about and implement revisions. But this was not true in my case. My major (re)-designs came for the spring semester when the memories of what did and did not work in the fall were still fresh in my mind.

An example of how I felt about this creativity occurred one Christmas morning at the YMCA Camp in Estes Park, Colorado. As I was waiting for the rest of the extended family to gather for the opening of presents, I had a pad of blank paper on which I was brainstorming with myself about how to organize one of my spring semester classes. My daughter, Cindy, came and looked at me with distain and said, "Dad, you are such a workaholic!" I replied, "This is the moment that I live for each semester." This is also an example of how much preparation goes into a well-run course.

Teaching Impediments

In addition to the creativity that goes with teaching—there is frustration. I find this frustration brilliantly described in Mark Edmundson's 2013 work *Why Teach: In Defense of a Real Education*[30]. Though he teaches at a different university and in a different discipline, his mantra rings true. Here are a few poignant excerpts.

---

[30] I highly recommend this work for anyone interested in education.

No surprise that when the kids got to the classroom they demanded a soft ride They wanted easy grading, lots of pass fail courses, light homework, more laughs. If the professors didn't oblige the kids flayed them on the course evaluations. Those evaluations had an impact on tenure promotion salary, and prestige. By and large the professors caved. [xi-x] Seldom caving in kept me on the dean's bad list.

Over the past few years, the physical layout of universities has been changing. Funds go to construction, into new dorms, into renovating the student union. A new aquatics center and ever improving gyms stocked with StairMasters and Nautilus machines, turning the universities into a sports and fitness emporiums. [Liberally paraphrased from p 12]

Teachers who really do confront students, who provide significant challenges to what they believe, can be very successful, granted. But sometimes such professors generate more than a little trouble for themselves. As did I. A controversial teacher can send students hurrying to the deans and the counselors, claiming to have been offended. (*Offensive* is the preferred term of repugnance today, just as *enjoyable* is the summit of praise.) Colleges have brought in hordes of counselors and deans to make sure that everything is smooth, serene, unflustered, that everyone has a good time. To the counselor, to the dean, and to the university legal squad, that which is normal, healthy, and prudent is best. [p 17]

Perhaps it would be a good idea to try firing the counselors and sending half the deans back into their classrooms, dismantling sports teams and making the stadium/arena [football in original] into a playground for local kids, emptying the fraternities and boarding up the student activities office. Such measures would convey the sage that American colleges are not northern outposts of Club Med. [p 26]

… why did the administrators who are coming more and more to dominate the academic scene come to academia in the first place? Why didn't they stay in business where the salaries are higher, the perks cushier, and where everyone seems to receive weekly and free of charge a zippy new handheld wireless device? [221][31]

Entry Into Teaching Technology

I spent portions of my early careers teaching and the last 17 years in full time teaching. In retirement I do miss the students and their successful projects and papers. I miss the *good* collegiality of academia. I truly enjoyed the teaching and the students. I received real satisfaction from attending graduation and seeing students who had blossomed from unpromising beginnings walk across the stage with their diplomas. For short times after graduation I kept track of a few students and visited them at their workplaces. I miss not being able to directly influence young people in how to properly execute and manage technology. But I do not miss any of it enough to even remotely consider going directly back into the administrivia (rampant bureaucracy).

After retiring, I did, however, apply unsuccessfully for an adjunct teaching position at a local community college. Unfortunately the types of classes that I would like to teach do not generally go to adjuncts—or to junior faculty for that matter. I do not have any interest in teaching an introduction to... course ever again. I would very much like to teach an advanced seminar—great way to learn and to keep up to date.

So in addition to enjoying the creative aspect of teaching technology another reason is to learn—from and about the material being taught, but maybe most importantly by the students themselves. After attaining my PhD, I attended a Department of Quantitative Methods seminar at the University of Cincinnati (UC) conducted by a well-known marketing professor. He said that when the Internet was coming into flower he wondered what it's impact upon marketing would be. So he thought to himself, "I should conduct a seminar." Together with an engineering professor and a group of graduate students, he held a seminar and explored the implications of the

---

[31] He neglects to mention that many administrators have been promoted to administration where the pay and perks are higher and the work is less—from the classroom.

Internet upon marketing. This is the kind of course that I would like to teach should I return to remunerated teaching technology.

Students were often fixated on how they would be graded and thus asked about my grading procedures. For example, Student: "How long does my paper need to be." My answer: "Long enough to get to the end." Student: "How are you going to grade our project?" My answer: "Partially on how much I learn." These answers, while meaningful, somewhat frustrated the students and most importantly placed the learning responsibility on them.

Another teaching anomaly had to do with the red pen. Students would notice that they received a C, for example, on an assignment with very few red marks, while another student receive a higher grade with many more red marks on their assignment. When they challenged me on the supposed discrepancy between the red marks and the grade I replied, "The higher graded paper has much more potential that I am trying to move along, than does yours." This again was not exactly the answer that they expected or wanted to hear.

Learning from the students was often as important as their learning. One of my best learning experiences was when a student encountered an obscure paper on computer system flexibility, which was and is my research interest, which led me to contact Peter, its author, in Vienna, Austria and form a collaboration. I met with him in Vienna, he came to Cincinnati twice, and we presented a joint paper in Hawaii. Very successful learning experience engendered by a student.

I am a strong believer that a solid background in programming is highly beneficial for students and employees in the IT field and for IT applications. This belief is based on my extensive experience with programming, programmers, and in the IT field. Programs underlie all of IT. Today everything has a program, often multiple programs: for example your car, your cell phone, your DVD recorder, microwave, and the annoying answering systems that you use to interact with your world. In one-way or another, programmers developed all of these programs. Early in my career at Procter & Gamble (P&G), General Computer System Corporation (GCSC), and Thoman Software, I worked directly with programmers and, managers who, with a few exceptions, were or had been programmers. However, later on in my career it was much different as I experienced more and more *technical distance*. At Billboard, and during much of my time as an independent contractor I worked with managers who, at best, had limited knowledge of programming and related technology. I worked with consultants from the then great eight accounting firms who took great pride in not getting their hands dirty programming. My Xavier colleagues teaching IT along side me had limited or no programming experience and did not believe it was necessary for them or for our students.

My success and the success of the businesses mentioned above were highly correlated with the programming experience, the technical knowledge, of those with whom I worked. Also my job satisfaction and professional growth were much higher in those organizations.

My view of the importance of programming experience is definitely in the minority. Maybe even a minority of one[32]. But, in spite of that, I go even further in stating that programming experience should include a machine or assembly language. Not understanding the inner workings of the computer can be a significant handicap. For instance, in a computer there can be several ways to represent data. Each representation has a unique set of machine level instructions to process its data. Processing floating-point data with a packed decimal instruction causes a data exception. So when a student's program written in a higher-level language gets a data exception a student without close to the machine experience does not understand what happened and may not be able to fix it.

While gaining an understanding of technology is the primary benefit of computer programming experience, discipline is another benefit. To be successful at programming one must be disciplined. Such discipline carries over into other aspects of work and life. I also found that military experience was an important contributor to the success of those I worked with and those who worked for me. We can all agree that experience is important. The question is what kind and how much? When I was teaching at Xavier University I encountered an interesting phenomena. My students had trouble obtaining positions due to their lack of experience. On the other hand, I was unable to obtain a position that reflected my wealth of experience. No organization wanted to pay that much, they wanted

---

[32] This is one of the reasons why I call myself a curmudgeon or more properly a CRUDmudgeon.

some experience—but limited experience which would enable them to limit the pay.

But I Am Ahead Of My Self. How Did My Teaching Technology Start?

I started with Procter & Gamble (P&G) July 1, 1962. For the first nine weeks I was in programming class with approximately 20 other new programmers. We started with the IBM 705/7080 Autocoder programming language for the first several weeks and then switched to the Common Business Oriented Language known as COBOL. Autocoder was the native language of the 705/7080 hardware, while COBOL was a "higher level" language designed to run on any computer after being compiled into native machine language.

Our class was all lecture instruction without actually writing and running computer programs until about the 6th or 7th week. When we did write programs and try to run them we used COBOL not Autocoder and thus we did not really gain a first-hand understanding of the 705/7080.

The 7.8 Computer

The next year, I was assigned to teach the Autocoder portion of the class. By the beginning of the second day I had the students writing programs, which were executed by the computer. While, at the time, we actually wrote our programs in COBOL (we switched to PL/I later) we made minor changes, called patches, to our programs in 7080 machine language because the COBOL compiles were expensive and time consuming. The 7080 instruction format was complex— converting an alphanumeric operation code into one digit, squeezing the addressing of 160,000 positions of memory, and 15 registers plus indirect addressing into 4 (6-bit or binary digit) positions. Thus we used an expanded-load patch format, which did the conversion. This was much easier and much less error prone than the fully manual process.

The 7080 had an intricate Input/Output) (I/O) structure that required a long learning curve to understand and master. But since I wanted the students to write and execute actual computer programs

147

from day one, I needed to overcome this complication. Thus I simplified the 7080 I/O by writing a wrap-around system. This caused the 7080 to mimic the 1401 (where I/O was to and from fixed positions of memory) so that the students could concentrate on processing and decision-making instructions. With this simplified machine which I called the 7.8, all the students had to do while programming in expanded-load patches was to branch to a designated position of memory and data would show up in specified positions of memory. After their program executed, their results were left in memory and displayed via a memory print.

The 1401, a companion machine to the 7080, was so named because the original machine had only 1401[33] positions of memory. It had very simple input/output. (I/O) Cards were read and punched from specified positions of memory (0-79 and 100-179 respectively). Lines were also printed from specified positions of memory (200-332; 1 position for the carriage control character and 132 positions for the print line itself).

When I explained my expanded-load patch approach to Walt H, the machine language instructor from the prior year, he said to me, "But you have no program to patch." My response was, "Hey, it works as long as we do not tell the computer that there was no program to patch." While the 7080 had a clear (portions of) memory instruction, the fact is that there is always something in memory, even if its is spaces, blanks, or zeros, and all new programs or data are loaded over what is already there.

By engaging the students with the computer much earlier in the class, this approach helped catch and keep their interest and thereby improved their performance.

Teaching As Learning

Another reason to teach is to learn. I learned an enduring early lesson while teaching the 7080 Autocoder class. Being new at teaching and professional programming, I was pressed for time and took a short cut. I used the mid-term Autocoder exam from the prior year—the one I had taken when I was in the class. But during the interim, P&G

---

[33]   1400 actually.

had completely switched from the 705 III with 80,000 positions of memory to the 7080 with 160,000 positions. Thus, while 705 III compatibility was maintained, additional instructions and memory caused the addressing structure to differ significantly. Many of the exam questions, which had been valid the prior year for the 705 III, were not only very difficult to solve but were meaningless when solved for the 7080. This invalidated a significant portion of the exam. The lesson here was "always develop the answer key BEFORE giving the exam—not after!" From here on out I followed this mantra rigorously.

When I taught P&G's Autocoder programming class, I was aware from the previous year's class of the difficulty of using and interpreting the IBM Manual for the 7080. To overcome this, I produced my own manual for use by the class. For each instruction, in alphabetical order, I produced one succinct paragraph describing its operation along with the operation code and the format of its operand(s). This was typed up and copies made and distributed—before word processing. This proved to be of real and continuing value, not only for the class, but also for the entire department. Well into the 1980s, as long as the 7080 was in use, my manual was the primary source of reference information for 7080 Autocoder programming and patching replaced the IBM manual. I wish that I still had a copy!

705 To 7080 Computers

When I started as a programmer/analyst at Procter & Gamble and when I did the bulk of my teaching, P&G was in the process of converting from the IBM 705 III to the 7080, which, in most ways, was really a 705 IV. So while 7080 programs would/should execute programs written for the 705 I, II, and III, they required testing. The original 705 (really a 705 I) had 20,000 addressable memory locations each with five six-bit characters with an instruction structure as follows:

|O|NNNN| with a one position operation code (O) and a four position address (NNNN) capable of addressing 0000-9999 or 10,000 positions of memory. To address the additional 10,000 memory positions, a zone bit

was added to one end of the address. So instead of an 1111-address location—it had J111 to address position 21111.There also were 15 registers (1-15), called Auxiliary Storage Units or ASUs, which were addressed via zone bits in the middle two digits— thus 1AA1 would address position 1111 augmented by ASU 15. Note that in the binary coded decimal (BCD) representation of 1, 2, 4, 8, only four bits (binary digits) of the six are needed to represent the numbers 0 through 9. The other two bits 5 and 6 are called zone bits and are used to represent alphabetic and special characters.

One of the zone bits on the high order of the address was used to indicate indirect addressing. (Which means don't use this address in your operationgo to the address specified in this instruction for the "real" address of the data to be processed.

The 705 II had 20,000 positions of memory with the same instruction structure as the 705 I. Then came the 705 III with 40,000 positions of memory requiring a second zone bit to add another 20000. Thus when one got to the 7080, with 160,000 positions of memory, a 3rd zone bit was required to address up to 79999. An additional instruction was required to enable addressing all 160,000 positions.

705 I 00000-19999 (R999) with one addressing zone bit + 10,000
705 II 00000-29999 (I999) with two addressing zone bit + 10,000 +20,000
705 III 20000-79999 (I99R) with three addressing zone bits + 10,000 + 20,000 + 40,000

At this point, all the bit positions of the 4-digit address have been used (remember one bit on the high order portion of the address was reserved for indirect addressing and thus not available for direct addressing) and there still were 80,000 positions of memory to address. So a new instruction, enter upper memory, was added:

When an enter upper memory instruction was executed, 80,000 is added to the address of the next instruction.

7080 80000 -159999 (A99J) with three addressing zone bits + 10K+20K+40K + enter upper memory

Thus an address like IIII preceded by an enter upper memory referenced an indirect address at memory location 159999 augmented with ASU 15.

I continued to teach at P&G on and off. And from time to time I taught courses during the General Computer Services (GCSC) years, most often on the use of basic functions[34] as a design technique and our basic function implementation software tools. But on the whole formal teaching was not a part of my activities during the middle years of my careers.

FORTRAN For Small Machines[35]

I did a modicum of teaching after I was made manager of Procter & Gamble's Winton Hill Technical Center Regional Data Center (the longest title in the company at the time.) I even produced a publication. In addition to Winton Hill, P&G had another technical center that also had an IBM 1800 computer, which was run by the Mathematics and Statistics Group —not Data Processing Systems Department. There was complete cooperation between the two centers and quite a bit of interchange of clients. But because of different reporting lines and development history the two centers had slight differences in operating procedures, which sometimes caused confusion. So the other manager and I decided to develop documentation of our procedures. We saw no need to necessarily operate exactly the same way—but felt it very important that the differences be clearly spelled out for our clients. So we met regularly and developed *FORTRAN for Small Machines*. The document became part of official P&G operating policy signed by my boss Bob, the corporate operations manager. The really

---

[34] Basic Functions are covered in chapter 6 P&G/GCSC Basic Functions

[35] I wish I still had a copy of *FORTRAN for Small Machines*.

fascinating thing to me is that when it was all said and done—we had made the procedures for the two data centers exactly the same! Where differences had existed we found that it was easier to resolve (dissolve?) them than to go to the trouble of explaining them. This was an entirely voluntary effort.

Most of my work on this manual was done at army reserve meetings. There was not really much to do or that had to be done at these meetings. I formed my company and took roll call at the beginning and end of each meeting and did the collection of the vending machine receipts, bookkeeping, and disbursement of the unit funds for the reserve center. Most of the meeting was usually wasted and I did not want to be tapped for any busy work. So I took my *FORTRAN for Small Machines* project with me and did most of it there. Right after forming the troops and checking the vending machines I settled down with my manual project and looked busy. Several of the enlisted members of my company approached me with the compliment, "Captain Johnson, you are the hardest working officer in the unit."

Hankering To Teach Full Time

As time wore on and I experienced management and technology problems, I acquired a hankering to teach full time. Hoping that I would be able to help a new generation of managers and technicians to do it right,—to overcome technical distance (see 5). I had even considered applying for a university teaching job in Idaho —but it was only a one-year sabbatical replacement appointment at a significant reduction in pay with no chance of renewal.

But over time I drifted into adjunct teaching at local proprietary schools and community colleges. This drift was made possible by the fact that I could teach adjunct during the day. While adjunct teaching fed part of my teaching hanker, it did not feed my wallet. The pay for adjunct teaching was, and to my knowledge still is, abominable. But apparently there were enough people like me who are qualified and willing that the supply outstrips the demand. This is true even at real universities and can be good or bad depending upon the qualifications of the adjunct and the prevalence of the practice. Generally a master's degree is required and the Civil Engineering masters that I received while waiting for my wife to get her BA enabled me to obtain adjunct positions.

I taught first at proprietary schools: Southern Ohio College and Bets Business College. Subsequently at Raymond Walters Branch of the University of Cincinnati, and finally at Xavier University where I became a full time faculty member and was required to pursue a terminal degree, a PhD, in order to obtain tenure. I was appalled at the low level of instruction at the proprietary schools. Shortly after I started teaching at Southern Ohio (before I knew their flaws) I was chosen by the administration to be interviewed by an accreditation team. I did not realize until afterwards that it was a set up in that I could say nothing bad. I had not been there long enough to know of significant shortcomings in their offerings. I left Betz suddenly when one of their officers, a physician, on drugs, in a fit of anger, punched holes in an office wall in my presence. I was scared. Would I be punched next? I left immediately after receiving my paycheck for the week. The instruction at Raymond Walters was first class and very rigorous.

A memorable incident while teaching adjunct at Southern Ohio College again shows the need for preparation, in this case proper preparation. I was asked to substitute for one session of a remedial math class. So I decided to go for the basics and a special interest presentation. As the subject was fractions, I brought a pie and necessary accouterments to serve it to the class. We counted the people in the class including me, discussed how to divide up the pie, divided up the pie, and ate it. My special interest presentation was on the operation of the abacus. The pie operation did not take much preparation, but I carefully practiced the abacus operation walking into class sure that I had it down cold. But nothing worked. I fumbled and it was almost like an electronic computer that had decided not to boot up. So I aborted my presentation and we went back to the fractions. Somewhat later the nature of the problem hit me—operator error! At home while practicing I had been holding the abacus to face me, in the class I had been holding it away from me toward the class. I suppose being left handed with dyslexia and aphasia did not help.

Making The Jump To Xavier
I had done quite a bit of teaching in industry and several times considered switching to a teaching careerbut could not afford the cut

in pay. When our son and daughter finished college and were off the payroll I was able to take the jump to Xavier.

In the summer of 1982, I taught two classes at Xavier as an adjunct: COBOL programming for the Information and Decision Sciences department and FORTRAN programming for the Computer Science department. I was lucky to have taught adjunct as I got to know a little bit about the faculty, the department, and the students. In fact, I flunked the son of a colleague who subsequently became my department chair, co-author, and associate dean. However there were no repercussions— his mother knew her son did not do well and deserved his F.

My summer teaching was helpful when it came time to choose an office. I knew to avoid sharing an office with a faculty member whose desk was piled high sloping (slopping) from the ceiling to the floor— reminding me of the Swedish slip circle that is used to determine the maximum angle of repose of the hillside above a highway cut that we had studied in Civil Engineering.

While teaching adjunct at Xavier I learned another lesson from/ about teaching: "It is (almost) impossible to answer a question that has not been asked." Since, while teaching summer classes, I did not yet have an office or access to secretarial help, I would prepare handouts at Xavier's computer center and then print a copy for each student. On one of the first days I had several pages of fan-fold green-bar computer print out which included material needed for different portions of the 3-hour class. When I handed out the listing I said to the class, "Please ignore the stuff on all but the first page—we will get to pages two and three later." I no sooner launched into the first material to be covered and a hand went up, "What is this stuff on pages two and three?" I again said to the class, "Please ignore the stuff on all but the first page—we will get to the rest of the listing later." I again launched into the material and another hand went up. Same thing, "What is this stuff on pages two and three?" After a few rounds of this I was able to get on with the class. But I had answered the question too soon—the students had not yet asked, "What is this stuff on pages two and three." And they were not paying attention to my answer to their question, which they had not really asked yet. In retrospect I could have separated the pages and handed them out one at a time.

Unexpectedly, in the spring of 1982, due to a last minute resignation of a faculty member due to her spouse's transfer, a full time tenure track position in Information Systems and Decision Sciences (IS/DS) opened up at Xavier, a mile or so from where we lived in Cincinnati. I applied for the position, was interviewed, and conducted a mock class for the faculty, and was rejected for the lack of the PhD terminal degree. Meanwhile I was attending classes at UC as a benefit of my teaching adjunct at Raymond Walters and had decided to pursue a PhD. UC adjuncts could take one course for credit free each quarter at the University and I was never one to look a gift horse in the mouth.

But Xavier was unable to find anyone else to fill the position on such short notice. Therefor I was hired into a tenure-track position with the understanding that the terminal degree, a PhD in a business subject, would be required for tenure. By both working toward the terminal degree and teaching full time, my lucrative independent data processor freelance computer professional business was no more. As a result I took a big hit in remuneration. Xavier was paying me about a fourth of what I had been making as a free lancer. I went from around $100,000 per year to $25,000 for eight months. I worked up to around $52,000 by the time I left. The going rate for my rank and degree for someone from the outside at that time was well over $65,000. Because I was a local prophet without honor, Xavier knew that it did not need to pay me the going rate. In addition to not needing to pay me the going rate, Xavier did not have to pay for my medical benefits, as my wife's benefits with the Cincinnati Public School System were a better deal. However, to Xavier's credit instead of just paying me the adjunct rate for my summer classes, I was paid the full time rate.

Xavier's Information Systems/Information Technology Program

When people say "Those who can do and those who can't teach," are not altogether serious. But frankly several of my colleagues at Xavier could not do—so I guess that why they were teaching. I knew that I could and was anxious to pass it on as best I could under the circumstances.

Xavier's Information Systems/Information Technology program was embedded in the business college, which, in turn, was embedded in a Catholic Jesuit Institution. I was a token Protestant and my first department chair, who was Jewish, called himself a "Jewish Jesuit."

Liberal arts and business courses filled a great deal of the curriculum for IS/IT majors. Thus IS/IT course work was limited and therefore Xavier's IT courses should have been much more rigorous.

I concurred whole heartedly with the general set up of the curriculum often saying, "What will serve you better 30-years from now, COBOL or philosophy or literature or psychology?"

When I came to Xavier I had strong feeling about what was required to prepare students for industry. I immediately detected several shortcomings in our course offerings and textbook choices. For instance, the introductory textbook being used was written by a Xavier faculty member—who had written many textbooks—but had never really been in industry or done any computer programming. A FORTRAN program listing in his book was erroneously identified as a COBOL program.

While I did not succeed in making Xavier's IT program rigorous, at least my classes were rigorous which from time to time was a source of conflict. Much of the time I was the only faculty member with actual industry and programming experience and I felt that the rest of the faculty did not know what it took to be an effective IT professional in the real world.

For example, one of our faculty members had a PhD and a MBA in management—but there were no openings in management, so she was assigned to teach IS/IT. First she had to become American Association of Collegiate Colleges of Business (AACSB) accredited. I reviewed some of her classes (particularly in database design.) I found to be another case of a straight though PhD instructor who had no practical experience in the subject. He/she just passed on what they had learned when he took a similar course (which I did not even believe was correct). I call this hand waving, not teaching or learning.

Such straight through, PhD professors often to the third generation were a bug-a-boo in my PhD program as they, lacking actual experience, could not see my point of view. Early on in my PhD program I made the first case analysis in a marketing class. As soon as my solution deviated from the professors, professors, ... I was done. From then on I did not bother to answer.

Here is another example of the impact of the lack of industry experience and rigor. Surreptitiously two members (including the one mentioned above) of the department received approval from the college curriculum committee for a combined C and COBOL course. Neither of them knew either language and were not willing to accept the fact that students could not even master COBOL or programming in one semester—much less combined with another unrelated language. They declined to teach the course, even if it was their ill-conceived idea. I knew COBOL—but had never studied or used C or any of its derivatives: C+, C++, C#, B-. I was assigned to teach this course before I even knew it existed. I protested mightily—both the very existence of the course and my being assigned to teach it. My protests fell on deaf ears and I was forced against my better judgment to teach the class.

As was to be expected, the course went badly. There was no way to overcome its ill-advised existence in the curriculum. Two male students sat in the back of the room and continually talked and disturbed the class. When I could not alter their behavior I escorted them out of the classroom. All hell broke loose, the dean and the department chair came down heavily on me. In the chair and dean's words I was, "Treating Xavier students as children." And they were right. I was treating them appropriately. As my wife said, "They *were* acting as children."

About half way through the class there was a mutiny. Some of the students were with me and some of the students were vehemently against me. As a result the class/course was abandoned and turned into two tutorials. Another professor was assigned to manage one tutorial for the students who were against me and I managed a tutorial for those who were still with me.

While Betts Business College and Southern Ohio College were somewhat weak in their preparation for all fields including computer programmers, Raymond Walters branch of UC was very, very rigorous and I identified with their approach. They had a three quarter programming sequence in a specific language. The language was BASIC when I came and was switched to Pascal about the time I left. But the point was that in the sequence students were learning to program—the emphasis was on programming—not the language. The rigor of this sequence was demonstrated by a 50% failure rate from each class so that theoretically only one out of eight students would successfully complete all three. However due to students repeating one or more of the courses the actual numbers completing the sequence was somewhat higher.

Once through the three quarters, students were deemed to know how to program and thus subsequent courses in specific languages such as COBOL or FORTRAN were one quarter long and dealt only with the language not with programming as such. Xavier, unlike Raymond Walters, never decided whether we were teaching programming—or just specific language syntax—and there is a distinct difference.

An example of the rigor that I carried into Xavier, at first, was due dates and times for programming assignments. A computer science professor at Raymond Walters, whom I respected, would stride from his office into the class room a few minutes before the class convened and announce that at the bell he would place his notes on top of the computer printouts that had been turned in for the week's assignment—and that any listing on top of his notes —did not exist.

When I tried that at Xavier I was immediately reprimanded and told that that approach was unacceptable. I had to accept late assignments—but in the name of academic freedom I could discount them as much as I wanted—above zero. The University of Cincinnati, where I was working on my PhD, was funded by the state with tuition providing only about 20%—where as Xavier was just the opposite— tuition driven with more than 70% of our income coming from tuition. We had to treat the students with kid gloves.

The importance of this difference in funding source was driven home dramatically to me during a summer class I took for my PhD. On the first day the professor announced, "One half of you must drop out or flunk. We do not have the funds for this may students." I made damn sure that I was in the half that stayed.

Having had extensive industry experience, I was of the opinion I knew what was required to be successful on the job. Thus I was more rigorous than the Straight though PhD professors who spent all of their time in academia.

This rigor came into play in the area of cheating. We had a business professor, who was also a lawyer, who consistently said in faculty meetings, "You cannot accuse a student of cheating. He or she may sue you." Well I ignored him and when I thought that I had encountered cheating—I confronted the student—and, in every case, they backed down and admitted cheating. I don't have any idea of how many cheating incidents I missed—but I never made a false accusation—and was never sued.

While grading programming assignments, it would at times dawn on me that I had seen the same bad (wrong) answer several times. So I went back and checked. First of all I was amazed at how consistent I was in giving similar grades to each. I then set the plagiarized assignments aside and when I was done I took the few points that these assignments had earned and split them among all the authors—the original (which I did not know) and the plagiarizers. Generally the plagiarizers would come to my office and confess their transgression and I would give them a zero and the original author the total amount (often only 3 points out of 10—because of the wrong bad answers). I was amazed at how many students copied bad programs. Maybe others copied good correct programs—but they were much harder to detect and I seldom detected one. How many undetected plagiarisms existed is not known.

Cheating In Academia Is Still Not Handled Properly

A school's commitment to integrity must aim to change not just students' attitudes but also those of faculty. Right now, faculty are a big part of the cheating problem—with students commonly reporting that teachers and professors let cheating go on. Many teachers don't seem to think that policing integrity standards, and all of the hassles that entails, falls under their job description. But obviously it does. Schools must make it clear to faculty that keeping students honest is as important as their other obligations, such as teaching and publishing. Schools should measure whether faculty live up to that obligation, just as they measure performance in other areas. [Callahan, 2004, p 288]

According to a June 2, 2013 article in the Denver Post, the situation has not changed in the almost 10-years since the above was written.

It is hard for anyone who has not taught in general or technology in specific to grasp the amount of work to prepare courses and classes, much less keep up with the technology. Even those teaching other subjects often fail to appreciate what is required. The Dean of the College of Business for most of my time at Xavier was a management professor and a green eyeshade accountant. He did not need to spend much time keeping up-to-date in his field(s), which had not changed significantly since the time of Pacioli in the 16th century nor did he use computers or related technology. Thus he had no appreciation for the fact that IT faculty were often on multiple technologies in any given day and that from day-to-day our technology was changing and we had to spend time and effort to stay up-to-date. Just working on several different keyboards and operating systems in a given day could be a challenge. Often when new technology showed up unexpectedly we had to call the computer center and ask, "Where is the on button?"

Professional Programing In Cobol

Having spent many years programming COBOL and related languages (such as, PL/I, FORTRAN, and SPL for the Hewett Packard H3000) I was extremely disappointed in the COBOL textbooks that were available. I collected an entire bookcase full—yet none satisfied me. So I began to develop my own material, which eventually morphed into a textbook called *Professional Programming in COBOL,* which was published by Prentice Hall in 1990. But getting the book published was quite a struggle.

Initially Marcia, my coauthor, and I circulated the first and last chapters and some information about the book to publishers. They all rejected it. Later when we had a complete book, we again sent out to publishers— again all rejections. But now the rejections were more interesting. Many reviewers said it was just like all the other COBOL textbooks. This hurt. Some said it was a terrible approach and an awful book—but different from other COBOL books on the market. This was taken as a compliment. I knew our book was not the same—we were different and one could honestly disagree with our approach. The most interesting rejection came from Prentice Hall who eventually published our work.

Publishers, in my experience, don't actually evaluate textbooks. They send manuscripts out to college professors and practitioners like me. In truth, I have very seldom reviewed a manuscript that I recommended be published. Prentice Hall sent our manuscript to three reviewers. We shall call them A, B, and C. A liked the even numbered chapters and trashed the odd numbered chapters, B praised the odd numbered chapters and disparaged the even numbered chapters. C liked some chapters and disliked others somewhat randomly. Overall they recommended against publication and we were rejected. If one assumed that these reviewers were the world experts and we should follow their advice—what would we do? All we could do is to pick through the very few specific plus and minus and ignore their overall review.

Some time later after using the manuscript in class for several semesters and making significant revisions, we sent the manuscript around again to publishers—including Prentice Hall. Prentice Hall sent it back to the same three reviewers. Guess what they said this time? "The authors followed our advice and did exactly what we recommended. PUBLISH!"

After 35 rejections of our book, Marcia and I had an acceptance. Before the acceptance, we had resisted major additions or changes, but after acceptance the job was to sell as many copies as possible, so we added material, including material on interactive COBOL. The copy editor did a great job and we followed her recommendations for some major revisions—primarily moving material around.

While the book counted as a publication which got me tenure (after my PhD) and promotion to Associate Professor, it did not sell very well. I have always been puzzled as to why Prentice Hall published it in the first place. But I am grateful. They did not promote it. I think, because they already had a successful COBOL textbook on the market. But tenure and promotion were good enough.

The importance of having co-authors cannot be over emphasized. Originally I was working with a member of the Computer Science Department but then he left Xavier for a college in the Boston area and eventually went into industry. He lost interest and then I lost track of him. I then teamed with Marcia, a colleague who was a member of our department—the chair at one time, and associate dean of the college of business at Xavier during most of our collaboration. On my later work *Flexible Systems Design: Systems Development for Changing Requirements* presented the in chapter 6 (In)Flexibile Systems, I had three coauthors all making major contributions.

Marcia and I would get together most Monday nights at my home office—often with the Xavier basketball game on the TV or radio. I would write and she would read and critique. While her field was quantitative methods, she had started her career as a programmer—in FORTRAN for General Electric. Thus she had some programming and language credentials—but her most valuable contribution, and it was most valuable, was a fresh approach to making the material accessible to undergraduate students. She taught a subject that was difficult for most students, quantitative methods, and many of her students did not do very well; in fact, rumor has it that she flunked her husband—but they still loved her. She had a real gift for teaching, which she carried over into the book. As she read, she would often say, "Bruce, what is this %$#@?" I would take a look and become horrified at what I had written. "Geeze, I don't know what I had in mind, but I will redo it for next week." She also did a superb job on the index, which is a really difficult task.

An interesting sidelight on our bookwork was what the spell checker did to our names. For Ruwe the spell checker suggested Rude. And for Bruce, it suggested Brute.

Just before I defended my dissertation, my department at UC had a seminar on publishing—both journal articles and books. I was so excited. Our COBOL book was about to be published and I so wished to share that fact. But I did not dare. I was afraid even more pettiness would rein down on me that if the department knew I was having a book published at about the time my dissertation was to be defended. I felt that due to a combination of jealousy and not spending 100% of my time on my PhD program there would be repercussions. An interesting part of this seminar was junior faculty members talking about how hard it was to accept their first few rejections. Sam, the senior member of the faculty, the only one present older than I was, piped up and said, "When do rejections stop hurting?"

Rejections are an important part of the publishing process as they imply persistence. If we had not gone through the 35 rejections, we would not have had our COBOL book published. Speaking of rejections, one of my scholarship problems while at Xavier, particularly after I received my PhD was not getting enough rejections—because I did not have sufficient submissions. After all, a non-rejection is an acceptance. To get published one needs to submit the same paper serially to several different publications and eventually it may not be rejected.

Resubmissions after a rejection, of course, should be revised according to reviewer's comments. However, all too frequently, I found that the reviewers did not offer constructive advice, and in fact, they often referred to unobtainable (non-existent?) literature. Believe me much of the literature was totally non-existent. A friend our ours was interning at the Xavier library and I made repeated requests for her to find referenced literature—many of which she determined after a very thorough search truly did not exist.

My main problem was that I would submit paper one and then go on to paper two. When the rejection for paper one came, usually after a long delay, I was engrossed in paper two. When I submitted paper two I went on to three instead of going back and revising paper one and resubmitting it. After I retired I did revisions and resubmissions after each rejection and eventually got most of our submissions published. Interestingly enough, Walt, Bo, my colleagues on the flexibility papers and book presented in chapter 6 (In)Flexbile Systems and I had several first time submissions accepted.

TEACHING EXPERIENCES
While at Xavier I had many teaching experiences mostly positive but some not so positive. The positive and negative incidents are interspersed below.

No More Engineer Bashing
One of my most satisfying teaching assignments was with the University of Cincinnati (UC) engineers. Xavier had an arrangement with the UC engineering college whereby Xavier business students would team with UC engineering students on projects funded by companies who expected to benefit from such collaboration. UC then passed some of the money to Xavier and Xavier paid an extra stipend to the faculty member coordinating Xavier's portion of the clinic. I used some of the money to obtain the most powerful PC at Xavier and the school's first installation of Windows.

The Xavier faculty member originally involved had been from the Accounting Department but at some point the Accounting Department decided that they were not interested. Since I had a reputation for working with teams, projects, and outside agencies I was offered the position and readily accepted. Little did I realize how much I had missed working with engineers after all this time on the business faculty? Even with two engineering degrees, I had fallen into the habit of engineer bashing. I hit it off right away with UC engineering faculty involved with the clinic. Here were colleagues with whom I could immediately identify.

This clinic was a huge success and I continued as Xavier's advisor for several years. In some ways this was a complement to the capstone senior project course, described below, that I taught for many semesters. I don't remember most of the projects, but one was a study of the costs and benefits of setting up staff so that they could, working at home, take trouble calls for a local utility and channel them to the proper service personnel. Other projects had to do with design of new or improved products or systems, including economic analysis.

Total Quality Management

As my teaching career progressed, so did my teaching philosophy. I became disenchanted with exams and I felt more and more strongly that students performed better with projects, hands on involvement, than from straight lecture or book learning. Projects, in which they worked in teams, were particularly effective. While I could not totally control the experience, the results for both the students and me were much more rewarding than exams. The business community was continually pressing academia, and specifically business colleges, to emphasize teamwork and communicationboth written and oral. Projects were ideal for this. As an example, I was part of a quality initiative grant. We integrated Total Quality Management (TQM) into our courses. My main focus was empowering students to control their own learning.

An example of how student empowerment did (or did not) work was an MBA class in IT and Quality. It was a totally project-based class and, in fact, the students' projects were subsequently published in booklet form [Johnson & Pinto 1992]. Some of the students were taking part in quality initiatives at their companies. These students reported that after each meeting at their companies, the participants rated the meeting on a scale of one to ten and made a short comment regarding their rating. They recommended that we do this for our class. And we did, using a 1-10 scale. I collected their ratings and comments at the end of each class and shared it with them the following week.

During class periods the students generally worked in groups on their projects and I wandered around keeping tabs, answering questions, checking on their projects, and observing their team operation. This was somewhat tension-filled for the students because; unlike "normal" classes they did not have specific, definitive assignments or lectures. They were empowered to control their own learning—a new experience. The ratings for these classes generally averaged from 6.5 to 7.5 showing, I believe, the ambiguity of the situation. From time to time, the students would come up with a question or a topic that they would like to know more in depth. I would prepare a presentation and during the next class part of the time would be spent in a more traditional lecture presentation format. Lo and behold, the ratings for those class meetings went up to more like 8.5 or 9.0. Interesting. This is one of several examples of how ambiguity affected students.

Another example of how ambiguity effects students come from what, in many ways, was one of the more successful semesters academically for the senior project class. But was also in many ways an administrative failure. One of the accounting professors and I often ate lunch together and I attended several of his seminars on chaos theory. As a result we decided to have our classes work together. His accounting students became the clients of my IT students. The accounting professor gave his students the features required for an accounting system and they, in turn, would relay them to my IT students—immediately creating industry-like communication difficulties.

This worked fine for my IT students even though it caused some frustration and exchange of information difficulties, which, of course, were designed into the learning experience. But the accounting students kept asking how they were being graded. They were used to specific numerically graded assignments. This was more ambiguity than they could handle. As a result they trashed their professor on the course evaluations. His department chair, the traditional eyeshade accountant, did not understand what we had done and so my colleague was reprimanded. This made him nervous about receiving tenure and a brilliant professor was lost to Xavier.

Walled Fiefdoms

The walled fiefdoms of academia in general and specifically at Xavier have always disturbed and frustrated me. I was and still am a strong advocate of interdisciplinary teaching. This was only one instance where I was unable to work with faculty in other disciplines.

I tried to start another multi-disciplinary class that never got off the ground. I was and am enamored with Gerry Weinberg's *Psychology of Computer Programming* [1973] and tried to interest a professor in the Psychology Department to jointly teach a class related to this topic—to no avail. The reward structure in academia is slanted toward ever-narrower slices of disciplines and multi-disciplinary teaching just doesn't fit into this model.

While I was frustrated at the lack of success these efforts yielded, I am encouraged by insights such as the following, "Multidisciplinary educations and research, the need of the day, is a worthy effort... ["Thinking about Washington State," 2005]"

Another example of the compartmentalization of academia: in my data structures course I would use (try to use?) calculus to show optimum data structures under varying conditions. The students would literally scream, "This is a data structures class—not a calculus class." And reflect the same on my course evaluations. While I insisted upon continuing to use calculus, I somewhat tempered their anxiety (and sold out to the system) by prefacing my presentation with, "Humor me. I am going to use some calculus here to make a point. But I will not, I repeat, I will not include this on the exams."

CAMPAIGN STORIES

I used to call them "war stories," but I don't really like the term war. How about campaign stories? The stories consist of real life business and technical experiences that those of us who have been out in the real world have experienced. I had many such stories that I felt enriched my teaching. But they were not well received by undergraduate students. They would just say or think, "Get on with the material Johnson, you are not going to include this on the exam. So why waste time?" The undergrads were primarily interested in obtaining credentials—a degree (the laying on of hands, I often called it), not necessarily real learning. However the MBA students literally hung on my every word as they were mainly out in the real world and wanted to hear about real life experiences. Of course campaign stories were not on their exams either.

Freshmen Boys At The Horse Race Track

Believing so strongly in projects, I even did them in the freshman introductory class, IS100. Three male students who approached me about studying parimutuel betting did the most memorable project from this time. I knew I was taking a risk. I could almost hear the department chair or dean saying, "Your students are out at the race track doing an assignment for your course!" But I agreed and several times they went to the track and were able to get access to the personnel running the computer operation. They turned in a stunning report from which I learned a great deal myself. It worked very well and I did not get in trouble—that time.

CAPSTONE COURSE

For several years I taught the Information Systems capstone course. No text, no lectures, just a team project. This course was very successful and I truly enjoyed teaching itbut there was tension and headaches. For example:

Stew In Their Own Juices

One of my early teams had a simulated ATM project, which was written in Digital Equipment Corporation's (DEC) VAX BASIC. They wrote it as all one program. This meant that for any change, the whole program had to be recompiled. This soon took over an hour, causing scheduling problems. I suggested, coaxed, and cajoled them to break it up into several independent modules. But they refused. I came close to ordering them outright to break it up—but resisted. After all it was their project and I felt obliged to let them stew in their own juices.

With considerable extra work, they finally got their ATM system to function correctly and completely. In their final report they stated, "If we were to do this again, we would follow your advice and make it into several independent modules." If I had forced the issue, I am not sure that they would have learned that very important lesson.

A Safety Net For Failure

Another team was getting absolutely nowhere and the relentless academic schedule was bearing down. I would work with them to try to get them to step back from their failed solution—but as soon as they thought that they had an idea of how to handle a minor problem, they would stop thinking and immediately go to the computer and start flailing away. Again to no avail. I even took them to another campus building away from the computer and terminals to meet with them and to try and get them to see the big picture—but even then they immediately got involved in minutia and made no progress. "What was I going to do? How was I going to salvage their grade? Their project was at the F level and declining as the end of the semester bore down."

I thought to myself, "Maybe I could ask them to write a paper on what has gone wrong—and what they learned—and what they should have done differently and, hopefully would do differently next time." But it was their project so, even while losing a lot of sleep; I did not force them to take any specific action.

But they did it on their own—they were missing sleep also. They essentially turned in garbage for their project. But they produced a brilliant paper analyzing what they had done wrong, why they had done it wrong, and what they should have done and would do differently next time. I gave them all Cs with a clear conscience. After all they had learned a valuable lesson—in academia—where there was a safety net for failure.

Enough Rope To Choke—But Not Enough To Hang

In the capstone course, I continually wondered, "what was the correct amount of intervention?" Like my Dad used to tell me, "Bruce, it is my job to give you enough rope to choke—but not enough to hang yourself." I felt that the students choking in pursuit of their projects was acceptable—but when to stop the choking? That was a big concern of mine.

One way to decide was to ask them—subtly. In most of my classes I tended to give a mid-term evaluation as part of the mid-term exam. This enabled mid-course corrections on either my part or the students' part. Students often said they needed to work harder or smarter—but occasionally I received some really useful advice. There were no exams in the capstone course—but I did the mid term evaluation anyway. One of the questions was as follows: "On a scale of 1-10 (with

1 being way too little and 10 being way too much) how would you rate my intervention on your project?" A few students rated me at 7-9 and few more at a 2-3 but the majority rated me at about 4-6. The average was in the 5 range. "You can make some of the students happy some of the time and some of the students happy at another time—to paraphrase our 16th President. I felt that I was doing OK."

The Churches

While many of the projects, both at the graduate and undergraduate level, benefited the actual business clients for whom the project was accomplished—the most rewarding was the churches. One semester during the database course several students approached me saying, "We will be in your senior project class next semester and we have been talking with Belermine Chapel here on campus about installing a computer system in their office. They already have authorization to purchase one or more PCs." This sounded like a great project for that group to do but it would not be a large enough project for the entire class.

I had been casually talking with Hal the minister at Mt Auburn Presbyterian church where my wife and I went about the possibility of installing a computer in Mt Auburn's office. I went to Hal and said, "Now is the time. I will have students in the upcoming semester. If we are going to do this we must move according to the academic calendar." I was somewhat ahead of him and the session, the governing body of the church, but I was determined to move. The academic semester was non-negotiable.

Progress went smoothly with the Belermine project because they had already done some planning. Mt. Auburn was falling behind on the project, while the academic calendar was whizzing bye. Something needed to be done to get the Mt. Auburn project back on track. Thus I sent the Mt. Auburn student team to a computer store with my credit card and they bought the computer and necessary software. Now they were able to install the hardware and load the software and get started with the church's operation. It took quite a while for the Mt. Auburn session to reimburse me.

Church administration software was installed at both locations and the students helped load the data and train the office personnel.

Both churches now have several computers and are running smoothly. A subsequent senior project (after I no longer conducted the course) installed major hardware and software upgrades to Belermine Chapel's systems.

SPECIFIC STUDENTS

"Professor Johnson you are not a racist... you just don't like me."

My most unpleasant experience came in the capstone IS course. One of the students was very disruptive. He would come to our team meetings late without knowing what had transpired before and attempt to take over the meeting.

This student was president of the Black Students Association. He had intimidated the faculty, and for almost four years no one had stood up to his intimidation—for fear of being called racist. I was not intimidated. I was not and am not a racist. After several warnings I asked him to leave class. He refused and I gently escorted him out and closed the door behind him.

Shortly thereafter, he came to my office and loudly threatened me. I was not intimidated, my action was entirely appropriatebut I was afraid for my physical welfare. However, I did not back down. In the process of threatening me he said an interesting thing. He said, "Professor Johnson, I know you don't like me. But I know its not because I am black. I see the way you treat other black students and how they respond to you. I know that you are not a racist."

Immediately after he left, I called the dean's office to report the incident. I was told to drop everything and write it up. "But," I said, "I am struggling with my dissertation. I do not have time for such distractions." "Write up anyway and write it up immediately." I did. Fortunately, I had witnesses. My office door had been open and my office was situated in a corner. The nearby offices were occupied at the time—and the occupants had over heard the entire exchange.

In spite of the faculty's failure to stand up to this student, the College of Business dean's office had been anxious to get rid of him for a long time. I had finally given them the ammunition. The university backed the business college's position and as he was about to be expelled, the dean of students intervened. He was worried about the hassle of a possible racial discrimination lawsuit. So a deal was brokered with The University of Cincinnati to accept this student as a transfer and to award him not an Information Systems degree but, a general studies degree. In the process he agreed not to take action against Xavier.

Xavier did not always take such decisive action. We had a female Latino student, who had the same last name as a Latin American Dictator. She continually flunked her IS courses and the faculty kept recommending her dismissal. She would disappear for a semester or two, and then be right back, with the same of lack of performance. Xavier could not offend a Latin American country, as Latin American countries were a fertile source of tuition-paying Catholic students.

Eight Ball COBOL Student

One of my COBOL students was a real eight ball. I had had him in other classes and he had not performed well and generally caused problems. At the end of the course I noticed a strange phenomena. His even numbed programming assignments received A's. His odd numbered programming assignments received D's and F's. He also did poorly on the exams. Thus his overall grade was computed to be a D. But I gave him an F because I just could not believe that the A assignments were actually his work. When he received his grade he came straight to my office to complain and to deny cheating. When I explained my actions and said they would stand he went directly to the deans office to complain.

Soon thereafter I received a phone call from the associate dean searching for a way to resolve the issue. She suggested that I assign him a program and follow his work closely and if he succeed, change the F to a higher grade. It was summer, I was not teaching, and my PhD tenure deadline was bearing down—I told her I just could not afford the time. She then asked if it would be OK if she oversaw his work—all I would have to do is to choose the program. After all, she and I were co-authors on the COBOL textbook being used for the course. "Great," I said and called her a few days later with the appropriate program. She called the student into her office; assigned him the program—and like the rider beneath the streets of Boston in the song MTA by the Kingston Trio—he never returned.

Who Carries The Weight?

In general, academics are conservative and don't like to take risks. But I have always been a risk taker (maybe that is one of the reasons why I did not exactly fit in the conservative academic environment). Here was a risk that really paid off. One of my students in the capstone course came to my office and said, "The other members of my team working on the banking system, are not carrying their weight. If I treat this as a team project we will not get it done. In order to get it done I will have to do it all myself." Having had her in several classes, I knew her dedication and ability I said, "I know that you can do the work so there is nothing for you to learn by doing it yourself. So how about you becoming a project manager and working through your other team members to get the project done? I will guarantee you an A. Now see if you can get the system developed by managing them." She did. They developed an A project. When she interviewed for the job she wanted at a local bank, she discussed the banking system and how she managed it. The interviewer was so impressed that she was offered a job on the spot and she accepted it.

Some of the more memorable, for better or worse, students were discussed above. A few other memorable students are discussed here.

M who was blind due to a swimming pool accident, graduated and obtained a good job. He had a service dog named D who generally slept under his chair or desk during class. Occasionally D would yawn which caused the students and faculty who heard about it to say, "Even D thinks your class is boring."

B was our departmental graduate assistant who had been a basketball star as an undergraduate. He called me "Professor J" which I really liked. His brother was a baseball star and I advised him to stay in good graces with him. He is now a basketball color radio announcer as well as a finance and insurance broker. He still called me Professor J when we flew with the team and supporters to a Thanksgiving tournament in Puerto Rico—which Xavier won.

Innovative Teaching

In addition to projects and papers I was continually trying new techniques to engage the students and further their mastery of the subject matter. Two of these used primarily in the MBA Introduction to IT course are described here. When a class meets weekly there is a delay between when an exam is given and the results are returned. And often by then students are somewhere else intellectually and emotionally and do not get the full value from the feedback on their exam. So by handing out two copies of the exam for them to fill out and only collecting one we could go over their answers in the same class period while the exam was fresh in their minds and they had a copy in their hands. This had an additional benefit. The answer key could be honed to account for ambiguity or clarification so that there were few appeals.

Another approach was to have the students make up the exam questions. For example, I had each student submit three true-false or multiple-choice questions on a diskette along with the answers. I told them that this was the database, the only source from which I would select the actual questions for the exam. Given that they asked me, "Is it OK if we distribute copies of our questions to the class?" I said, "Well this is an information class and that is information, go ahead." But the students did not blindly trust the answers provided by their fellow students so they thoroughly checked them out and as a result each student in the class received an A.

I had a least one class where each student did so well that they received an A for the course. I was concerned about possible repercussions from the administration. So I formulated a backup plan. If questioned I would have had the questioner select, at random, a paper, a project, and the midterm exam and see that all were A work. However I was never questioned.

Even without prior computer experience many of the MBA students executed outstanding projects. Several stand out. On student the chief operations officer at a hospital across the Ohio River in Kentucky implemented a computer project that saved thousands of dollars annually re positioning inventory to reduce access time. Another student entirely revamped the sales incentive system with a brilliant spreadsheet.

Xavier was often willing to try new things and, of course, not all of them worked. I was taking courses at UC during the summer 10-week quarter. I also wanted to teach summer courses at Xavier, but they were for longer periods of time, which would reduce our family's ability to do some summer traveling. Xavier agreed to let me teach a

10-week data structures class. Only about 6 students signed up which was not enough to create a critical mass for learning. The course did not go well. It was too concentrated. Students were unable or unwilling to spend the necessary out-of-class time to succeed in the class. Only one student received credit for the course and the evaluations were not good. The worst thing about the evaluations was the students comments, "This was an abbreviated summer course, yet Johnson did not cut back on what would be expected during the fall or spring semester!" The problem was I was already feeling guilty for easing up. After all they were receiving full credit for the course.

To accommodate students, Xavier had some 5-week summer classes, which I occasionally taught. These did not work well either, as the students could not accomplish the necessary out-of-class work. As a guide, students were expected to put in three hours of work a week for the 16-week semester for each credit hour. So a three credit hour course that met for 1-hour 3-times a week, requires 6 hours out of class per week or 96 hours per semester. Meeting for 5-weeks 2.5 hours 3-times per week, a student should put in 20-hours per week outside of class—equivalent to a half-time job. Students with full-time jobs and/or families could not or would not do this even to accelerate their degree.

Student Course/Instructor Evaluations
Xavier placed great importance on student course/instructor evaluations. The evaluations saved the department chairs and deans from really determining what good teaching consisted of or actually observing faculty in the classroom. The faculty fought them but to no avail. The students got tired of filling out four to six evaluations each semester—so they often did a slap dash job. Mine were not outstanding but they were generally better than my chairs and deans gave me credit for. There was one semester however, when to my surprise, I received really bad evaluations.

After I successfully defended my dissertation, I provided refreshments at the next class meeting in each course I was teaching. This consisted of chips, pretzels, soft drinks, and beer (which was against school policy)—but hey it was a real celebration. While I did not plan it this way, these meetings coincidently were only a week or two before the meeting in which the students filled out course evaluations. Thus one might think the memory of the beer and pretzels would be fresh in their minds and they would be positively disposed toward the course and me. This was not so. Apparently, with the tension and terror leading up to my dissertation defense, I had been a really lousy teacher. At least that is what the majority of the evaluations reported.

A class member took the completed evaluations directly from the classroom to the dean's office where they were keyed and statistics produced. It was some time before they were released to the faculty member. One year I received a letter signed by the chair (dictated by the dean) saying that my evaluations were sub par and that my merit raise would be negatively affected. I had 30 days to appeal. I asked to see my evaluations but was told that they were not yet available. Long after the 30-day appeal period was up I received the evaluations in the campus mail. They were much, much better than the letter had indicated. I immediately appealed and, of course, was told that the deadline had passed and my appeal would not even be considered, regardless of merit. When I said that the evaluations were withheld from me—I was ignored.

Summing It Up
In some ways I can sum up my experience teaching technology, particularly at Xavier with the comment I received on a student evaluation. "I never learned a damn thing from Johnson, I learned it all myself!" While I am sure that this comment was not meant as a complement and that department chair and dean docked my pay for it, I think it was a high complement. After all "Aren't we supposed to help our students to learn how to learn? We will not always be there."

Teaching Technology In Other Chapters
Basic Functions: chapter 6 (In)Flexible Systems

Chapter Bibliography
Callahan, David 2004 The cheating culture: Why More Americans Are DOING WRONG to GET Ahead, p. 288.

"Decline and Fall" 2005 *Interface* August.

Edmundson, Mark 2013 *Why Teach: In Defense of a Real Education*

Kerwin, Michael W. (2013). "Cheating Epidemic?" The Denver Post, June 2, pg. D1&6.

Johnson, Bruce, Walter W. Woolfolk, Robert Miller, Cindy Johnson 2005 *Flexible Software Design: Systems Development for Changing Requirements,* Auerbach Publications.

Johnson, Bruce 1992 *Information Systems Technology for Quality Improvement.* Editor with Sam Pinto.

Johnson, Bruce 1991 *Professional Programming in COBOL* with Marcia Ruwe. Prentice-Hall, 1991.

"Thinking about Washington State" 2005 *Washington State Magazine* Fall.

Weinberg, Gerry 1973 *Psychology of Computer Programming* Van Nostrand Reinhold.

CHAPTER 8
GENERAL COMPUTER SERVICES CORPORATION (GCSC) RISE & FALL

It was late afternoon on April 21, 1976, four months prior to his fortieth birthday, as Bruce Johnson (Johnson) sat in the library outside the president's office waiting for someone to come so that he could turn over the reigns of General Computer Services Corporation (GCSC). Early that afternoon a hostile board of directors had been elected which then voted him out as president. After dedicating over 8 years of his life to the company he helped found and serving the last two as president, Johnson had just submitted his resignations: as a director, effective immediately, and as an employee, effective July first. [From: Actual Case Study in Lieu of Final Examination, Bruce Johnson, University of Cincinnati, BA 22-405-805 spring 1983, Entrepreneurship: New Venture Formation.]

The following was written in June 1983 in lieu of a Final Examination for BA 22-405-805, spring 1983, as a part of my PhD and MBA class work. Minor editorial changes have been made.

Actual Case Study in Lieu of Final Examination

Bruce M. Johnson Jr.
BA 22-405-805 Spring 1983
Entrepreneurship: New Venture Formation

June 6, 1983

General Computer Services Corporation (GCSC)

It was late afternoon on April 21, 1976, four months prior to his fortieth birthday, as Bruce M. Johnson Jr. (Johnson) sat in the library outside the president's office waiting for someone to come so that he could turn over the reigns of General Computer Services Corporation (GCSC). Early that afternoon a hostile board of directors had been elected which then voted him out as president. After dedicating over 8 years of his life to the company he helped found and serving the last two as president, Johnson had just submitted his resignations; as a director, effective immediately, and as an employee, effective July first.

While the shock of what had happened had not really hit Johnson yet, he did

While the shock of what had happened had not really hit me yet, I did realize that it truly was "the first day of the rest of my life." In fact, one of the first things I did was to call my wife and say: "We are free now to do almost anything we want to do. We are not tied to the past."

As time wore on I began to look back and try to assess what went wrong and to ask myself, "What mistakes did I make?"

In 1965, after three years with P&G, I met George, who had a B.S in industrial engineering from McAllister University, St. Paul, Minnesota. George and I soon became close friends and associates. In early 1967 we began to seriously consider going into the data processing services business together. We spent many evenings and weekends developing a business plan, considering such things as: when, where (we both loved the West and were avid campers and backpackers and considered such places as Colorado, Oregon, etc.), how to fund the start up, how to obtain legal and accounting services during start up, as well as what services to offer, and how to build a clientele from scratch. During this time I began to feel that my compensation with P&G was not directly related to my performance. I have since said: "A major reason for leaving was: 'At P&G I could predict my salary years into the future.' Not being able to significantly influence my salary really bothered me." I wanted an online wallet— which I truly got.

In the fall of 1967, George and I were introduced to the three principals of the Halsey Corporation and began the negotiations that lead to the founding, in February 1968, of General Computer Services Corporation (GCSC), with headquarters in Middletown, Ohio. Roy and Ron Halsey were brothers. Roy was a CPA in private practice in Middletown, and Ron was an electrical engineer, ex IBM salesman, and a professor of computer science at Purdue University, Lafayette, Indiana. The third principal was Roger B. Turrell, an attorney in private practice. Both Roy Halsey and Turrell had worked for Armco Steel Corporation, which was headquartered in Middletown.

The Halsey Corporation was founded in 1966 to perform data processing services for banks, but ended up as a used computer hardware brokerage firm. As a sideline of their purchase and sale of used computers, the Halsey Corporation was often asked to provide programming and other software services. They had tried to do this by hiring programmers and treating it as a sideline. In mid 1967 they

178

began to look for some heavyweight talent in the software field to 1) relieve them of the management of that aspect of their business, and 2) to more fully exploit, what they believed to be, profitable opportunities in the software business.

GCSC was incorporated in February 1968 with Turrell, the Halseys, George and me as shareholders. The company was capitalized at $500 and received a $6000 6% loan from the Halsey Corporation. The company started with four employees: a programmer and a secretary-data entry clerk from the Halsey corporation, George as President, and me as Executive Vice President. One room and several desks were rented from the Halsey Corporation. Ron Halsey served as chief executive officer, Roy Halsey as treasurer, and Turrell as secretary. The three Halsey principals agreed to serve in these capacities for the first year, for a percentage of the profits.

The five founders of GCSC provided the range of talents required to successfully operate a computer services business. Turrell, an attorney experienced in corporate law; Roy Halsey, a CPA, experienced in cash management of undercapitalized companies; Ron Halsey the expansive talking wheeler dealer, ex IBM salesman; George, with 16 years experience in industrial management with P&G; and myself, with strong technical and creative talents in the software field.

Due primarily to existing Halsey contracts and contacts with Armco Steel, GCSC had an immediate backlog of work. By August GCSC had paid back the loan from the Halsey Corporation and had hired two experienced programmers. One was an ex P&G employee and the other was hired directly from P&G. The rented space soon became inadequate and the employees were playing musical desks. The building across the street, an old beauty parlor, was purchased and an auction of the contents raised enough money to make the down payment. In December, George and I, who had started with GCSC at our P&G salaries, received raises, and all five principals received bonuses based upon the first year of operation. At this time the Halseys and Turrell were placed on retainer as remuneration for their services.

The synergism between the Halsey hardware business and GSCS's software capabilities proved to be very beneficial, especially when applied to the Armco (International Division) contacts. Halsey sold computers to Armco International for installation in Germany, France,

179

Italy, England, and Mexico. GCSC handled the acquisition, shipment, and installation of these computers and trained the local staff in each country. In many instances, GCSC performed contracts to replace the acquired computer with a more powerful and/or modern system. Such as reported in the DMIOCS Four to Zero project in chapter 1.

Local domestic contracts also developed, but not as fast as the international contracts. Other Armco divisions provided a continuing source of work. After several unsuccessful proposals to P&G, and after GCSC had proven to be successful without P&G contracts, P&G awarded us several large contracts and may smaller ones. Up to 10 persons at a time worked on P&G contracts

Many persons who have asked me about GCSC's market assumed that we did computer systems for small to medium-sized companies who could not afford their own computer personnel or equipment. However, this was seldom true. The majority of our work came from large companies such as Armco Steel, Procter & Gamble (P&G), and Champion Paper, all of who had large staffs and a full complement of computer equipment. They generally contracted with us for one or more of three reasons: they currently did not have sufficient staff to take on a priority project, they did not have the necessary expertise and we did, or we were cheaper. The following incident contrasts the GCSC approach with the approach of these large companies.

P&G asked if we could do a payroll system for them. I met with six (yes six-persons) from P&G. I met with a person from payroll and his boss and a person from data processing and his boss, and a person from the group that served as liaison between payroll and data processing and her boss. My other five counterparts were out making money—designing systems and writing programs—covering the overhead of my sales call. Even though we were cheaper, P&G decided to do the payroll in house for confidentiality reasons. Salary information at P&G was top-secret information. But the fact remains that our overhead was much, much lower and not just because of P&G's benefits—as GCSC had full benefits.

Often we were the envy of some of our colleagues who were still at P&G. From time to time we were invited out for a drink with one or more of them who were considering going out on their own, as we had done. I think in every instance what we said discouraged them. They, like us, were technologists and knew technology but what we had stepped into was a business. Business acumen was primary—technology acumen was secondary. GCSC was lucky to last as long as it did considering our lack of business experience and knowledge. For an example of this see the Orange Juice Story in chapter 5.

GCSC reached maximum employment of 25 persons, performing contracts for a dozen clients. In 1972 we began recruiting on college campuses, in 1973 GCSC opened a branch office in Cincinnati, in 1973 we reported sales and earnings of $425,000 and $50,000 respectively, and in 1974 we established an employee stock purchase plan and profit sharing trust. With my desire to develop the loyalty of the professional staff, and to take the company public, I was responsible for the stock purchase and profit sharing trust plans. It was this broadened stock ownership, ease of issuing new stock, and resulting participatory management style that subsequently played a key role in the firm's demise. The very events that were mentioned above as providing growth and profit for GCSC also contained the seeds of the company's eventual destruction.

The Halsey Corporation went out on the limb and purchased, for speculation, a large computer system consisting of an IBM 7090 and an IBM 1401, which they were unable to sell. They tried to salvage their position by using the equipment to establish a data center, first in Winston-Salem, North Carolina, then in Rosslyn, Virginia, across the Potomac River from Washington, D.C. George and I spent alternate periods of time at the data center (often working around the clock) trying, unsuccessfully, to make it profitable. Eventually the IBM 7090 was sold at a slight loss and GCSC acquired the 1401.

After an exhausting 36 hours stretch of working in the data center, the GCSC principals' decided to acquire the 1401. I voted against the acquisition for many reasons. George was scheduled for an extended stay in Europe managing Armco International business, we had no business plan for a data center, and we had no data center customers. The responsibility to develop a data center business and to pay off the $250,000 debt incurred at 12% for the purchase the 1401, not to mention $600 per month maintenance fees to IBM, would fall on me and I was already overwhelmed with project and corporate responsibilities. George's closeness to Roger and the fact that three of the five GCSC principals were Halsey Corporation owners caused me to be overruled and left holding the bag. In spite of pouring an enormous amount of additional resources, mainly programming effort taken away from billable projects, into the data center it continually lost money for the company.

In 1970 the Halsey Corporation again found itself in trouble. Strapped for cash they looked to merge or to be bought out. Their initial deal with Transamerica Corporation fell through. In early 1971 the Halsey Corporation was sold to Fidelity Corporation, Richmond, Virginia. (Fidelity was an aggressively expanding insurance and savings and loan holding company.)

Fidelity acquired the 55% interest in GCSC held by the Halsey principals for effectively nothing, as a result of the Halsey's desperate negotiations with Fidelity. George and I held first rights of refusal on the GCSC stock held by the Halsey principals. We chose not to exercise that right when faced with the likely demise of the Halsey Corporation without the Fidelity buy out. And, of course, we had no funds with which to purchase the Halsey shares.

The Halseys' participation in GCSC affairs had been dwindling, and with the transfer of their stock to Fidelity they effectively disconnected themselves from GCSC. Ron Halsey subsequently divorced, moved to Michigan, and remarried. Roy Halsey subsequently purchased the Halsey Corporation back from Fidelity, divorced and moved his residence out of Middletown.

Fidelity's interest in GCSC soon waned. (Or were they really interested in the first place?) Our hands were tied. Fidelity owned a majority of the stock, appointed the auditors, and refused to make decisions necessary to prosecute the business. George was in Europe with Armco during most of this time, so I received the few perks that went with the Fidelity association, a week in Nassau in the Bahamas and several high-class business trips by corporate jet. In late 1972 George and I bought Fidelity's GCSC stock for $10,000 each, financed by 6% notes from the company.

By early 1972 strife between George, myself, and Roger Turrell began to build. The company was stuck with a number of bad contracts authored by Roger, and at my insistence he was subsequently fired as legal counsel. During this time he went through a bitter divorce. George and I were having severe disagreements over how to manage the business. George was a workaholic, aiming for the biggest possible gross income without regard to profit and the personal lives of the employees. I was interested in bottom line profit and building a stable, capable, and creative professional staff.

The conflict was basically a quality of life issue. I was willing to work hard during the profitable peaks, and to slow down and take vacation during the valleys. George continued to take on unprofitable contracts to try to cover the increasing overhead. The peaks became higher, and the valleys deeper. The peaks became more and more unmanageable, during which internal management (both long and short term) and marketing were ignored. The desperate and concentrated sales efforts during the valleys led to higher and less profitable and even less managable peaks.

George and I each had specific areas of responsibility, yet he continually trod on my turf. He was primarily in charge of Armco International work and developing and, when he was in the country, running the utility billing and other systems for the 1401. I was manager of the P&G work and the Cincinnati branch office.

Soon after start up, George and I recognized the infinite velocity, zero mass nature of our services business. Services cannot be inventoried in the valleys and sold in the peaks to help even out the workflow. In general, high utilization yielded high profits and low utilization caused losses. The unpredictability of contract awards complicated our efforts to balance periods of over and under commitment. The 1401 data center was used unsuccessfully in an attempt to stabilize revenues and profits; however, the investment never came close to paying off. We were unable to recover its high overhead or the continual investment to develop processing systems such as, payroll, accounting, and utility billing

Between mid 1972 and mid 1973 the moral of GCSC was severely depressed by the strife between George and I as mentioned above, and by George's marital problems which were manifest by recriminating phone calls to GCSC office personnel by George's wife and girl friend(s). I was out of the Middletown office conducting business from the Cincinnati branch office most of this time and was the last to know the seriousness of George's marital problems and liaisons, and their impact upon the company. George's work in was in Middletown when he was not abroad; I was in Cincinnati working mainly on the high-pressure System for Planning Electrical Construction (SPEC) project (See chapter 10). While we tried regular meetings, George was impossible for me to communicate and reason with. He continued to countermand decisions in my areas of responsibility, not for business reasons, but to do favors for Roger and others. He frequently did not show up for our meetings, or else was late and/or left early.

George and I both obviously changed a good deal since establishing our friendship. The tensions and pressures of the business were considerable. For example, we both went without pay for significant periods of time when there was not enough cash to fund the full payroll. But more than that, many of the employees suspected that some or all of these problems were due to personality changes in George, possibly due to the medicine he took to treat his foot condition. George suffered severe inflammation of the feet. Though he went to many doctors, tried various treatments, and wore special shoes, he did not find much relief. The medicine he took may have contributed to, or caused the personality change. Or could this have all been psychosomatic due to the stress? I don't think so. George never showed outward signs of stress and, in many ways, seemed to thrive on it possibly as a means of staying away from home.

In 1974 George proposed to the recently expanded, to include an ex Armco executive and an employee (added, hopefully, to stabilize the rapidly deteriorating situation), board of directors that GCSC open an operation Brazil. GCSC had several employees who had grown up in Brazil. Also, in 1968 GCSC had a project in Brazil, which George executed while he was in Mexico on one of the Armco International contracts. I again opposed the move, primarily because there were many profitable and better-understood business opportunities much closer to home. Most of the board felt that George's Brazil adventure was an attempt to escape from his problems.

George persisted and the board really had no viable alternative. So temporary peace was made and George was given a charter and a budget (including money he loaned the company) to go to Brazil and to establish a subsidiary of GCSC. His initial foray into Brazil occurred in late 1974. George's removal to Brazil did not solve the problems. He continued to demand scarce resources from the parent company, which itself was struggling, demoralized, and on the brink of bankruptcy. He often returned from Brazil (at great expense) to Middletown. His presence further demoralized the employees who felt that first of all the company could not afford his expensive comings and goings and more importantly when George was absent the company functioned peacefully.

In early 1975 the company came close to mutiny. Various factions of employees were meeting, plotting, counting their stock purchase plan and profit sharing stock shares, and attempting to elect new officers. Four, including myself, were vying for the Presidency. In a final attempt to make peace I was elected president, with George's backing in return for my agreeing to Roger's election to the board of directors as chairman. George's behavior was such that the board at this time offered to send him to a sanatorium, at company expense, for a rest and a checkup. He refused. It was during this period of time that he divorced.

By the time that I became president, strife and intrigue were such an integral part of GCSC that there was not much I could do to overcome it, even if I had seen it more clearly. I did not see it clearly for several reasons. I have already discussed George and I's difficulty communicating which was a large part of it. We also had an office manager who thrived on strife and kept things stirred up in the Middletown office where most of the employees were—but where I was not most of the time. But an even more basic cause is that I am a trusting person. Raised to be honest and forthright I trusted people, including George and Roger, and did not expect them to plot my overthrow behind my back. Thus I was unprepared.

Meanwhile George, in Brazil, had not followed the resolution of the board of directors. He established GCSC do Brazil, with himself owning 90% and GCSC owning 10%. He refused to account to the directors for the more than $40,000 in company assets that were transferred to him in Brazil. Based upon George's continued failure to explain or rectify the situation, the board, with Roger dissenting, voted to file suit against George for restitution of the assets he allegedly had misappropriated. When George and Roger subsequently took over the company this suit was dismissed.

Unknown to me and the other officers, during late 1975 and early 1976, Roger (while serving as a corporate director and board chairman) and George plotted George's return to take over the company, and to oust me, at the April 21, 1976 Shareholders' and Directors' meetings. The takeover and my ouster were facilitated by the fact that I was on vacation the week prior to the meetings, and by the fact that I was primarily operating out of the Cincinnati branch office.

Thus, in the early afternoon of April 21, 1976, with Roger presiding and voting George's proxy (which was subsequently proved to be stale and invalid), the shareholders voted to further enlarge the board (more effort to achieve stability?), and to delete, from the bylaws, the requirement that the president be a director. At this point I saw what was happening, but it was too late and I was powerless to stop it. The enlarged board elected George president, dismissed the suit against him, and increased the directors' fees. I announced my resignations, effective in 30 days, as had been predicted in the exchange of letters between Roger and George. George having already returned from Brazil was waiting in the wings and he and Roger immediately took over the company.

Why did George and Roger want to oust me? Why did the shareholders vote to enlarge the board? Why was George reelected president after my ouster? My ouster was to facilitate the dismissal of the suit against George, which Roger had apposed. The new shareholders were primarily the employees via the Employee Stock Ownership Plan who in my absence from the Middletown office had been poisoned against me by the office manager with George's help remotely and Roger's locally. Some of these poisoned employees were added to the board with the promise of director's fees.

On April 22. 1976 (the day after), I discovered that the meetings, which lead to my ouster, were illegal. I immediately asked for an injunction to overturn the meeting, which was denied. I subsequently filed a lawsuit against the company and the directors. As a result, I was summarily fired via a telegram received at 3am on April 23d.

Between April 22, 1976 and November 1979, I made several unsuccessful attempts to gain control of GCSC. I held a clear majority of the shares outstanding at the time of the takeover, but the hostile board led by Roger and George issued stock bonus shares to their group thus maintaining control with the watered-down stock.

During Thanksgiving week 1978, two and one half years after the take over and the filing of the suit, the trial was held. The trial consisted of more than two weeks of bitter recrimination and testimony, which proved conclusively that Roger and others, while serving as directors of GCSC, had plotted with George to take over the company and oust me, and to cover up George's activities in Brazil. The trial Judge, Paul E. Riley, (an aged visiting Judge from another County), very much wanting to avoid making a decision, forced the parties over and over again to try to reach a negotiated settlement. After almost three years this had proved to be impossible. The Judge finally ruled that the actions on and subsequent to April 21, 1976 were illegal, but refused to reverse any of the subsequent stock transactions. Thus it was an empty and worthless "victory." (Justice delayed, is justice denied.) I filed an appeal to Judge Riley's ruling, which was recorded in February 1979.

The following paragraph is taken from a letter from my attorney to the judge dated January 26, 1979:

"In effect, you have ruled that the defendants wrongfully opened the barn door by denying Johnson's option and electing themselves as Directors at the April 21, 1976 shareholders' meeting without a proper majority of the outstanding shares; yet you have not required them to return the horse they took (the stock bonus shares) while the door was open. Had this trial taken place on May 1, 1976, the Court would have enforced Johnson's rights and the Plaintiff would have properly had control of a majority of the outstanding shares at all subsequent shareholder meetings. This court of equity should not allow the delay in trial date to affect the equitable result of its decision."

Shortly after the trial, George and several others involved in the takeover left the company. I can only assume that they left because the strife continued. Quoting from the 1979 GCSC annual report:

"The year 1979 was without a doubt the most traumatic year in the history of our company.

With the departure of our President, Vice President and Secretary, on March 1, our management and marketing functions as well as nearly 1/3 of our professional staff positions were vacant."

In July 1980, with the appeal scheduled for the next month, all the parties to the litigation sold their stock to a third party for cash and notes, and agreed to drop, with prejudice, all litigation. By this time my legal fees were well over $20,000, of which I had paid approximately half. (With prejudice, means that the suit is dropped in such a manner that it can never be refilled.) Shortly thereafter GCSC ran into more trouble and the notes were defaulted upon. In 1982 GCSC filed for bankruptcy. In 1983 I received my last notice that my note was uncollectable.

The short-range effects of the ouster from GCSC were devastating. I had no plans, no money set aside (it was all in the company), and no car, since I was driving a company car (and had no money to buy one). For several weeks I doubted whether I would get the pay and benefits due me from GCSC. The upheaval caused severe unprofessional disruption to several of GCSC's clients, including P&G's engineering division, for whom I had been project manager. P&G awarded me an $8000 personal services contract through July 5th to bring the project to an orderly turnover to client personnel. This financial and personal support did a great deal to put me back on my feet.

Roger Turrell was killed September 29, 1989, in Newcastle, Indiana, in the crash of a private plane that he was piloting; the locations of the other three principles are unknown. George remarried in Brazil and was living in Chicago at the time of the trial. It is believed that he subsequently moved to California.

No facts relating to this saga have been knowingly misrepresented, however they are presented from my point of view, and should be understood in light of my intimate and personal involvement in the case.

I was fortunate to have had the opportunity to be an entrepreneur, I decided not to do it again. It was an exhilarating and terrifying experience, which continues to have an impact upon my life. As can be seen from the above, the personal price of entrepreneurship can be high. For example, all four of my associates were divorced during the GCSC years. My family and marriage, while still going strong, suffered significant trauma during and after the GCSC years, due to the pressures and demands of the business. The long hours, uneven income, teeth gnashing tension brought home to the wife and children caused pain to us all. I took some of my anger at George and others out on the family and often even when physically present I was not mentally there for the family. But they forgive and forgave me and helped my get though it all and we are stronger for the experience.

While I was ideally suited for the technical challenges of the business and handled them well and thrived on them, I was short on other desperately needed talents. I was not a salesperson; I was not able to handle office politics especially in such a close and in what became such a tense and poisoned atmosphere. While being able to handle the technical challenges, their all-absorbing nature diverted my attention from what was occurring elsewhere in the business. The stand out lesson from this period is one that many others have learned and that many warn us about—business ruins friendships. It is still hard to imagine how close George and I were and what bitter adversaries we became. When we set up the business we appeared to be on the same wavelength—but slowly and inexorably that changed and lead to the downfall of an organization that we had both worked so hard to build, that provided meaningful services to many firms, and provided well paying interesting professional jobs to more than a dozen persons.

Chapter Bibliography

Johnson, Bruce 1983 Actual Case Study in Lieu of Final Examination, Unpublished case study for BA 22-405-895 Entrepreneurship: New Venture Formation, University of Cincinnati, Cincinnati, Ohio June.

CHAPTER 9
GENERAL COMPUTER SERVICES
DAYS AND NIGHTS

At GCSC we had many all-nighters and I soon learned that the day following an all-nighter is not what does one in. It's the next day. This has been driven home many times in my career and has been validated by persons, such as physicians, who have experienced the same phenomenon.

Introduction

General Computer Services (GCSC) days ... and nights... were some of the most intense, stressful, and interesting periods of my life. In many ways it all blends together—the projects, the people, the terror, the excitement—the stress on my marriage and family life. The rise and fall of GCSC and some insights into the nature of the business were presented in chapter 8. This chapter presents my life during the existence of GCSC—from 1968 to 1976. The succeeding chapter covers GCSC's largest project System for Planning Electrical Construction (SPEC).

During this period I learned extensively and grew much. I learned and relearned that I had extensive technical skills and insights. And while I never became really good at dealing with adversity, I improved a great deal. My people skills improved marginally—never, however, coming up to the level required. I expected (and still do expect) people to be honest and forthright—to be upfront with their feelings and beliefs. I found that I was just too trusting and was often taken advantage of. There are a number of persons whom I don't believe can honestly look themselves in the mirror in the morning when the comb their hair. But I can.

The black and white thinking of an engineer often does not work in business or personal situations.

While GCSC was absorbing my being I also had other things going on in my life. This was a period where IBM dominated the IT field. Their hegemony was complete. Acquire equipment from another vendor and have problem and you were out of a job. Fail after acquiring IBM equipment and you could try and try again and again. IBM's hegemony over the IT field was replaced by Microsoft, which is handing it over to Google. Though, at least to me, Google's hegemony seems much more benign that IBM or Microsoft. And Google seems to have much more competence.

At GCSC I continued to demonstrate my technical skills that had started with Procter and Gamble (P&G) with the 7.8/1401 simulator on the 7080, with code relocation without index registers, and with the development of the Winton Hill Data Center time share and accounting system.

General Computer Services (GCSC) was founded in February 1968 with five principals—I was one. Initial contracts were with divisions of Armco Steel and later with Procter & Gamble. The state of the business waxed and waned until about 1975 when factions formed and then a boardroom coup in April 1976 was the beginning of the end.

The GCSC case in chapter 8 provides detail on the formation, operation, and destruction of the company. Reading the case before continuing with this chapter will give the reader additional background. Chapter 10 describes SPEC (System for Planning Electrical Construction), GCSCs largest project, which I managed.

While at times we were marginally profitable, in truth we had to watch every penny. When business was going well and we were relatively flush with cash was when we were most conservative. We were afraid of running short of cash and when clients paid ahead we had money we had not yet earned. However when business was not so good we often felt freer to spend money that might bring in new business.

Aged accounts receivable are a common financial management tool. GCSC went a few steps further than just aging our receivables. We aged our payables as well and had hierarchical payroll system. We learned which supplier would tolerate how much delay in their payments. Also when short of cash we would meet payroll from the bottom of the organization chart up—often officers' pay was significantly delayed—but we eventually received it all.

The pressure to meet project deadlines in order to get cash to meet the payroll and other expenses was so intense that often I only had bowel movements on Sundays. And frequently I was tense and difficult to get along with.

CULTURE

As with many start up and under funded operations, we worked long hours. When GCSC first began I lived on the Eastern edge of Cincinnati and our offices were in Middletown over 40 miles away and for more than half of the distance there was no interstate. Thus it was an hour and fifteen minute drive—if all went well. In those days there were no cell phones and portable/car phones cost several hundred dollars a month. So I was between a rock and a hard place. If I called to say that I was on my way home I would invariably get interrupted and not get away for an extended period of time. If I just left when I could get away and before the interruption then my family did not know that I was on my way.

I often had to come in on weekends to try and catch up, but even then there was a catch twenty-two. I would often get phone calls from clients or vendors that would require actionso I would not get my work done. I needed to answer the phone in case the call was from the family. But eventually this was solved. We obtained a phone system that had three lines xxx-0703, xxx-0704, and xxx-0705 with roll over so that if 3 were busy 4 would ring, and if 3 and 4 were busy 5 would ring. So I had the family directly call me on line 5. The other callers were not aware of 4 and 5 so I just did not answer them on weekends or evenings. This was also before answering machines were in common use.

Our Salesman

The working principals of GCSC were computer programmersnot business or salespersons. This presented problems in obtaining new business—particularly via cold calls. So we, or should I say George, hired a salesman. This endeavor was not successful. We had great hopes that this would bring in profitable new business. When my wife expressed concern that that salesman was making more money than I, the Executive Vice President, I said, "Wouldn't it great if I made more than I am now due to increased sales?" She then understood the logic—but it did not work out. While he had good contacts, he, not being a programmer and anxious to garner new business, would consistently underestimate the amount of work involved in executing a contract—thus causing us to loose money on the job. I have come to believe that salespersons are basically unmanageable and this one certainly was—and we had to let him go—an expensive lesson.

Back Side Printing

Another of our cost saving procedures was printing program listings and the output from test runs on the backside of outdated production printouts. Today many of us do this regularly with sheet feet printers but we did it with an IBM 1403 continuous feed printer. We just turned the separate runs over and taped them together until we had a box full and then used that. With careful taping we seldom had a jam. We did not specifically think of this as environmentalism—as recycling—but it was reuse, which is a step before recycling.

354 Call—Customer Satisfaction

I suppose that many service organizations have trouble keeping their clients happy—even when doing good work. At GCSC we learned this the hard way. We would have a crew at a client's sight working diligently on their system in plain sight yet hear complaints like, "Your people are in our way. Why are you charging us so much and you are using our office space?" and so on. Then on the other hand sometimes it was best to develop the system at one of our offices and then deliver and install it at the client's site. During such an operation, since our programmers were not visible, we could hear, "Where are your people? We don't know if our system will be done on time or done right!"

As a result we developed a tradition which we called the 354 call. Our time at work was recorded on time sheets using work codes to indicate the type of work performed. The code was of the form xyz. Where x = 1 was billable, x = 2 was non-billable administrative or overhead work, and x =3 was sales related—also not billable. The y was used to indicate the skill level and thus the rate to be charged for the work being performed. Y = 1 was consulting, y = 2 was analysis, y = 3 design, and so on down to keypunch and clerical.

Z was used when a finer xy breakdown was needed. The 354-work code stood for "a drop in unannounced visit at a client's sight by a person not involved in the project." This would generally involve an informal visit by an officer not assigned to the project with key client personnel over a cup of coffee. In this setting the client personnel would often drop hints of problems brewing with the project. These early warning signs could then be reported to the project manager who could take steps to defuse the situation before it became an issue.

Thus 354 calls became standard operating procedure, which vastly improved our customer relations.

Projects Are Finished On Fridays

Another tradition or maybe it was an observation was that projects only get finished on Fridays. I am not sure what the cause was or when we observed this but it was so real that we had many a push to finish on Friday or else the project seemed to drag out for another costly week.

We were so fixated on this that occasionally we called not an all nighter but an all weekender, particularly on 1401-oriented projects. We had the project team come in the Middletown office for the weekend with food, sleeping arrangements, and the like. I remember one particular project where the team was blaming their lack of progress on lack of machine availability as well as operator error. So I operated the 1401—thus the team had no recourse but to make progress. The project was not completed over the weekend but many impediments were out of the way and it was up and running by the following Friday.

Inventory Policies

Nominally I was in charge of the Middletown office but I was often only there for a few minutes per day so things could get out of hand. One troublesome problem seemed to be our supplies management.

We would continually run out of things (nothing like a reorder level seemed to work) so I informally adopted the policy that when we ran out of something we would automatically order twice as much as we had ordered the time before. This was somewhat uneconomical and certainly violated the economic order quantity (EOQ) that I heard so much about later during my PhD studies, but we significantly reduced the outages. I chuckle to think that when the company blew up we had a whole case of extension cords.

Nepotism

When one has his or her own company, hiring family members can aid the family income. Also family members tend to be known quantities. Our son Russell served as janitor for a while. He would come into the office on weekends or evenings after school and clean the place up a bit. This would not have been very interesting if it were not for the chads from the punched cards.

Middletown had some trouble at their football games and as a result instituted what they called the Yellow Hat brigade. Members of the community would go to the games wearing yellow hats, which made us conspicuous as we were sprinkled throughout the stands. We had no police power—but our presence appeared to quell disturbances before they started.

Since I was going to the game anyway, I took our kids: Russell, our daughter Cindy, and our foster son Timmy. Russell collected the chads from the card machines in our office and packaged them in Baggies and sold them at the game for a nickel. He tried to get Baggies from his mother via our kitchen—but since he was selling them and making money she made him buy his own. He made reasonable money for not much work. But it was Timmy, the true entrepreneur, who really cleaned up. Russell sold the bags of chads for confetti at five cents and created a demand, which was still present when his supply was exhausted.

Timmy would then scrounge the stands for discarded Baggies and chads and repackage them and sell them for a quarter. So with even less work he could make more money than Russell.

I wanted to hire my wife Carmen as she has good organizational skills and work habits. In a pinch I could get her to do small tasks for us. But, at the time, she was not interested in computers and did not want to work for me, which was probably a good thing because we are still married as my sister-in-law says "almost 60 years."

Fire At The Backup Location

Both of our Middletown buildings were wooden structures and we were quite concerned about the effect fire could have on our business and our records. Halsey Corp, our sister company, had some space in downtown Middletown, Ohio in a brick building, which we used, as a backup location. We kept backup tapes and some important archival data and records that we only had one copy of there for safekeeping. One day we were informed that the furniture store in the building next to our Halsey backup location was on fire and that the backup sight was in also in danger of catching on fire.

We rushed down town and got as close as we could to the fire and watched as the fire department struggled to bring the fire under control. All the while we were worried about our backups—but we could not get access to them because the area was blocked off for fire fighting. The good news is that the Halsey location did not burn and our backups were safe and more importantly so were our archives. After this we took them to our Cincinnati office, which was a much safer location.

OFFICES

As GCSC progressed and business expanded our office space profile developed.

Musical Desks

Roger, our lawyer and one of our principals, owned office space in a converted house in Middletown, which he and Roy our accountant (another principle) shared. They had an extra room, which they rented to GCSC. Space was very limited and on days when several of us needed to be in the office, one had to be sure to get work early—or be without a desk. When one of us left for a client's site etc. his or her desk would be taken over by another employee.

The Beauty Parlor

As GCSC expanded musical desks became more and more of a problem. Fortunately the building across the street went on the market. It was a house that had been converted to a beauty parlor. But we had no cash with which to make such a purchase. Roy, our accountant, who was experienced with undercapitalized firms, went to work. He had the building appraised—for more than the purchase price and obtained a 100% loan.[36] We then sold off the beauty equipment and thus we had the building and cash with which to purchase office furniture. We had one of the settees in our home until we left Middletown. Roy again came to our aid. He obtained the services of his brother-in-law, who was an electrician, to modify our third floor into an office, library, and conference room.

Nothing in the third floor was square or true. A carpenter would have had a great deal of trouble handling it. But not Roy's brother-in-law, so we ended up with very functional space.

Odd Fellows

After several years we out grew the beauty parlor building and were able to purchase the building next door. However, our purchase was significantly delayed while we applied for a natural gas hookup. Since the building had not been totally utilized, we had to apply for a new hookup and there was a supposed shortage of natural gas. We did eventually obtain a natural gas hookup with which to heat our offices. While it was a two-story building the first floor was leased for the next 10-years to the Odd Fellows. As the Odd Fellows were a secret society, we were not allowed to access their space.

We remodeled the second floor into several offices accessed via an outside stairway. We had both of these building for the life of the company.

Cincinnati Branch Office

From early on much of GCSC's business came from Cincinnati. I drove the hour plus each way most days and some of our employees lived in

---

[36] Can you imagine that happening today?

the Cincinnati area. But we could not always obtain adequate office space at our clients thus it became necessary to obtain office space in Cincinnati.

The Cincinnati branch office, which we rented, had office space for the manager, along with a large work area with several desks for programmers and a conference room. It was located in the same office complex as a P&G data center that we used for any of our P&G projects.

In addition, off and on, we had space with one or more of our P&G clients generally in connection with the Personal Records System (chapter 3) or System for Planning Electrical Construction (chapter 10).

RELATIONS WITH IBM
As IBM was the dominant force in the industry during this period, GCSC had numerous dealings with IBM—some business related, some technical in nature.

Inadvertent Financing
A computer must be kept continually under a manufacturer's maintenance agreement to keep its value in the second hand market Thus we had a 1401 maintenance agreement with IBM that cost us about $600 per month. Making this payment often presented a problem. IBM's accounts receivable system allowed us to fall three to six month behind before they even began to question us. We could then stall them for another couple of months while we worked with them to straighten out the bills and statements.

Several times GCSC offered to develop a viable accounts receivable system for IBM—but, of course, they ignored us. But, to me, this is just one example of how the shoemaker goes barefoot— or the computer system supplier does not use the computer to it's advantage.

Software Bugs
Several time we were bitten by bugs in IBM's operating systems particularly when we bid a fixed price job which require extra work and time due to bugs in their software.

At this time IBM had a mantra: "IBM does not make *undetected* errors." This is a philosophical discussion that should only be continued over a few brews.

Early on IBM's S/360 disk operating system (DOS) would not sort zero records. We wrote a system to maintain a mailing list for an industry magazine. The list was maintained in zip code sequence. Thus when a subscriber moved from one zip code to another, realignment was required. The realigned record was written to a work file, which was then sorted by zip code and merged back into the main file. But when in a given update run no one moved between zip codes, an empty realignment resulted and the job crashed. So we had to write a dummy record and then bypass it during the merge. While IBM claimed this was the way a sort was supposed to work and initially did not consider it to be a bug, they eventually fixed the sort to not crash with zero records.

IBM did not make all the errors. In this very system we made our own errors. Each address/label had a computer-generated match code with a check digit that was used to update its information. At one point in the development of the system we generated a batch of bad match codes. When we went to update these, the transactions were kicked out because the check digit did not compute. So we had to add code to have a check digit override until the bad match codes were eliminated.

BUREAUCRACY
Several examples of dysfunctional governmental regulations and intrusions into our business are reported below.

Spouse's Salary
The Ohio legislature passed a law that income tax withholding was to be based upon the combined income of the employee and his or her spouse. To me this seemed ridiculous. We had no business knowing what an employee's spouse made. I sent a memo to our staff saying that under no circumstances was any employee to divulge their spouse's salary, and that if there were any repercussion I would take the fall.

I was soon exonerated. One day while on site at P&G I became aware of a P&G memo that essentially said the same thing as the memo that I had written. The law was soon rescinded.

Who Is Responsible For The Financials?

As GCSC issued public stock, we had to have our books audited. Since Haskins and Sells (H&S) were auditing nearby Armco Steel's books and since Armco was an important client, we had H&S audit our books and certify our financials. For this we paid an outrageous sum and then when it was all over I, as president, had to sign off on the financials.

I believed at the time and still do that my neck was on the line for the accuracy and fairness of the financial reports. But now in light of financial scandals such as Enron, WorldCom, and elsewhere it appears that chief executives can plead ignorance—even after they have signed testifying their veracity. Finally recent federal legislation has apparently given the CEO signature on the financial statement the status that I thought it had back in the 1970s when I believed that I was signing my life away. Our financial performance was not uniformly good—but our financial reports were always correct and honest. You bet my life.

I just don't follow it. How can many of today's CEO can get off scott free when their firms cook the books? The following is from *Business Week* (May 23, 2005): "One measure would require CEOs to personally certify their companies' tax returns, with penalties for perjury." That is what I thought that I did in the 1960's and 1970s?

There were two interesting sidelights to H&S audits. One was their opinion of GCSC as a going concern—they said that we were not—we were too undercapitalized to continue. Yet, while we often struggled financially, we managed. It was not finances that caused GCSC's demise. Also as we wondered why it took the auditor, who was from Cincinnati, so long to audit our meager books we found at that he had a girl friend in Middletown.

Wage And Hour Laws

P&G had data center managers, who were managers and thus exempt from wage and hour laws, work the overtime to circumvent wage and hour laws; GCSC circumvented them also. We hired the college-educated daughter of one of our principles. She had been working at a local amusement park for a dollar an hour in a job with no future. We started her out as a data entry clerk and she quickly rose to programmer. Since the amusement park was not in interstate commerce it did not have to pay the $2.50 minimum wage. But since GCSC was in interstate (actually international) commerce we were supposed to—although her abilities did not yet warrant that amount of pay. We started her at an effective $1.50 per hour a 50% increase with advancement opportunities. But what about the $2.50 minimum wage? She just reported three out of every five hours that she worked until her pay was raised to $2.50—an example of a bad regulation.

While in the past I have opposed the concept of minimum wages, I now support current attempts to raise the minimum wage both at the National level and here in Colorado. Times are different and there is much more exploitation of workers and excess pay for CEOs and other corporate officers.

The IBM 1401

The circumstances and conflicts regarding the 1401 purchase are presented in the GCSC case in chapter 8—here are some additional situations dealing with the GCSC 1401.

IBM 1401 and the Investment Tax Credit

Roy, who was both an accountant and one of our principals, was experienced handling finances for under capitalized companies. Being near to Armco also helped us learn a few additional accounting tricks as reported below.

GCSC obtained a used 1401 from Halsey Corporation early in the 4th quarter. GCSC's purchase was contingent on upgrading the computer's memory and adding additional tape drives. These additions brought us almost to the end of the calendar year (which was also our fiscal year). If we could get the 1401 operational before the end of the year, we would reap a financial benefit from the investment tax credit. We pulled some strings with IBM and one of our clients to execute a production run and get paid for it before December 31st. Thus we collected the investment tax credit. But it was several more weeks before the machine was really in production.

Armco did the same thing with their new rolling mill. They rolled an iron ingot through their mill before the end of the year—pulling it through by hand. One of the accountants that we worked with at Armco said only half jokingly, "Our objective is not to make steel. Our objective is to collect the investment tax credit."

IBM 1401 Incidents

While our 1401 operation ran quite smoothly, we did suffer a few glitches. One was a significant spike in voltage feeding the 1401. This was finally discovered after we suffered occasional sudden outages over a long period of time. IBM placed a voltage monitor on the line, which documented large variations in voltages.

But until we discovered the problem the machine would shut down and often damage tapes. It turned out that the voltage spike occurred during the late morning when the grade school across the street turned on their ovens to get ready to serve lunch. The problem was solved when the power company placed a device on the power line feeding the 1401 that caught and stopped the voltage spike.

Another incident had to do with preventive maintenance. Several times data center personnel cancelled scheduled preventive maintenance (PM) due to a heavy processing schedule or because the machine was lightly loaded. This came home to haunt us. Because during a peak load period we would experience a hardware problem, which may have been avoided by the cancelled PM.

Thus we implemented the policy: "PM is never cancelled for any reason. It we are busy enough to consider canceling—that means that the machine must be in top working condition. If we are not very busy, that is a perfect time so give the machine to IBM for PM."

DEALING WITH LIMITED STORAGE

Today computers have essentially unlimited storage both internally and externally, thus we forget that originally storage was very limited. For example, the IBM 1401 of the 1960s was named after it's original memory size of 1401 positions. The first 1401 that I worked upon had

4,000 positions of memory each with 6-bits which could contain data or (part of) an instruction. It was eventually expanded to 16,000 of these 6-bit positions.

In order to overcome this limited storage all kinds of programming techniques were taken. A few of these are listed below.

Add Feed-A-Card To Counter

The 1401 had a variable length instruction format. I assume that this was designed to, at least partially, overcome the limited storage. Thus instruction could be one, four, five, six, or seven characters. An instruction always had a one (6-bit) character operation code (op-code), some instructions had one three-character operand address and some had two three character operands. The five and seven character instructions had one-character modifiers in addition to their address(es). A special seventh bit in each position called a word mark was used to determine the length of the instruction—each op-code was designated with a word mark. The end of each data field was also designated by a word mark.

Unit record (card read/punch or print) I/O (input/output) was to or from fixed locations in memory; thus unit record I/O only required a one-character instruction. In the case of feed or read-a-card the op-code was a one (1). Thus one way that was utilized to save memory was to provide a data name such as feed-a-card to an instruction to read a card and then use that as the literal or constant one (1). This is shown below (note that the operation code for Add is A, and that counter is 4-digits and is located in memory position 363-366 and that position 363 has a word mark):

Memory Label Op-code Operand1 Operand2
Address
...
0366 Counter(4)
...
0501 feed-a-card 1
Process card just read
.....
.....

      1143 Accumulate A feed-a-card counter (autocoder format)
            A 501 366 (assembled machine
            instruction)

    ....

The astute reader may have observed that we can't address 1401 or 4,000 memory positions, much less 16,000, with 3 digits which only address 1,000 (0-999) positions and thus may well be doubting the presentation. This observation is only partially correct. Note that only four of the six bits in each position are needed to create the digits 0 thru 9. The four bits represent the binary powers of two (1, 2, 4, 8) and with various combinations of these we can actually create the decimal digits 0 thru 15. So the remaining two bits in each position were used to cumulatively add one, two, four, or eight thousand to the address and thus we can address, when the machine is so configured up to 16,000 positions (0-15999). This is related to the 7080-addressing scheme shown in chapter 7.

    So back to feed-a-card to counter. While this may save a position or two of memory often more is needed. This leads us to additional approaches described below.

NOT A Millennium Bug!

It was techniques such Add feed-a-card to Counter and the two-digit year that lead much later to the Y2K problems. And, as you remember, they were often called "bugs" or programming errors. As you can now see, they were not bugs at all—but necessary techniques to handle the disparity between the programming needs of the day and the size and power of the hardware of that era.

    In the 1960s and 1970s and even later it did not seem necessary to have a four-digit year—particularly when storage was at such a premium. With a two-digit year and a date format of YYMMDD, a date took six positions, saving two positions on external and internal storage for each occurrence of a date. In fact, in some cases we used a five-digit date of the form YYDDD where DDD was the day of the year up to 366. Of course for human interpretation and display this had to be converted to something like May 6, 1965 by a routine, which took some storage but could be used over and over.

Much worry and some panic accompanied the transition from 1999 to 2000 or 99 to 00. I offered via the Internet and several other sources to work 12 hours on Wednesdays to help organizations with the transitions. No offers! The few responders wanted 100-hour weeks. I had had enough of those.

Card Overlay

At this time programs were written on coding sheets designed for each specific computer language. Next they were keypunched onto punched cards. These cards were then run through a compiler or assembler, which produced a deck of cards called an object deck that would be loaded into the computer to run the actual program.

Good writing has a beginning, middle, and end—the same is true of good computer programs. A common computer program pattern executes the beginning to do initial program housekeeping, and then does its main work in the middle, and when it is done it cleans up by executing the end of the program code. The work done in the middle is most often the largest and most time consuming portion of the program and generally consists of accomplishing the same processing for each incoming set of data (for example a customer record).

Serial (one after the other not included in a loop) processing segments can be loaded into the machine, executed, and then overlain by the next segment. This certainly applied to well-designed beginning, middle, and end code segments, all three of which do not have to reside in memory at the same time. The middle can overlay the locations used by the beginning, and the end can overlay the locations utilized by the middle (and before that the beginning).

Not requiring the entire program to be in memory at once obviously allows one to operate larger programs. We are limited here by the size of the largest of the beginning, middle, or end or any serial segment that we may need again as the card reader cannot be backspaced. This piece is generally the middle. In fact the middle is often by far the largest segment of the program. This means that while the partial card load approach gains more memory than the add feed-a-card to counter or the two-digit year approach it still can be quite limited since portions of the program must be loaded in the sequence that they are executed and once executed we cannot return to them

Obviously code that we needed to go back to could be duplicated as many times as needed but this could create an unwieldy maintenance burden when code must be kept the same in multiple places or expands the size of the overall program. There is, at least a partial, solution to this problem—that is the tape overlay approach presented next.

Tape Overlay

Since tape can be searched both forward and backwards (by backspacing or rewinding) segments of code from any portion of the program can be identified and copied from their cards (which were output the compile or assembly) to tape.

A portion of memory can be set aside for such code and when a particular routine is required, if it is not in memory, then the tape librarycan be searched and the segment loaded and executed. This is how the sawing MATRAN described in chapter 1 worked, except that the MATRAN program was stored on a permanent library tape.

This adds complexity to the designing and writing of the program. The program must be designed and written so that the library modules can execute independently. A program librarian sub system must be incorporated and the program must interface with it. And searching and loading takes time and if done too often slow operation will result.

However, in spite of these limitations, very significant programs were operated which without such a technique would have far exceeded the memory capacity of the 1401.

This 1401 computer did not have a disk drive which would have made the operation faster and easier and the actual operation would have been much like today's disk operating systems. Nor did the 1401 have a tape library as such—there generally was not a tape drive available—they all had to be used for processing. See also Sawing MATRAN and Scatter Read in chapter 1.

PROJECTS

GCSC practiced management by notebook. As new projects came in they were assigned a project ID and a notebook was established to keep track of documents relating to the project. Several GCSC projects are presented in the following sections. Two especially important projects, SPEC and Mexico are presented separately. (Mexico in a section of its own below and SPEC in chapter 10.)

Federal Home Loan Bank

GCSC did data conversion for the Federal Home Loan Bank (FHLB) branch in Cincinnati. The FHLB contracted with savings and loans in the region to do their processing online interactively at their facility in Cincinnati. I never understood this because it appeared that a (quasi?) governmental agency was competing with private data centers. The systems of these S&Ls ranged from completely manual to locally hosted online systems. The project consisted of taking the S&L's existing system data, in whatever form, and converting it to the FHLB's system's format. Over time, GCSC developed a stable of routines for various kinds of conversions. One of the most significant of these was shortening names. If the S&L's system allowed 60 characters for a name and the FHLB system allowed only 30, a smart algorithm was required to shorten the name without ending up with obscene or uncomplimentary words.

The first thing that we did when we received data from a S&L was to produce a print out of all the data in all the files. Yes all. We learned that at any time we might need to be able to see what the data actually looked like. This proved very valuable and avoided several potential disasters. We developed and tested our conversion programs and procedures with data, which, once supplied, was quickly out-of-date. When we had convinced ourselves, the FHLB, and the S&L that we had successfully managed to convert all their data correctly, the actual conversion took place. The S&L would close their books on a Friday and get their data to us. We would do the conversion Friday night and/ or Saturday and deliver the converted data to the FHLB. They would add it to their system and bring the new S&L up in time for Monday morning online processing.

If their system was totally manual, we would have the names and address and account information punched and ready to have current data added. Manual systems often caused the most difficult scheduling —but in general these were the smallest S&Ls.

Marrying Republicans

Using some of the data conversion and matching routines from the S&L system, we put together a slick system for political mailings—as I remember it was for the Republicans. Through our client we obtained tapes with the names and address of registered voters in Hamilton County, Ohio. The job was to produce labels for mailing political literature. We added a twist that saved the client more money than our processing cost. When two persons at the same address had the same last name we married their labels and produced only one label thus saving significant mailing and printing costs. GCSC appears to be the only firm that practiced this efficiency as we regularly receive two identical mailings, which could easily be avoided.

Fuel Oil

GCSC developed a fuel oil accounting system. It kept track of degree-days (derived by adding the number of degrees that the average temperature was below a cutoff for each day since the last delivery) indicating when deliveries should take place, recorded the deliveries, produced bills, and posted payments. We intended to sell the system to multiple fuel oil dealers, however only one dealer was acquired.

Bed Sheet Ballots

I became a member of the Accuracy Certification Board for Hamilton County, Ohio elections. At this time Hamilton County (Cincinnati) used very large ballots, called bed sheet ballots that were marked with florescent ink and then stacked by precinct and mounted on a pallet, which was subsequently fed into a Coleman vote tabulation machine. The Coleman was a very large machine, which read the ballots, tabulated the votes for each candidate or issue and punched a deck of cards that summarized the results for a given precinct. The cards were then taken to a central computer where all the precincts were tabulated and countywide totals were produced. Since issues and candidates had to be rotated by precinct there was a punched paper tape for each precinct. This tape unscrambled the results into the punched cards with a consistent placement of candidates and issues.

Our job on the Accuracy Certification Board was to take a stack of pre-counted ballots and the associated tape to each machine on an hourly basis and tabulate the ballots and check the results with the pre count. The Coleman bed sheet ballot system proved over several years to be extremely accurate. We never encountered a problem with the equipment and/or procedures. Unlike in today's elections there never was a question about the validity of the outcome. But, the Coleman system, with all its steps and manual handling was terribly, terribly slow and Hamilton County was invariably the last county in the state of Ohio to report results. This caused unbelievably bad press and much pressure on the country commissioners to do something different. The press and the general public were more interested in speed than accuracy and validity. The system was replaced with an all punch card system and I was no longer involved.

The Storm

We thought that GCSC had a good chance to land a significant project with a firm in Erie, Pennsylvania. We had experience in their industry, so George and I drove up to take a look.

As usual we had been working around the clock so we took turns driving and kept the radio off so that the other person could catch up on his sleep. However, during our drive a violent storm of which we were not aware raged near us. We had seen black clouds to the south of us but we were not concerned. But our families were. They were desperately trying to find out where we were in relation to the storm. Of course this was before cell phones.

We were safe. But our experience in Erie was not good. The firm was all tied up in the recent purchase of one of the magical methodologies a 12-volume set of manuals on how to and what to do to develop a computer system. Of course these magical methodologies assure that nothing goes wrong—because nothing gets implemented.

George wanted, in some way, to incorporate the author of these 12 volumes into our business. I thought he was a blow hard and I told George so. I said no deal until he presented a solid business plan. Well he never presented a plan of any kind—solid or otherwise—and one disaster at least was avoided, but unfortunately as reported in chapter 8 GCSC had others.

Local Outsourcing

Several years after GCSC installed the 1440 described in DMIOCS and Four-to-Zero in chapter 1, Armco decided to transfer the computer processing from their Washington Courthouse plant to their Middletown headquarters. Armco chose to contract for the transfer and requested bids. Since GCSC had performed the conversion that installed the current computer system at the plant and had extensive experience with the headquarters main frame, we felt uniquely qualified to bid on the project. We invested significant resources into preparing the bid, planning the work, and estimating the timetable and costs involved. We submitted our bid and were counting on it to bring the company out of its doldrums.

While working on another project for the plant at the courthouse I found a copy of GCSC's proposal in the files of another firm, which was also doing work at the plant. Armco had disclosed our bid and accompanying plans to another firm recently formed by the IBM salesman on the Armco account. This information enabled them to undercut GCSC's bid by utilizing our strategy and thus they were subsequently awarded the contract. During their execution of the contract they developed a Database Management System, which became a significant product that launched a very successful company.

Roslyn Data Center

GCSC was an outgrowth of The Halsey Corporation whose main business was buying and selling used computers—primarily IBM computers that had been under continual IBM maintenance.

Two of the Halsey computers were purchased from a bank in Winston Salem, North Carolina. Instead of reselling these computers, an IBM 7090 and an IBM 1401, Halsey set up a data center in Roslyn, Virginia right across the Potomac River from Washington, D.C.

But first a story about Roy's acquisition of this 7090—Roy was in the bank's conference room with several bank executives. They had come to a tentative understanding of the conditions of the sale and purchase. But the executives wanted to take a break to talk to the head office and get its OK. They asked Roy if he would like access to a phone so that he could check with higher authority and obtain the necessary approval. Roy said, "I have already checked with higher authority (me) and I have approval to go ahead with the deal as constituted." Halsey purchased the system from the bank and installed at Roslyn.

GCSC personnel did most of the data center operation for Halsey, though it was not a very lucrative arrangement. GCSC just received salaries, expenses, overhead, the use of a car, and obtained some systems work as a result of being there. Halsey kept an apartment in a nearby apartment house, so that lodging was free and we could cook some of our meals.

Another interesting aspect of Roy's financing operation was the handling of airplane tickets. Round trip tickets of limited duration (two weeks?) cost less than one way or tickets with a longer duration. At each location—Middletown and Roslyn—a pile of return trip tickets was kept and whoever was traveling checked to see if there was a appropriate ticket in the pile.

Some of the processing at the data center was for Armco Steel back in Middletown. This included an international, multi-division, statement consolidation with currency conversion utilizing a FORTRAN program written by Ron. GCSC also did some market analysis from Dunn and Bradstreet (D &B) tapes that Armco had purchased. During this time I developed a strong dislike for D&B, a grudge that holds to this day. A faulty tape drive damaged one of the D&B tapes. D&B adamantly refused to replace the damaged tape without charging for repurchasing the entire set. So the analysis excluded what ever was on the damaged tape.

While GCSC was tending the 7090 data center in Roslyn, Martin Luther King was assassinated. The District, right across the Potomac River from the data center, literally exploded with violence. None of the cleaning crew (primarily African Americans) showed up that night or for several days. We were mildly frightened—but nothing much happened in Roslyn. From the roof of the 11-story building we saw many fires burning in the District.

Some time later, while the situation in the district was still tense, I had a scary adventure. I, by myself, drove the Halsey Cadillac into the District to see a movie. When I got out of the movie it was dark and I could see that I was in a colored neighborhood. And I was lost. I kept driving in circles—the Washington DC roundabouts had me completely confused and then I noticed that I was low on fuel. I had the windows rolled up and was afraid to ask directions either to a gas station or on how to exit the neighborhood. I finally found my way to a busier section of town, purchased gas, and found my way home. Whew!

MEXICO
A major GCSC project was the installation of a 1410 at a subsidiary of Armco Steel in Teleplante, outside Mexico City. Jack, our representative, was there almost two years and I went down twice.

Bitrate Zimblast[37]
A 1410 had been purchased used in the USA and required an export permit to be shipped to Mexico. In filling out the papers I came across a section where I was to enter the Bitrate Zimblast.[38] I knew not what it was, and to this day don't believe that it exists. So I left that section blank. The permit was rejected because I had not completely filled out the form. The Bitrate Zimblast was missing.

So, being a good engineer by training, I made a scientific wild assed guess (SWAG) as to what might get by and entered an entirely made up number. The permit was approved and we shipped the 1410 to Mexico.

IBM And The Seven (Deadly) Lies
Our competition for the Teleplante project was IBM itself. They wanted to install a new S/360 for a great deal more money than our (their?) 1410 would cost. In their proposal, among other things, IBM made seven lies regarding our project. Unfortunately, I cannot remember them all—but we documented each lie as a lie by using IBM's own publications. The ones I remember are:

---

[37]   This could also go under the bureaucracy heading.
[38]   I don't remember the term exactly—but the rest is factual.

1. Lie: The 1410 was no longer being manufactured. Rebuttal: An article in an IBM publication describing the manufacture of 1410s in India.
2. Lie: Mexico did not have any customer engineers trained to maintain the 1410. Rebuttal: We had one under contract.
3. Lie: We would be unable to obtain a maintenance contract on the 1410.[39] Rebuttal: We already had a maintenance contract signed by the IBM office in Mexico City.

Data Center Construction

The 1410 required a controlled environment to operate. So we sent drawings for a controlled environment data center in Mexico. But our communication was not up to Mexican standards.

When Jack, our representative, arrived at the data center he found that there were doorways but no doors. When he enquired as to the problem, the locals responded with, "Oh! You wanted a doors in the doorways." We had not been explicit enough—assuming that doorways had doors.

The data center was to have raised flooring so that the cables connecting the modules of the 1410 could be out of the way. When they installed the raised flooring it was not even. So they obtained a heavy-duty grinder and ground the floor level—instead of using the adjusting mechanism under each floor section. Of course, this made a real mess—so they had to take up the flooring to clean out the metal grindings from the room. But now the floor sections were no longer interchangeable parts. So each section had to be identified as to its exact location in the room—a very large complex jigsaw puzzle.

Almost Lost That Customer Engineer

The infamous data center was on the second floor. Thus a section of the wall was removed and the computer components were lifted by crane into the second floor. The hole in the wall was then covered

---

[39] In order to be marketable in the used computer market, the computer must have been under continual IBM maintenance. Our 1410 had been under continual maintenance and would continue when installed in Mexico.

with a plastic sheet until such time as a permanent wall could be re-instituted. This would, of course, be mañana, as this was Mexico.

One day while the IBM customer engineer was working on the 1410, he backed up—right into the plastic sheet and having nothing to hang on to he began to slowly fall through. Very fortunately, one of the data center employees witnessed this and was able to come to his rescue and grab him and pull him back in to safety. The next day turned out to be mañana—plastic sheet was replaced with the permanent wall.

Out For Lunch

I went to Mexico twice to assist Jack. One time it was to install the 1410 FORTRAN compiler and to develop instructions for its use. I don't remember what the specific assignment was the other time. But I do remember the executive lunches.

Lunch was a two-hour affair. We first met in a lounge for cocktails and hors d'oeurves. This was a social time. Then we went into the big dining room. The men (all the executives were men) sat around a long oval table according to their pecking order based upon their rank with the company. The senior executive on sight that day sat at the head of the table, the remaining executives arranged themselves clockwise starting at his left. And I, as guest of honor, sat at his right hand.

The food was fabulous and fresh. I was really impressed with the very large bowl of fresh strawberries that was passed around. The conversation, of course, was in Spanish so I could understand very little. Except occasionally I would pickup the word "Senorita" and then there would be racus laughter. I assumed that an off-color joke had just been told.

Hombre Record

The installation had several programmers trained in COBOL and Jack taught them GCSC techniques including basic functions[40]. Of course the key words in the COBOL statements were in English (MOVE, READ, WRITE, etc.). But the data names were in Spanish.

---

[40]   Chapter 6.

So we had statements like. MOVE HOMBRE-RECORD-IN TO HOMBRE-RECORD-OUT.

Electric Power

Electric Power in Teleplante was very erratic. It went out almost every afternoon during the daily thunderstorm. Power outages were particularly difficult to handle, as the 1410 was a tape-oriented machine. When the power went out, the job had to be restarted from at least the beginning of the last step. So whenever a storm was eminent, the current step was finished and the 1410 was powered down until the storm passed and the power came back on.

Ugly Americans

When I went to Mexico I stayed in a local motel that was used primarily by Mexicans. It was not a tourist hangout. The only meal I had there was breakfast, but the breakfast menu was in Spanish. I had a very helpful waiter (who spoke English but tried hard to hide the fact). He made sure that I ordered in Spanish and that I knew what I had ordered.

Several days into one of my visits, two matronly U.S. American women showed up and sat several tables away from me. They immediately complained about the menu being in Spanishgrumbling, "Don't these damn people speak English?" In their presence my waiter knew no English and was not at all helpful.

"I Have No More Relatives."

While Jack was in Mexico, he was contacted by P&G and referred to the Mexican TV and communications conglomerate. P&G de Mexico was advertising on their stations and their advertising agency was supposed to get a commission based upon the TV commercial costs. But the agency had not been billed for TV time—so the agency could not get paid. P&G asked GCSC to look into it.

Jack went to the firm's offices and met with their President who was reluctant to have us get involved—but finally agreed to have Jack do a study to see what the problem was. Jack interviewed several managers and studied their systems and came to a conclusion as to the cause of the problem—there was no one in charge of data processing. The organization chart had a missing name on it. Jack had difficulty presenting his report. The president was (almost) always off the coast of Mexico in his yacht. When Jack was finally able to pin him down, he asked about the missing position. "Why don't you have someone in charge of data processing?" "Because I have no more relatives," was the response.

That was the end GCSC's involvement. I have no idea what happened, except that we did receive our fee for the consultation.

TIMELESS TIMES
While the following incidents are from this period they are actually timeless.

"Dad this is too much work!"
Since I had unfettered access to the 1401, which had a FORTRAN compiler, I thought that I would teach our children a thing or two about computers. So I had them take some of their algebra problems and convert them to FORTRAN, write them on coding sheets, keypunch them, and run them on our computer. When they got their answers from the computer I asked, "How do you know they are correct?" So they had to sit down and do them by hand. When their results checked out they came to me and said somewhat sheepishly, "Dad, we don't want to do this anymore. You make us do it by computer AND by hand. Our teacher only makes us do it by hand. I said, "At least now you won't blindly believe that computer output is always correct."

Which price is correct?
The above lesson reminds me of a time when I went to a local hardware store and the item I wanted to purchase was on a top shelf so I asked some employees to help me get it down. A young women and a young man—both probably college students—came to help me. When we got it down we noticed that it had three different prices marked on it. Two were handwritten and one was computer generated. When I

asked. "Which price is the correct one?" the young woman answered. "The computer generated one, of course." The young man said, "No I don't trust computers, I'll bet it's one of the handwritten one." It was one of the hand-written ones.

Grinvelopes[41]

Roger, a lawyer, one of the GCSC principles had a client, Artie, who was getting out of jail on parole and Roger wondered if GCSC would have a job for him. Artie was married and had two small children. Twins? But he had no real skills—not even a high school diploma. We gave him a job as a go-for in the firm with all kinds of opportunities to learn about computers. But first he had to earn his way as janitor, delivery person, and errand runner—a gofer.

Artie was a talented artist. He drew what he called grinvelopes which were humorous caricatures and the like. They were quite good and original and he wanted to go into business producing and selling them. His idea was a large operation with him having a swank office and perks. But we advised him that he had to start small and, if successful, work up to that. We offered him after hours use of any and all facilities of the office. But he did not avail himself of our offer.

To start Artie was paid the minimum wage of $2.50 per hour. When he received his first weekly paycheck he was aghast. It was not for $100 ($2.50 x 40) but for something like $75 or $80. He immediately started arguing and I had to explain about taxes, social security and the like to him. I said, "How do you think your jail was paid for? Where did the money come from to take care of your wife and kids while you were gone?"

For a while Artie worked out well, but then he began to come in late, looking droopy and beat up—from drinking. When, after several warnings, the situation did not improve I contacted his probation officer and said "I need help here. I have a job that Artie can do and grow in—but he has to come on time and do the job. But I am not a social worker."

The probation officer almost immediately contacted Artie and told him to quit. "Johnson is a troublemaker." He quit and got a job

---

[41]   This incident could also go under the bureaucracy heading.

(through the probation officer?) with Armco Steel in the mill—a job with no future but one that paid $4.00 per hour. That is until he got laid off—this is when I lost track of him. I cannot imagine a very favorable future for he or his family.

Getting Out of the Army

After moving to Cincinnati I was assigned to the 311th Field Hospital to fulfill the remainder of my Army reserve obligation. I attended weekly evening meetings and all day one Sunday a month. The pay was a nice adjunct to my P&G salary—but to exercise my independence, I made sure to miss one meeting per quarter.

Annually I was given a contract renewal which was a chance to sign up for another year. The year in which my obligation was up, I checked the box that said, "I opt to leave the reserves as soon as my obligation has been fulfilled." When the eighth anniversary of my joining the reserves came in April 1976, I requested that I be discharged. At that point I was told, "Sorry Captain Johnson, last January you sighed up for another year. You may not be discharged at this time."

My reply was, "Please check my 'contract renewal' of which I have a copy in my safe deposit box if you don't. I opted to be discharged on my anniversary date." They checked and I was discharged. The following October while driving home from work in Middletown to our home in Cincinnati I heard on the 10 o'clock radio news, "The 311th Field Hospital has been called to active duty and is being sent to Vietnam." I stopped my car on the freeway exit ramp and invented the Subaru add—where the person gets out of their car, jumps up and down and hollers, "Whoop de do for my Subaru!" It pays to read the fine print. Since I had just started my own company, it would have been a bad time to be gone for an extended period. I later avoided another potential long absence when I was excused from jury duty because I was a company owner and had an advanced degree.

The army reserves could have been a good deal—theoretically only 12 more years and I could have received a military pension. But almost everyone I knew had been cheated out of a year or more of service and thus I was looking at maybe 15 more years. And I would have gone to Vietnam. Good decision.

Fink/Unfink: Early Hacking?

This story came from Purdue University via Ron, one of our principles. At Purdue as elsewhere computer jobs were prepared on punched cards, which were then converted to tape in a card to tape operation on a computer such as an IBM 1401. The tape was then taken to a large computer, in this case an IBM 7090 and run. The output then went to tape which was taken back to the 1401 and printed out and sent to the submitter along with their cards.

This often meant that there was a long delay between the time the job was submitted and the results were received. To shorten this time, some computer science students modified the 7090 IBSYS operating system to recognize a new control card of their making—the FINK card—and flush the rest of the jobs. Thus the jobs before the FINK card would be returned sooner. But, of course, there is a side effect. As more persons learned about the FINK card there was more chance of your job being behind a FINK card and being FINKed and not run at all. The obvious solution, of course, was another new control card of their making—the UNFINK card which then enabled subsequent jobs to be run (until another FINK card was encountered). When everyone placed an UNFINK card before their job the installation was back to where they had started. The final saga was an operating system modification that caused a FINK event when an UNFINK card was encountered when the system was not in the FINK mode.

This sounds to me a little like today writing of viruses and worms, etc.

TECHNICAL LEADERSHIP WORKSHOP

In 1975 Jack and I attended a Technical Leadership workshop in Tarrytown, New York, conducted by two well-known IT gurus, Jerry Weinberg and Don Gause. Several incidents from that workshop are memorable. There we 16 of us carefully chosen attendees who arrived at the conference center on a Sunday, checked in and then met for our first session. This workshop was paid for out of our 200 hour bonus. As George was constantly causing us to work long hours I prevailed upon the board to pay us an extra $5.00 for each hour over 200 a month, 168 being the standard 40-hour week.

Seating Chart

Weinberg and Gause immediately began to develop a seating chart. We repeatedly lined up by height, gender, age, and whatever else they could think of and we obediently let ourselves be herded around until Weinberg said forcefully, "What is the matter with you folks? You are adults, you have paid dearly for this workshop, why are you letting yourselves be herded around like cattle, just because you have become students?" That was only the beginning of their surprises and a small insight into their approach to the seminar.

Dossiers

In order to be accepted (we thought), we filled out an extensive dossier regarding our experience, education, and the like. We quickly found out that this was not so. The group was not all that exclusive—the dossiers were used to organize us into groups of two, four, or eight with certain compatibilities or often incompatibilities.

Write A Program: What language?

The first night, after a short organizational session—without a seating chart actually being implemented, we were broken up into groups of four and given a programming assignment. Right away we saw the dossiers at work. None of the four of us shared a common computer or programming language. It was very stressful and it got to the point where I was ready to punt and go to bed without a program being developed, as it was getting very late. We were very incompatible and really getting on each other's nerves. We finally did bat out a bad program (on paper) in FORTRAN as I remember, but I am sure that it would not have worked had we keypunched it and tried to run it.

Workshop Format

For the rest of the week we met at 7am for breakfast, had workshops till noon, had lunch together, then more workshops, supper together, more workshop and off to bed about 10pm. Very long, very intense, and very interesting days—to say the least.

Working In Quiet Isolation

With two to eight groups performing workshop projects, our assigned room could get quite hectic. I thought for some assignments that a quieter workplace would be nice so I arranged one evening with the facility to obtain a separate room. Our group of four went there to work out our assignment. What a bummer! We did not solve hardly any of the problems at hand—but the other three groups got almost all the way through. Why was this? As the other groups worked in the same room they would ask Jerry or Don a question (which they may or may not have answered but the back and forth gave the other groups information that turned out to be useful for carrying out the assignment.) While Jerry and Don wandered in and out of our room and we had the ability to ask them questions (which they may or may not have answered) we had not overheard the tidbits of information that were floating around from their interactions with the other groups.

Teamwork: Bowling

There were no workshops as such on Wednesday night —it was a social time. We had a luxurious dinner with plenty to drink. We were supposed to get better acquainted with our workshop mates. One way was to reveal something intimate—so we told each other our mother's maiden names (?).

We also had some interesting exercises in teamwork as opposed to competition, which we eventually carried to the bowling alley. Instead of bowling individually and keeping our own scores, we each bowled one ball and tried as a team to maximize the overall score for each line. This proceeded successfully for a while, as for several games our total score increased. But, it then began to fall off. Jerry and Don suggested that adding new members to a team might energize us and that we should go out into the conference center and recruit bowlers from other groups at the center. We did this and the mostly high-powered business execs that we recruited got a kick out of the crazy programmers, so several agreed to join us. Then came an interesting part.

Our order of bowling as a workshop group was alphabetical by our mother's maiden name. So in order to fit the new team members in the lineup we had to know their mother's maiden name. This caused some embarrassment and more thoughts of crazy programmers but we eventually got the information and inserted them into the line up.

And sure enough, our team scores went up indicating that adding new persons to a team may improve performance. But our scores only went up for a while, as eventually fatigue exacerbated by all the beer took over and our scores began to fall drastically and we called it a night.

Strength Of Conviction

During one of the workshop sessions, Jerry was emphasizing that it was not only what you believed that was important—but also how strongly one believed it. So he said something that sounded reasonable and asked, "Who is willing to bet $10 that X[42] is true?" Almost all of us raised our hands. (We believed that this would be real money, so we were thoughtful.) He then asked, "Who is willing to bet $50 that X is true?" Only about half of us, including yours truly, raised their hands this time. When he got to $100, my hand was the only one up. I was sure that I had won $100 dollarsand if I had lost I was on an expense account and I thought my loss would count as a workshop expense. Well, it turned out that I was wrong. But Jerry refused to take any money from me. He said I had already paid enough. I have often wondered it there is any relation between that event and my son from time to time saying, "Dad, you may be forceful—but you are wrong!"

In 2005 I contacted Jerry Weinberg regarding our book *Flexible Software Design* identifying myself with this story. He vaguely remembered it after 30 years.

Ping-Pong Balls And Punched Cards

As two teams of eight we built a large structures out of punched cards. Then we tried to destroy the other team's structure with ping-pong balls. We felt that this would be very easy—after all the structures were, in reality, houses of cards. But! Just try and throw a ping-pong ball—straight. Actually I just did and it seems quite easy. But that day, at least, it was nearly impossible. (Maybe they were trick balls?) But our houses stood and another lesson was learned. Even if you are

---

[42]   Too bad I cannot remember what X was.

weakyour adversary may be even weaker. Don't know the exact value of that but there it is. I find this to true often in tennis.

PUNCHED CARD DAYS

Punched cards were the norm in the GCSC days. They, of course, were used for program code and for data. But they were also used for notes. GCSC designed our own card, which actually served as our business card. As shown below one side is for punching, the other side is for taking notes.

The GCSC period coincided with the transition from punched cards to online entry. The transition was not easy but it was welcomed.

GCSC office in Cincinnati was across a parking lot from a 12-story building. Our client P&G had a data center on the ninth floor where we took card decks (often boxes or trays) for transmission to the mainframe downtown and received our printouts back. One day while walking across this parking lot in the rain with a tray full of cards, I slipped and fell. The tray went out in front of me and the cards flew all over. They were now wet and could no longer be used. We had to revert to the back up deck and make the changes necessary to bring it up to date.

When P&G acquired TSO (Time Sharing Option), we loaded all our cards on disk as card images. They then could be edited via a typewriter terminal using TSO. Also batch jobs could be submitted though TSO. This was not without troubles—as several times early on all or our card images on the disk were lost through operating system errors. We then had to bring our decks up to date and reload them. SPEC alone was over 20,000 cards.

223

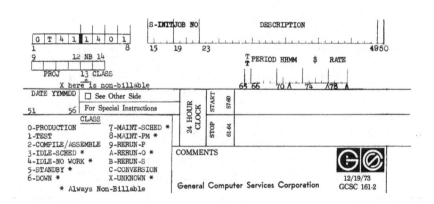

Card Capacity/Card Production

At this time, IBM had a virtual monopoly on the production and sale of punched cards that may be while they are still called IBM cards. If one bought punched cards from IBM and had problems, ones employment was still secure. Save money by purchasing punched cards from another vendor and have trouble, you were out on the street without a job. At least when using IBM card on IBM hardware running IBM programs you knew who to call when problems occurred.

The government sued IBM and forced them to divest themselves of sufficient capacity so that they had less than 50% of the USA card capacity. Note the keyword here—capacity. This backfired on our government—IBM ran their plants overtime and still sold over half of all punched cards.

This is similar to the SOHIO (Standard Oil of Ohio) BP (British Petroleum) situation. When BP began using Alaska Oil their costs were significantly reduced and they were selling gasoline at ten cents a gallon less than anyone else and still making bundles of money. So one branch of our government sued them for unfair competing (underselling the other companies) and another branch sued them for making excess profits. So they did the smart thing to get one agency off their back—they raised the price of their gasoline. So the consumer lost, not only having to pay more to drive but also having to fund two government agencies that were at cross purposes with each other.

Almost To The PC

GCSC ended before the advent of the personal computer. But we were right on the verge. The Mits/Altiar came out at the end of our existence. I sent the programming staff to seminars presenting the machines. We could not figure out how to make use of them. One of the challenges regarding their use was that their input and output was through console switches and lights—in binary mode. It was really just a hobby computerbut it helped start the microcomputer revolution.

The next chapter describes GCSC's involvement in the development the SPEC (System for Planning Electrical Construction).

CHAPTER 10
SYSTEM FOR PLANNING
ELECTRICAL CONSTRUCTION

If the wiring in the Glass Tower building in the movie *The Towering Inferno* had been configured according to System for Planning Electrical Construction (SPEC) there would have been no movie, as the tower would not have become an inferno. Butthe wiring was not done SPEC's way, thus an exciting movie. [Picture credit thetoweringinferno.info[43]]

Though my role ended in 1976, 22 years before I retired, System for Planning Electrical Construction (SPEC) is certainly one of my most significant career accomplishments. SPEC was done for the engineering division of Procter & Gamble (P&G), a very demanding customer. SPEC was done on a tight budget and time schedule, actually on tight schedules and budgets—as we generally preceded incrementally $25,000 at a time through many deadlines and budgets. While this start-stop hectic environment is, unfortunately, not unusual for IT projects, what was unusual was that this was also a leading-edge endeavor in which the implementation team had little or no application knowledge and the client team had no experience in developing computer systems.

My involvement with SPEC and its predicessors spanned almost 20 years and several advancements in technology. While at P&G downtown in the early 60s, I was asked by the Engineering division to consult on the design of Electrical Design System (EDS) which they were developing in house. EDS, and subsequently EDS II and SPEC, managed the routing of electric wires through a network of

---

[43] But it does not appear to be there any more.

conduits. When the engineering division's EDS development team ran into trouble routing wires, I was contacted. I saw their problem as similar to the routing of highway traffic though the Washington State Highway system so I helped them use the Moore shortest path algorithm developed at Wayne State University in Detroit as I had done for my Civil Engineering Master's Thesis at Washington State University.

EDS involved laying out a network of electrical devices, such a motors or switches, connected by wires routed though conduits, which resemble pipes and are used to protect the wires. The devices were manually converted to node numbers, which were the connecting points in the network. Nodes were numbered sequentially by hand. The data was then entered onto coding sheets and subsequently punched on to cards. The setup was very laborious and tedious and thus fraught with errors. As a result EDS was difficult to use and therefore had limited success. The system was written in 7080 autocoder, which was a second-generation relatively high-level language specific to the IBM 7080 hardware.With the advent of the S/360 and PL/I, the engineering division undertook a rewrite—essentially a redevelopment and selected our company, General Computer Services (GCSC) for the implementation of the system dubbed EDS II.

In 1970 GCSC was asked to bid on EDS II. The engineering division wanted a fixed price contract. I told them that it would be at least $20,000 but that they needed to budget $24,000 because I had to charge the engineering division for our time spent estimating change orders. P&G's engineering division was famous (infamous) for asking that we estimate what it would take to "add this or that" feature to their project—and then choosing not to implement "this or that." Thus we spent time associated with their project that we did not get paid for. I also offered them a time and materials alternative (T&M) with each of us doing what we would do best and most efficiently for which I gave a $16,000 estimate. They accepted the T&M proposal and as a result of full cooperation, we ended up under budget. EDS II was somewhat easier to use—primarily due to the automatic assignment of node numbers. However, it did not accomplish the full range of tasks that the electrical engineers needed done and thus was again a somewhat limited success. Some time later this led to the full redevelopment of the EDS II system with another techological advancement leading the way: Time Sharing Option (TSO) within Operating System 360 (OS360).

A significant difference between the EDS systems and SPEC was the development of an online interactive frontend data entry module whereby engineers entered specifications for the electrical network in a computer language specifically designed for SPEC to match their way of thinking and operating. This was facilitated by P&G's acquisition of TSO which supported on-line interactive processing via the use of typewriter-like terminals.

SPEC processing began with engineers entering raw electrical design specification data directly from their drawings using the frontend described above. Once the data was entered, SPEC was a batch processing (with no human interaction) serial sequential (executing data records one after another in a given order) system with limited random access direct processing (accessing specific records by computer address). The raw input data and the final field reports were the only data maintained between runs, which represented design versions of the specified electrical network. Each run compared its output to stored results from the previous run and noted differences. Intermediate data representing stages in processing was kept only for the duration of the processing as needed for its passage through 36 program modules including sorts.

SPEC was a large system and initially I was developing it alone. When GCSC hired Linda, our first college recruit, she was assigned to the project as the only other full-time GCSCer. Linda was a bright, talented addititon and was basically on the SPEC project for the duration. SPEC was being developed out of the Cincinnati branch office and thus she did not get to the main office in Middletown much and, while removed from the strife covered in chapters 8 and 9 she often said that she could devine the state of the business by how and how much I smoked.

P&Gs engineering division had several engineers interacting with us on SPEC starting with Jim, the project sponsor. As I subsequently learned in my PhD Project Management Course, a key to success for any IT project is sponsorship—maybe EDS and EDS II lacked powerful sponsors. After a long struggle, SPEC was a rip roaring success due in large part to a very strong sponsor and overall project manager, Jim. He was a hard charging, no-nonsense electrical engineer who would seldom take no for an answer. If he asked you to do something and you said "No," he would then ask, "Who is your boss?" even when what he asked was against company policy. He invariably followed through with his threat if you did not comply. Working closely with Jim were Dick and Ron, also experienced electrical engineers who were with us for the duration.

Dick was the primary technical liason/consultant who guided the testing of the system as it progressed. But, as we shall see later, he was not always attentive. Ron, was not a direct P&G employee—but a contract engineer who had been under contract on and off for some 20 years. Ron was an interesting case, single, footlose, and fancy free: from time to time he would take off on his motor cycle for several weeks and tour various parts of the country. I do not know what happened to Jim, Dick, and Ron as P&G phased out their in house electrical design operation and outsourced it.

Chuck, another much younger engineer, was not around long and most of his help was performed remotely. Prior to GCSC's involvement Chuck had been developing the frontend subsystem for entering the data into SPEC. The frontend was supposedly finished when Chuck was transferred to Boston. But, as we shall see, it needed much more work and we needed Chuck's help. He had access to the P&G TSO system in Cincinnati via dial up. We designated a file that both he and I had access to and I would type questions into it and then he would access it and add comments and answers. This helped in the beginning. As Chuck became more and more into his new job, he became increasing removed from SPEC, losing interest, and eventually dropping out of the picture entirely.

Our long distance computer based communication with Chuck was ceretainly an early very basic form of email which placed us ahead of our time.

GCSC was engaged to write the backend, which took the network specifications entered interactively by Chuck's frontend subsystem, analyzed them, converted them to data processing records, and produced reports that were used to bundle wires into groups with similar routing, install conduits and electrical devices, pull the wires through the conduits, and connect the wires to devices.

But, in reality, the frontend where wire, load, device, and conduit data were entered in an engineering format was not satisfactory.

Because the backend was not in operation, the engineers continually refused to stress test the frontend to identify kinks that could have been worked out while Chuck was on site. GCSC was developing the backend under tremendous schedule pressures. As we fed data to the backend from the frontend, the engineers found many things that they did not like about the frontend. Thus we had to stop our work on the backend and delve into the frontend code with which we were unfamiliar and by this time Chuck was in Boston with his involvement waning. This lack of testing of the partial system caused delays and loss of rapport between the engineers and developers. Also as the development progressed, the specifications changed and were added to causing continual stress.

I have encountered this unwillingness to interact with an incomplete system—to prototype—many times in my career. This was a ever present source of technical distance. It may be, however, with the advent of the PC and the Internet there is much more understanding of computer systems and a willingness on the part of clients to get their hands "dirty" earlier. This certainlly is a form of Technical Distance.

SPEC was much more complex than EDS or EDS II—and the engineering division wanted it yesterday. This led to several simultaneous activities: design, ementation, GCSC learning about the application, the engineers learning about communication, and other issues involved with computer system development. Another complication was the the engineers total process orientation—they focused on the processing—what SPEC had to do and how it would do it. GCSC's design philosophy concentrated on the data—what information we had to have at various points in the system so that the appropriate processing could take place. We needed to understand the data: such as where a conduit or wire began and ended, its size, what was it used for, even what color in the case of a wire. So the tail (process) was wagging the dog (data). This was an additional source of tension between GCSC and P&G.

An important tool to deal with this dichotomy of approach was SuperRecord which is presented in chaper 5 CRUDmudgeon.

As SPEC development proceeded, Jim became more knowledgeable regarding the process of developing a system such as SPEC. This resulted in specifications being periodically delivered to us in spiral bound books each version with a different color cover. The contents of these books: words, diagrams, tables, charts, etc. were all written (printed) by hand by Ron based upon feedback from engineers in the field chanelled thru Jim and Dick. Ron's "font" was as good as any printer. As new books were due we had minor ceremony to choose the cover color of the next issue.

While I did not add it up at the time, over the three years of development, I estimate that GCSC received $500,000 (1976 $) in fees for developing SPEC and its total cost including the time of the P&G engineers and computer charges, was well over a million dollars. While this indeed was a significant amount of money, the painful part was that it came in $25,000 increments. That was all that Jim's organization could authorize at one time without going to the Board of Directors. So we would agree to "finish" SPEC for $25,000 more and shortly thereafter the engineers would suddenly get smarter and realize something more that SPEC should do and out would come another colored-cover spiral-bound book produced by Dick. But with its revised and expanded specifications, the just authorized $25,000 could not "finish" SPEC.

So soon thereafter we would be back in a hard negotiating mode. "You said you could finish this quarter for $25,000 more." "Yes, but since that time and cost estimate you have added several features, including radial routing—not just shortest path." And after some hand wringing on both sides, out would come another $25,000 and soon thereafter another Dick produced spiral bound book with a different colored cover would show up. This cycle, almost an endless loop, went on for several years.

Much later in life (during my PhD studies) I took a course in project management. But at this time my project management knowledge was experiential—often learned the hard way. Wanting to measure progress on the SPEC project objectively, Jim and I instituted the following system.

When the engineers found a problem they would report it to us and we would then attempt to fix it and report back. Initially our rate of fixes was quite high and we, by that measure, were looking good. But I began to notice that the more fixes we made the more problems we had. We were making the fixes too fast without regard for their side effects. I convinced Jim of this and we went back to a more reasonable pace and actually made more progress while making fewer fixes. In computing, like in medicine, one must be aware of the potential side effects.

There were three versions of SPEC—today they would be called alpha, beta, and shipping. We used the alpha or programmer's system to test our individual programs. When we thought that they were OK we would "move them over" to the beta or engineer's system and they would run their tests of the entire system. When they came up with a version they trusted they would then move all the programs over to the production system and, in essence, ship it! SPEC was actually in production—shipped in many versions, supporting the electric design of new manufacturing plants, long before it was "finished."

SPEC was a fast moving target. I tried to keep Dick, our primary contact on the development and testing, up to date. I had the first page of the SPEC printout produce a list of the last 100 changes. I used a 100 record direct access file to keep this list. When 101st-change record came in it overlaid 1, etc. But I did not think Dick was reading these messages so I added a record that said "Dick, if you read this and call Bruce he will send $25 to your favorite charity." You guessed it. I still have that $25. This is only one example of the project communication issues. I have frequently done similar things, particularly at Xavier. I still have all this money.

GCSC, often to the chagrin of P&G's corporate Data Processing Systems (DPS), did a lot of work for various P&G departments. So DPS often went out of their way to criticize our performance. One of their criticisms was, "You folks are always around. Don't you ever finish a job?" The answer was, "Yes. But we did such a good job that we were called back to add features or to do an entirely different project." This is one of the phenomenon that led me to the myth of the successful system.

Managers are often uncomfortable with change, because it tends to upset both people and computer systems. This yields *the myth of the successful computer system.*

Myth: Successful computer systems usually generate few, if any, modification requests.

Reality: Successful computer systems generally generate continuous demands for modification.

Often an unsuccessful system is mistaken for a successful one and *vice versa.* This was particularly true of SPEC given the nature of its incremental funding. The system that is unused does not generate requests for the system to do more or to process differently. On the other hand, the system that is really being used effectively is subjected to high levels of customer demand. "If you can produce my design report, why can't you also calculate shop times?" And once that has been done, "Why can't you make materials order lists by supplier?"

Since such systems are "never finished," they are often looked upon as failures. The truth is "Use it or lose it"—successful computer systems generally generate continuous demands for modification. Thus, it is a counterintuitive managerial truth that being bugged for money and resources for modifications is really a sign of a successful, not a failed, system. A system "success metric" that includes the level of usage and modification requests by system customers would be a useful indicator of inflexibility in successful systems. What we are really saying here is that "a flexible system is supposed to be modified."

While we are at it, here is another myth pertinent to SPEC the *myth of parallel perceptions.* In the daily pressure to get things done we often fall victim to the *myth of parallel perceptions.*

Myth: Managers, customers, and technical staff have shared perceptions of the business, the technology, and their interaction.

Reality: Managers, customers, and technical staff speak widely different languages and have different views of both the system that is being computerized and the computer system itself.

This myth is different. We *say* that we don't really believe the myth but we *act* as if we *do* believe it. We operate as if we understand each others point of view, but in reality we don't really understand each other. Furthermore, although we say that we understand that there are serious communication difficulties among managers, customers, and technical staff, we often don't try hard enough to overcome them.

In designing SPEC I encountered the following situation. "We need long descriptive wire names," Dick said. "How long—twenty or thirty characters?" I asked. "How would I know? They need to be long and descriptive," replied Dick. This dialogue (two monologues?) went on without resolution for some time. Finally I produced sample reports with wire names. When they got to the wire name "CONNECTOR BETWEEN AIR CONDITIONER AND EXHAUST FAN IN THE WOMEN'S WASH ROOM ON THE SECOND FLOOR NORTH WEST CORNER" Dick said, "That's too long!" SPEC wire names ended up being 60 characters long.

The applications being computerized are perceptions. Moreover, they are someone's perception of what is necessary and important to transform the application's requirements into the computer's terms. Compounding this situation, the computer system is based on the implementer's perception of the designer's perception of the customer's perception. Information can be, and often is, lost during each transfer. These myths are particulary applicable to SPEC as it was a large, complex project plowing new ground requiring significant computing resources. SPEC's 36 programs including sorts eventually reached 20,000 punched cards, which we kept in specially designed file drawers. To modify a program we withdrew its cards from the cabinet and placed them in a punched card box and took the box to a keypunch to make the modifications.Then the box with cards was carried across the plaza from our office to the building where P&G had a data center and up to the 9th floor. This procedure was fraught with danger. Cards could be misplaced, damaged, or the ultimate disaster—dropped in a rain puddle, which happed more than once, when the person carrying the box of cards stumbled and tripped.

When P&G acquired Houston Automatic Spooling System (HASP) which permitted remote batch job entry, we loaded our PL/I program cards on disk as card images. They then could be edited via a typewriter terminal using TSO. Also batch jobs could be submitted though TSO. This was not without troubles as several times early on all our card images on the disk were lost through operating system errors. We then had to bring our decks up-to-date and reload them. This, however, was much better in the long run than dealing with individual cards.

Not only did SPEC challenge the abilities of the people involved, but also it often challenged the capacity of PL/I (the language in which SPEC was written) and OS/360 (the operating system used by the computer on which SPEC was executed). At one point as the program steps grew we exceeded the space allocated by the operating system for Job Control Language (JCL) the language which indicated to the operating system the sequence of computer programs to perform to execute SPEC as well as what files to process. SPEC was too big; it had just had too many JCL statements. We tried to think of how to break the batch (backend) portion of SPEC into two or more separate independent jobs—but this did not work. We eventually found a way to make two programs do the work of four by combining initial and final wire derating and raceway sizing into the same programs thereby reducing the amount of JCL.

As power wires carry current they cause a magnetic field and create heat, which reduces their current carrying capacity. Thus there is a limit to how many wires may be together in one conduit and depending on their electrical load, number, and placement the wires may need to be made larger than originally specified. This is called derating—decreasing the current carrying capacity for a given size of wire.

Wires were first derated based on their initial placement in conduits by the routing algorithm. Then the conduits were sized according to the number and size of wires routed through them, but if there are too many wires to fit in one raceway SPEC generated one or more parallel raceways and re-routesed some of the wires through them. But now the wires could be in a more favorable environment (fewer wires) and thus they could be made smaller, in other words re derated, and more may fit in a raceway—but if they were combined they again would not fit, a never ending cycle. Not recombining the raceways avoided this and thus allowed convergence We originally planned to have four programs do these steps—but to save JCL we used the same program twice with a control which told the programs

235

via JCL parameters which derating and conduit sizing calculations were to be performed.

From time to time we had difficulties with aspects of PL/I that did not function as advertised. But these were minor compared to the JCL crises. Actually things could have been much worse if it were not for Phil. At the time GCSC was heavily involved in SPEC, which involved sophisticated use of PL/I, OS/360 and its job control language and their interactions, the person to get answers from was Phil. We and others at P&G had significant challenges in getting these interactions to work. But when we turned to Phil downtown in the P&G corporate Data Processing Systems (DPS) office we would get answers without significant delay. Phil had extensive knowledge of the area and a direct pipeline to IBM.

But in inimitable P&G fashion it came time to promote Phil. To do so they sent him to Baltimore and "replaced" him. Now the answers stopped coming as readily and the struggle intensified. This was unaceptable so we found out how to contact Phil in Baltimore.

Gradually as more departments found out how to contact Phil, he again had a full time job consulting on PI/I and its interfaces—albeit from Baltimore. What is more, he was not getting his new job done. So at least P&G had the wisdom to transfer Phil back to Cincinnati to his old job —hopefully with a larger salary and title. Competence has is price, which I call "the curse of competence," which is more common than reconized. Many times people become "indispensible" and thus lose out on promotion and pay increases. Phil was very competent and I trust that he was adequatley rewareded. Long after SPEC I ocassionally saw and talked with him at University of Cincinnati gatherings. He seemed to be getting along fine. He was an advid automobile rally fan in his vintage Porsche.

For three years, from 1973 to 1976, SPEC consumed GCSC. My involvement was near total. Linda was full time for the duration. Many other GCSC programmers were pulled in from time to time. My heavy involvement contributed to the political problems that brought GCSC down as described in chapter 8: The Rise and Fall of GCSC.

As the project neared its completion I was nearing the end of my wits. The tensions mentioned above, communicaton, schedule presure, constant difficult negotations, and long hours took a toll. As a way of dealing with the pressure, I did a therapeutic art piece about SPEC. I have a photo of it hanging in my office today (shown below). I gave the original to Jim at our completion celebration. The piece, a collage, is called, "The Essence of Communication." It shows wires; parts of punched cards; parts of printed reports with red markings on them; phones; start, stop and off buttons; an electrical device, and my favoritea glass of scotch. (It's hard to find, it's just to the left of the middle of the long wire near where it says 100A.) Note that the word communication in punched card at the bottom has only one "m." Given the way that the word is punched two "m"s would not fit

When the project was officially complete, Jim held a celebration party for the entire team both GCSC and engineering division and their spouses at a nice restaurant. That really healed a lot of wounds. In many ways the project was very acrimonious, while we had a common goal of a working system, P&G's demands and GCSC's capabilites were often not compatible and we were not always able to amicably resolve them. The dinner also drove home what I said about Jim not taking no for an answer. Not knowing what the party would cost, Jim asked P&G's treasury department for a blank signed check made out the restaurant. Treasury's reaction was, "We don't do that" Jim's response was, "Who is your boss." Jim got his blank signed check and used it to pay our bill.

However, my involvement with SPEC was not entirely over. During the turnover to the engineering division I kept copies of the SPEC program listings in the trunk of my company car. As production versions were modified and new listings produced I would receive the just out dated listings. Thus I was often able to help engineers to fix problems over the phone. One time when the SPEC engineering team was in Louisville, Kentucky using SPEC to design the wiring for a new manufacturing plant, they called me down to consult. I drove down, spent several hours helping them to get the system working correctly and then drove back.

As SPEC became a routine production system, P&G changed their focus and began to down size their electical engineering department and outsource their electrical design work. Although SPEC had saved P&G a million dollars or more, as this outsourcing accelerated, SPEC became less and less important. One of the ramifications of this decrease in importance was the proposed licensing of SPEC to GCSC.

GCSC would take over SPEC making it available to any firm doing electrical design—the system would run on a service bureau such as McDonald Douglas' McAuto, since GCSC did not have the computer capabilities required to run SPEC. GCSC in turn would earn consulting fees and take a cut of the computer charges. This was a new type of venture for P&G and the negotiations were long and drawn out and the deal was never certain. But when GCSC went through the boardroom coup described in chapter 8, the deal was off. P&G did not want to be involved in such instability. I truly believe that if GCSC had stayed in existence and liscenced SPEC that we all would have become (pre) dot com millionaires (billioniars).

About the time SPEC was finishing up, the movie *The Towering Inferno* came out. When negotiating with P&G to market SPEC, the company gave each GCSC employee money to see the movie with their spouse or friend. The subject was apropos to SPEC, as the wiring in *The Towering Inferno* was not done the way SPEC would have had it done. The movie would have made a great marketing pitch had GCSC stayed together. As it turned out GCSC was the towering inferno.

As reported above successful systems are often continually modified—such was the case with SPEC. In fact SPEC spun off a companion system called Construction Electrical Planning System (CEPS). CEPS utilized SPEC's results to produce materials lists. GCSC was only in on CEPS at the beginning. I spent several days in a conference room with client personnel designing CEPS as a series of linked basic functions[44] sketched on a white board. GCSC then provided the appropriate number of basic function punched card decks in PL/I and from there on our involvement was only an occasional consultation.

Jim, the SPEC P&G champion, was appalled with the circumstances around the GCSC break up and my departure. He was upset enough to provide a significant personal services contract for me to make major modifications to SPEC based upon P&G's experiences using the system. This was partly business for Jim and P&G and partly a show of appreciation for my significant part in bringing SPEC to fruition.

This again was a rush, rush project that had to be completed within a short time frame. Thus I missed our family vacation that year. My family went on a Sierra Club service trip without me. But at least we had food on the table when they got back. This was my final involvement with SPEC except for brief look at the DEC system when I was at Xavier.

SPEC was transferred by P&G to a local engineering firm that used a Digital Equipment Corporation (DEC) computer operating system version of PL/I that did not have the seveal features that we relied

---

[44]   Basic Functions described in chapter 6 (In)Flexible Systems, consist of seven patterns that encompass all computer processing.

heavily on. Hours and hours of work were required and hundreds and hundreds of lines of PL/I code had to be added by brute force. I offered to consult with them to find an easier way—but they were unwilling to pay.

I know not whether SPEC or CEPS still exist. They don't even show up on a Google search! But they still exist in my memory, DNA, and experience. What a ride!

CHAPTER 11
SOME ADVICE

In this final chapter I will present some advice. While most of this advice is appropriate for those who are still in the trenches, some is more appropriate for your children or grandchildren. But before I cover more specific points—the myths.

BE AWARE OF IT MYTHS

Much of IT's "conventional wisdom" consists of myths. My colleagues and I have documented many of them in our paper [Johnson et al 1999] and book [Johnson, et all 2005]. A few of the most important myths that have not been presented in earlier chapters are set forth below with their corresponding reality.

Some of these myths are:
- The myth of perfect knowledge
- The myth of methodology
- The myth of reuse
- The myth of the solution
- The myth of the isolated system
- The myth of the naive customer
- The myth of outsourcing
- The myth of classification
- The myth of rapid application development (RAD)
- The myth of OO as a new technology and a silver bullet
- The myth of retroactive documentation

These myths are discussed in more detail in the referenced works.

The Myth Of Perfect Knowledge

Myth: With enough effort, we can attain essentially perfect knowledge of a system's requirements.

Reality: The real world changes, so knowledge of a system's requirements is necessarily imperfect since significant parts of the requirements lie in the future and are not available at the time the automated system is developed.

Accuracy today has virtually no effect on synchronizing with change tomorrow. This myth has led to the industry wide focus on improving requirements determination and its corollary myth: the myth of methodology.

The Myth Of Methodology

Myth: Good methods will produce good systems.

Reality: Good methods can and do produce bad systems, when the system perfectly fitted to current requirements cannot be efficiently adapted to unknowable future requirements.

Systems developed with such great precision or often inflexible and can be ruinously expensive to maintain.

The Myth Of Reuse

Myth: Once reusable code is written it does not have to be modified and thus reuse is free and easy.

Reality: Side effects, unintended effects, outright errors and the need to document and catalogue means that reuse is not free or easy.

Code must be found to be reused, to be found code must be documented and catalogued, and the catalogue must be accessible and up to date. This fact requires a certain amount of overhead—and thus is not free nor necessarily easy. In addition the cost of writing a module increases exponentially with its breath of use. To have it used by a colleague doubles the cost over using it yourself, for your work group the cost is ten times, for your company one hundred times, etc.

The Myth Of The Solution

Myth: Information systems are solutions to business problems.

Reality: Information systems simply offer fast, cheap, and accurate automated assistance with business functions.

Substitute the concept of "automated assistance" whenever the term "solution" is used when considering systems investments.

The Myth Of The Isolated System

Myth: We'll develop the new project control system for the engineering department. Then as we get requirements from the other departments, we'll evolve the system and roll it out across the company. This evolutionary approach will be cost effective and will not commit us to too big a development piece at any one time. We can develop systems one at a time and fit them together into an integrated whole as we go along.

Reality: We can build an organization's systems one at a time, but the underlying information structure for all the systems must be *analyzed and designed* first if integrated systems are to result.

Once a single coherent stable data structure has been developed then and only then (sub)systems can be fit into that structure

The Myth Of The Naïve Customer

Myth: Customer perceptions of what it should take to implement systems modifications are grossly unrealistic; they do not appreciate how complex automated systems are. Thus, IT together with their customers need to educate themselves in this matter.

Reality: Customer perceptions of what ought to be the cases are realistic. What they do not perceive correctly is the inflexibility and fragility of current systems. IT must learn how to develop flexible and stable systems.

Systems should be built consistent with the customer's perception that modifying an automated system should be no harder than changing the real-world system.

The Myth Of Outsourcing

Myth: We can hire an outside firm with the appropriate expertise that will manage our information technology cheaper and better, and we won't have the management headaches.

Reality: It's your business—you must manage it —including the IT component and IT professionals.

The transformation processes leading to successful IT systems require diligent effort, proper project management, and just plain hard work by all they players including: management, system customers, and IT professionals.

A realization of this myth by some firms may be behind what appears to be a significant bringing back onshore projects and processes that have been outsourced abroad.

Often my firm or me was the beneficiary of outsourcing. In these cases we were most successful when the client exercised strong management over our work. Case in point, SPEC. Sometimes the client did not initially know how to manage us—in these cases we set about to teach them how.

The Myth Of Classification (Also the myth of sub type or the myth of sub category)

Myth: Customers cannot dynamically manage classification or typing.

Reality: Classification and typing can be dynamically managed through regulation with techniques such as the Generic Entity Cloud [Johnson, et al 2005]

The Myth of Classification states that customers cannot dynamically manage *types at run time. (The * here means any of the multiple possible levels of typing.) Thus the concept of a *class manager that enables the dynamic management of *types by adding, deleting, or changing *types becomes an absolute impossibility. In a nutshell, this imaginary limitation revolved around the fact that subclasses had to be determined at design time. This is now overcome with the Generic Entity Cloud.

The Myth Of Rapid Application Development

Myth: The race against change is won by going faster—Rapid Application Development.

Reality: Rapid Application Development may simply lead to faster development of inflexible systems if adaptability to future requirements has not been considered.

Rapid application development cannot be applied to the 60 to 100 percent of IT work that is maintenance—where the real leverage is. Systems maintenance can be compared to a minefield where as system development is more like a greenfield.

The Myth Of OO As A New Technology And A Silver Bullet [Johnson, et al 1995, 1994]

Myth: Object Orientation is a new and different silver bullet.

Reality: Object orientation is old technology in new wine skins.

"Current approaches to computer science and programming resemble Middle Ages alchemy. They are faddish, changing with any new gurus, trends, or fashions that come along. They operate on concepts and definitions without unified classification. The search for something that will turn base metal to gold goes on. The newest fad is OOPSObject-Oriented Pieces of Something"

The Myth Of Retroactive Documentation
Consider the case in which an existing automated system is, for whatever reason, to be replaced with a new one. Management's desire to completely understand existing system leads to the myth of retroactive documentation.

Myth: The most important step in developing a replacement system is to "document the existing automated system."

Reality: The existing real world system is usually distorted by the presence of its entrenched automated component.

When an automated system has been in place for some time, it usually represents past versions of the business system—it is literally an accident of history. More important it has fallen farther out of synchronization over time, it has increasingly over-constrained the current business system, which must be bent in various ways to circumvent the limitations of the automated system. When coupled with the frequent breakdowns of the current automated system during modifications, the resultant unpredictability leads to fear of the system and an understandable reaction to counter this by completely understanding the old systems system before attempting to replace it.
Managers must realize, however, that documenting the existing system will perpetuates the distortions into the next generation.

The following additional myths have been included in the chapters where they related specifically to the material.

- The myth of the successful system
- The myth of parallel perceptions
- The myth of comparative evaluation
- The myth of modularity

SOME WISDOM

Based upon "wisdom" gained from experiences in my careers and IT industry evolution, I present here some guidance for those who follow. I would have done better and had an easier time had I known and/ or followed a number of these during my careers. As I review these points of guidance they seem somewhat simplistic and obvious—but I think when one digs deeper one finds that if they are followed, they are followed more in theory than in practice. To summarize, they are:

- Get an education—not just training.
- Continue your education and training.
- Be ware of technical distance
- Never be bored.
- Have fun—enjoy what you do—and be good at it.
- Learn and practice the first law of wing walking.
- Keep on top of technology progression.
  - ○ Look for the constants in ever-evolving technology.
  - ○ Don't be afraid to start over.
  - ○ Design for Flexibility.
- Choose the right bosses.
- Follow stupid rules exactly.
- Be patient.
- Pay attention to detail.
- Don't get outsourced.

Get An Education—A Broad Education—Not Just Training

The United States is rapidly falling behind other countries in math and science, which does not bode well for our high-tech industries nor protect our jobs from being shipped abroad. Many writers are lamenting the "ambition gap" between U.S. students and students from and in other countries. Don't fall into this trap. Ambitiously take all the math and science that you can. As noted below the must have degree has shifted from the MBA to computer science to engineering.

Education has always been important—but never more so than today. And I mean education —not training. Training teaches you a skill —how to do something. An education not only enables you to know something, but also enables you to know how to acquire and apply knowledge, and most importantly how to think and judge. In today's world of fast moving technology and outsourcing, skills can fast become obsolete. Education, on the other hand, lasts.

On one of my evaluations at Xavier, a student wrote, "I never learned anything from Johnson—I learned it all myself!" I am sure that this was not meant in a positive sense and I know that this detracted from my merit rating. But, on the other hand, it sounded like the student learned how to learn—and, after all, is that not the job of the teacher?

At Xavier our IT students took many more classes in liberal arts than they did in IT. Some thought this to be wrong. But my thought was and still is "What will be more useful to you in 10-20-30 years COBOL or philosophy, data base design or the classics?

My "education" was in Civil Engineering, which while in itself is not very broad, provides a great foundation, in math, science, and logical and critical thinking. Somehow I recognized this lack of breadth beyond the hard sciences—maybe because my father was a Civil Engineer and his interests did not seem very broad. So while working on my bachelor's degree in Civil Engineering I took an overload of courses so that I could include some of the liberal arts— literature, sociology, economics, psychology, biology, military science, and extra mathematics. Yet this smattering of liberal arts courses may not be enough to serve as a broad education today. The extra courses lowered my grade point average—but it was worth it.

Being an engineer I am biased toward engineering. engineering, science, applied math, and liberal arts should be fields of choice for today's college students. I could not have had a better education for the various career paths that I traversed. Civil Engineering studies worked very well for me. Even though I taught for 17 years in a business college, I do not recommend business as an undergraduate subject. In my view, business courses better fit the genre of training than education. They are mainly "how tos." How to keep books, how to market, how to finance an operation, how to develop and manage a system of machines and/or people, and the like. Once a person has an education and some work experience, then studying business and obtaining a Masters of Business Administration (MBA) may make sense—even though the MBA is vastly overrated and, to some degree has been supplanted by computer science degrees, the degree of choice today is/should be an engineering degree. The MBA serves as even more of a screening device than does an undergraduate degree. It can or at least used to lead to mighty high pay for one just starting out.

A problem with undergraduate business programs is that they are, all to often, weak in science and math. For example, at Xavier an undergraduate business student did not have to take a hard science such as chemistry or physics but could take general science or astronomy or some other hand-waving science to meet the science requirement. When I used calculus in class, which all students were supposed to have had, I was met with, "What are you doing Professor Johnson—this is a data structures class—not a math class?" But then lack of integration across the disciplines is an age-old well-recognized phenomenon.

Continue Your Education And Keep Your Training Up To Date

It is not enough to get a degree—even an advanced degree. One must continue their education, continue to obtain training and keep to it up to date. Many business writers lament the lack of adequate continuing education and training conducted by most organizations.

The shortage of on the job training was stressed over and over again in the courses that I took while obtaining my MBA and PhD. I also experienced this shortage often during my career. The lack of support received from P&G management for our FORTRAN course at Winton Hill serves as a prime example. I volunteered to develop the course on my own time, students agreed to take half of it on their own time. But P&G did not support the on-the-job portion—because the students had "no immediate need for FORTRAN."

Even though GCSC was a small often-struggling company, we conducted a great deal of training. We wanted all our analysts to use common techniques, such as basic functions, how to design with them and also how to implement them in each of environments in which we operated. In addition, GCSC conducted courses in system design, program design, and coding.

In addition, GCSC had an open-ended tuition remission program. Our employees were reimbursed for any college course, including basket weaving. While it was technically a reimbursement program paying the cost of tuition after successful completion, we provided payroll advances for the tuition when the employee did not have funds for upfront tuition payments.

Whatever you know and whatever you can do may well become either obsolete or outsourced or both. Whether or not I may still be the world's best 7080 programmer is irrelevant just exactly because 7080 machine language programming has long been irrelevant. I think I have done a reasonably good job in keeping up to date. I have an extensive personal library of technical and managerial books and read journals and magazines extensively.

Hands-on computer programming is a necessary skill and skills are important. I have gone from 650 machine language, to SOAP (An old kind of SOAP—Symbolic Optimized Assembly Program, not the new kind —Simple Object Access Protocol), FORTRAN, COBOL, SPS, several Assembler and macro languages, PL/I, SPL, B-, C++, and Java and others.

The best bet is to look for companies that have active on the job education and training programs. If it is not there then see if you can get your company to develop a program, and in all cases do some study and learning on your own. It is your responsibility!

Be Ware Of Technical Distance

What I have dubbed technical distance has followed me —no hounded me—all of my professional life. A prime reason for going into academia was to try and counter the technical distance problems from both sides—try to improve the technical knowledge of managers and to improve the capabilities of technical personnel. Technical distance was instrumental in my being fired from Billboard Publications.

Technical distance is the gap between a decision maker's knowledge of technology and the technical knowledge required to make an informed and intelligent technically involved decision. The prime example is the demise of the space shuttle Challenger on January 28, 1986. Low temperature caused O-ring failure, which lead to the shuttle exploding and killing all aboard. The technically knowledgeable persons who knew that the O-ring was not designed for such a low temperature were not empowered to make the decision as to whether or not to launch. And the managers with the decision-making authority did not have the knowledge that an O-ring failure was likely at the temperature at launch time—nor did they have the willingness to listen to and take the recommendations of their technologists! Thus disaster.

Another example of technical distance closer to home was the Billboard warehousing and IT consultants—when Billboard's managements followed the recommendation of the warehouse consultant even though Billboard had a world-class warehouse manager who disagreed with the consultant's findings. Yet they did not follow the recommendation of the IT consultant whose recommendations agreed with their IT staff who, while not as world-renowned, were imminently competent. Both previously successful operations suffered significant decline and were shuttered and moved to New York. Yet, given the technical illiteracy of Billboard management, there was nothing the in-house staff could have done to save their jobs or these operations.

Of course, politics gets mixed up with technical distance, again as shown by the Challenger explosion—not launching with all the hype and media presence would not have been a politically popular decision —hence the technicians were ignored.

I am not sure that my foray in to academia did much, if anything, to combat technical distance so maybe I am not qualified to address the issue. But technical distance was the subject of my PhD thesis and much class work and several class papers. I was unable, however, to get any of these papers published. The reviews themselves, negative and recommending against publication, were near perfect demonstrations of technical distance—totally dismissing the existence of such a phenomena.

So how does one avoid technical distance caused disasters? I say education. Educate your boss on technology? Educate yourself and your subordinates on the management and political issues involved with technical decisions. This can be delicate and difficult – particularly educating your boss. Here is where an engineering background is a mixed bag and may contribute to technical distanceas an engineer I tended to see things in black and white, while decision-makers and managers tend to see things in gray—but even worse important technical details often elude them.

I have made financial investments in companies based primarily on the fact that at least some of the top executives and board members were engineers and/or technologists. This has paid of handsomely— helping me to retire and to stay retired.

While one may not have much control over who is picked for your bosses, it is important from several standpoints including technical distance to do your best to find out the level of technical knowledge and interest that your bosses have—even several levels up. And where possible, upgrade their understanding of technical issues regarding the decisions they make related to your job. While I strongly recommend this, I was never very successful at it. In most cases, my bosses were just plain not interested.

Never Be Bored

Terrified yes! Bored no! Tends to summarize my careers. I probably had more terror than I would choose if I had to do it over—but I am truly thankful that I have never been bored. I think that in order to avoid boredom you must at least occasionally have a job that is over your head.

When I was assigned the role of Motor Officer in my reserve unit my wife said, "You know nothing about trucks, motors, and the like!" I responded, "You have seen my commission from Congress—it says that I am qualified for any and all jobs that a U.S Army officer can hold." I quickly introduced myself to the Motor Sergeant, who based on long experience in the motor pool knew the ropes, by saying, "Hello! I am Captain Johnson. I am the new Motor Officer; if you need anything let me know. Otherwise I will stay out of your way and let you run the motor pool. And oh by the way I would appreciate it if you would help me learn how to operate the equipment." He did and I drove some on our convoys.

The army is unique in that the responsible commissioned officer generally has experienced backup through warrant and non-commissioned officers and other enlisted personnel. This does not generally happen in business. This may help ameliorate technical distance in the military —but, remember, the officer is still responsible and has the ultimate decision making authority.

When one gets a job that is over ones head there are several ways to grow into the job. Pick the brains of your predecessor. Search out a mentor. Read, observe, and in many cases your subordinates can help you and occasionally even your boss can help.

Another part of this admonition is to recognize those about you who may not be as lucky; who may have a repetitious, boring jobs. This was the case at Billboard when I attended the potluck lunches and raved about Sue's brownies and Maggie's Lasagna. In the immediate picture of my job, I did not have time. But in the larger picture, I need to recognize that their jobs, unlike mine, lacked psychic income (of course their jobs also lacked the terror) and that their self-worth came from the cooking they shared. Since such satisfaction did not come from their routine clerical jobs. I do not mean to demean any type of work——all work can be necessary and important.

Have Fun—Enjoy What You Do And Be Good At It

I was also lucky to have jobs that I basically enjoyed. Of course not all of every day was a picnic and the terror certainly was not fun. But I was generally good at what I did: programming, designing systems, teaching, mentoring. I was not good at dealing with politics and bureaucracy—and the record shows that. But I did not set out to be a politician or a bureaucrat.

While studying Civil Engineering (CE) it did not look like practicing Civil Engineering would be much fun. Too many CEs worked for other CEs and this kept the salaries down. But, more importantly, there appeared to be a long apprenticeship—literally at the drawing board, which I would not have enjoyed. Programming, problem solving, seeing the results of your efforts run on a computer seemed like much more engaging. And as it happened, it was also more financially rewarding.

From what I read and hear, many initial career choices are being made today based on financial reward and not the more intrinsic rewards—such as having fun. Think about this as you make decisions regarding your first or nth career choice.

Remember, burn out is just waiting to happen when you don't love what you do.

Learn And Practice The First Law Of Wing Walking

One is supposed to have another job before he lets go of the current one. This I did not do. For speaking out I was fired several times without having another job in hand. I let go with one hand without having a hold with the other hand—a definite violation of the first law of wing walking. These "falls" were tied up with technical distance, engineering black and white, and my lack of political savvy.

But I never suffered irreparably from the violating this law. There was intermediate trauma while I was without a job—collecting unemployment—but in each case I shortly ended up better off both financially and professionally. But you may not be so lucky.

What to do? At least in the era of word-processing you can keep your resume up to date in real time. I am retired and I still keep my resume up to date with my publications and work in Java. Also keep your antenna tuned to your industry and related industries, and keep your contacts current. Each better job that I obtained was through professional contacts not though resume spreading.

Keep On Top Of Technology Progression

This is about more than education and training, one must have one's antenna out for developments near and far. One must be willing to try new things and to see where new technologies can apply to one's job or one's firm. I was the first faculty member at Xavier to have Windows, which I paid for myself and placed on their machine. While doing this, one must be aware of the following.

Look for the constants in our ever-evolving technology. There is no doubt that technology is evolving and at an apparently ever accelerating pace. But in many ways it stays the same. For example many of the latest methodologies appear at first glance to be new approaches to old problems. But often on closer look they are really just old wine in new wine skins. See the Myth of OO above for an example.

Today because so many computers are hooked to the Internet, malicious persons take advantage of system vulnerabilities to introduce viruses and the like. One of these system vulnerabilities—buffer overflow, sounds like vulnerabilities experienced way back in the 1970s with sector overflow on the IBM 1800 which made our system crash.

The hardware gets faster and the storage larger at ever decreasing prices—but even with outsourcing—developing software is still very expensive and prone to malfunction. Which, by the way, as the myth above says—outsourcing may be a reason that developing software is expensive and prone to malfunction

The corollary to this is: Be aware of IT history. I have made many presentations of IT history and I am apparently much more interested in the subject than my students were. But I believe that if you are in the field it is very helpful to know at least a bit of its history. And, frankly, you won't be in it long until you have actually observed a great deal of history. I have often given a history of technology PowerPoint presentation.

Don't be afraid to start over. We all have a desire to salvage pieces of failed or failing projects. But, as I have found several times, throwing the remnants of the old project out and starting with a clean slate and new ideas can be the way to a better product delivered faster. Reread the Myth of Reuse above and see if you can see any connection to this piece of advice.

Design for flexibility. Many of the items in this book have to do with change. Change may be the only constant. Thus whatever you design, what ever you build, ask yourself how can it be modified when the environment around it changes. My experience in the flexibility area has to do with computer software systems. Recently I was talking with an engineer who has designed corn mills for many years. All of which have had to be radically modified to meet the changing nature of the market for his products. Due to built-in flexibility most of the modifications have been made reasonably easy without drastic interruption to production or major scrapping of equipment or facilities.

Choose The Right Bosses

Of course one does not always have say over who your boss is or will be. But it pays to be aware and when possible steer yourself to a boss who will help you grow and who will support your advancement. I was very, very lucky in my career—particularly early on—to have bosses who were leaders, not just bureaucrats or administrators, and that I respected and learned from, bosses who gave me a great deal of freedom and responsibility, who supported me and supported my ideas and proposals. Certainly in retrospect I owe much of whatever success I had to my early bosses. I salute them. And hope that you have similar bosses. Later on my bosses who were actually administrators who were not as supportive, talented, or honorable.

Remember: Managers manage people. Leaders manage change. Try to pick leaders for your bosses.

Follow Stupid Rules Exactly

I gave examples in earlier chapters of what happens when good, conscientious, people, knowing that a rule is stupid choose not to follow that rule. But what happens when this is done? The rule remains. By following stupid rules exactly their stupidity will become known and, hopefully, they will be changed.

Be Patient

I should be talking about patience! But even though I have difficulty practicing patience —I know its value. Often things work out if one just steps back. With patience life is much less stressful. But as with almost anything too much may be nearly as bad as too little.

Pay Attention To Detail

The saying "the devil is in the details," is all too true particularly when it comes to technology. For the want of a period the computer program crashed. Because one subsystem was built in English measure and another in metric—serious life threatening problems resulted. So whenever possible go one level deeper, ask one more question, take one more measurement.

Don't Get Outsourced

So in parting, keep your education and skills up to date or ahead of the technology curve. And, wherever possible, take to heart and heed the advice and "wisdom" set forth herein.

AGAIN

Remember, just because I occasionally got away with not following the advice and wisdom given above and did not get outsourced does not mean that you will be as fortunate if you "break the rules."

It's been a great ride and, of course, now that I am retired, the trenches don't seem as deep. But I still relish most of my experiences and am glad that you are still with me. I trust that you have enjoyed these reminisces and have been able to profit from them.

REFERENCED WORKS

Callahan, David 2004 *The cheating culture: Why More Americans Are DOING WRONG to GET Ahead*, p. 288.

"Decline and Fall" 2005 *Interface* August.

Drucker, Peter 1974 *Management, Tasks, Responsibilities, Practices* Harper & Row, Publishers.

Edmundson, Mark 2013 *Why Teach: In Defense of a Real Education*

Johnson, Bruce, Walter W. Woolfolk, Robert Miller, Cindy Johnson 2005: *Flexible Software Design: Systems Development for Changing Requirements,* Auerbach Publications.

Johnson, Bruce 2005 "On Drucker" *Wall Street Journal* November 22.

Johnson, Bruce, Walter W. Woolfolk 2001: "Generic Entity Clouds: A Stable Information Structure for Flexible Computer Systems" *Systems Development Management* October.

Johnson, Bruce, Walter W. Woolfolk, Peter Ligezinsky 1999: "Counterintuitive Management of Information Systems Technology," *Business Horizons* March-April.

Johnson, Bruce 1992 *Information Systems Technology for Quality Improvement*. Editor with Sam Pinto.

Johnson, Bruce 1991 *Professional Programming in COBOL* with Marcia Ruwe. Prentice-Hall, 1991.

Johnson, Bruce 1990 *The Interaction of Equipment and Process Technology Knowledge and Decision-Making Methodology,*

Unpublished PhD dissertation, University of Cincinnati, Cincinnati, Ohio.

Johnson, Bruce 1984 "Data Processing—Out of Control." *Operations Management Review* Volume 2 Number 2 winter.

Johnson, Bruce 1983 Actual Case Study in Lieu of Final Examination, Unpublished case study for BA 22-405-895 Entrepreneurship: New Venture Formation, University of Cincinnati, Cincinnati, Ohio June.

Johnson, Bruce 1962 *Determination of Intercity Travel Desire Factor by the Digital Computer* Unpublished Master of Science thesis Washington State University, Pullman, Washington.

Kerwin, Michael W. 2013 "Cheating Epidemic?" *The Denver Post* June 2, pg. D1&6.

Miller, Robert W., Bruce Johnson, Walter W. Woolfolk 2002: "UniverSIS: Flexible System, Easy to Change", *Educause Quarterly,* Number 3, Fall.

"Thinking about Washington State" 2005. *Washington State Magazine* Fall.

Weinberg, Gerald M. 1973 *Psychology of Computer Programming* Van Nostrand Reinhold.

Weinberg, Gerald M. 1992: *Quality Software Management: Vol. 1 Systems Thinking,* Dorset House.

Woolfolk, Walter W., Bruce Johnson 2001: "Information Free Identifiers—A Key to Flexible Information Systems Parts I and II," *Data Base Management* July, August.

Yourdon, Edward 1992: *Decline and Fall of the American Programmer,* Prentice Hall.

Printed in the United States
By Bookmasters